ESSAYS IN THE ECONOMICS OF CRIME AND PUNISHMENT

NATIONAL BUREAU OF ECONOMIC RESEARCH
Human Behavior and Social Institutions

ESSAYS IN THE ECONOMICS OF CRIME AND PUNISHMENT

Edited by
GARY S. BECKER
University of Chicago and
National Bureau of Economic Research

and

WILLIAM M. LANDES
University of Chicago and
National Bureau of Economic Research

NATIONAL BUREAU OF ECONOMIC RESEARCH
New York   1974
Distributed by COLUMBIA UNIVERSITY PRESS
New York and London

HV6030
.B42

379283

Relation of the Directors to the Work and Publications
of the National Bureau of Economic Research

1. The object of the National Bureau of Economic Research is to ascertain and to present to the public important economic facts and their interpretation in a scientific and impartial manner. The Board of Directors is charged with the responsibility of ensuring that the work of the National Bureau is carried on in strict conformity with this object.

2. The President of the National Bureau shall submit to the Board of Directors, or to its Executive Committee, for their formal adoption all specific proposals for research to be instituted.

3. No research report shall be published until the President shall have submitted to each member of the Board the manuscript proposed for publication, and such information as will, in his opinion and in the opinion of the author, serve to determine the suitability of the report for publication in accordance with the principles of the National Bureau. Each manuscript shall contain a summary drawing attention to the nature and treatment of the problem studied, the character of the data and their utilization in the report, and the main conclusions reached.

4. For each manuscript so submitted, a special committee of the Directors (including Directors Emeriti) shall be appointed by majority agreement of the President and Vice Presidents (or by the Executive Committee in case of inability to decide on the part of the President and Vice Presidents), consisting of three Directors selected as nearly as may be one from each general division of the Board. The names of the special manuscript committee shall be stated to each Director when the manuscript is submitted to him. It shall be the duty of each member of the special manuscript committee to read the manuscript. If each member of the manuscript committee signifies his approval within thirty days of the transmittal of the manuscript, the report may be published. If at the end of that period any member of the manuscript committee withholds his approval, the President shall then notify each member of the Board, requesting approval or disapproval of publication, and thirty days additional shall be granted for this purpose. The manuscript shall then not be published unless at least a majority of the entire Board who shall have voted on the proposal within the time fixed for the receipt of votes shall have approved.

5. No manuscript may be published, though approved by each member of the special manuscript committee, until forty-five days have elapsed from the transmittal of the report in manuscript form. The interval is allowed for the receipt of any memorandum of dissent or reservation, together with a brief statement of his reasons, that any member may wish to express; and such memorandum of dissent or reservation shall be published with the manuscript if he so desires. Publication does not, however, imply that each member of the Board has read the manuscript, or that either members of the Board in general or the special committee have passed on its validity in every detail.

6. Publications of the National Bureau issued for informational purposes concerning the work of the Bureau and its staff, or issued to inform the public of activities of Bureau staff, and volumes issued as a result of various conferences involving the National Bureau shall contain a specific disclaimer noting that such publication has not passed through the normal review procedures required in this resolution. The Executive Committee of the Board is charged with review of all such publications from time to time to ensure that they do not take on the character of formal research reports of the National Bureau, requiring formal Board approval.

7. Unless otherwise determined by the Board or exempted by the terms of paragraph 6, a copy of this resolution shall be printed in each National Bureau publication.

(Resolution adopted October 25, 1926, and revised February 6, 1933,
February 24, 1941, April 20, 1968, and September 17, 1973)

Acknowledgments

Many individuals contributed to the entire manuscript and we should like to thank them for their efforts. Robert Michael, in his capacity as Acting Director in 1972–73 of the National Bureau's Center for Economic Analysis of Human Behavior and Social Institutions, actively encouraged the collection of these essays into a single volume and gave valuable advice on the organization of the manuscript. Bruce Ackerman of the University of Pennsylvania Law School and Guido Calabresi of the Yale University Law School generously gave their time in reviewing all the essays. Eugene P. Foley, J. Wilson Newman, and Alice M. Rivlin made helpful comments as members of the Board of Directors' reading committee. Skillful assistance in the preparation of the manuscript was provided by Ruth Ridler in editing the essays, H. Irving Forman in charting the graphs, and Elisabeth Parshley in typing.

The program of research in law and economics at the National Bureau has been funded from its inception in 1971 by the National Science Foundation, whose support we gratefully acknowledge. The views expressed in these essays are, of course, not attributable to the National Science Foundation.

GARY S. BECKER and WILLIAM M. LANDES

Permissions

Our thanks to the following journals for permission to reprint material previously published by them. From *The Journal of Political Economy,* we have chosen three articles: Gary S. Becker, "Crime and Punishment: An Economic Approach," in Volume 76, No. 2, March/April 1968; copyright 1968 by the University of Chicago, all rights reserved, and printed in the United States. George J. Stigler, "The Optimum Enforcement of Laws," in Volume 78, No. 2, March/April 1970; copyright 1970 by the University of Chicago, all rights reserved, and printed in the United States. Isaac Ehrlich, "Participation in Illegitimate Activities: A Theoretical and Empirical Investigation," in Volume 81, No. 3, May/June 1973; copyright 1973 by the University of Chicago, all rights reserved, and printed in the United States. This last, somewhat revised and expanded, appears here as "Participation in Illegitimate Activities: An Economic Analysis." From *The Journal of Legal Studies,* we have chosen two articles: Richard A. Posner, "The Behavior of Administrative Agencies," in Volume I(2), June 1972; copyright 1972 by the University of Chicago, all rights reserved, and printed in the United States. William M. Landes, "The Bail System: An Economic Approach," in Volume II(1), January 1973; copyright 1973 by the University of Chicago, all rights reserved, and printed in the United States. From *The Journal of Law and Economics* we have chosen one article: William M. Landes, "An Economic Analysis of the Courts," Volume XIV(1), April 1971; copyright 1971 by the University of Chicago, all rights reserved, and printed in the United States.

Contents

Contents

Preface

The relationship between law and economics has long been a subject of study by economists. At least since the time of Adam Smith's analysis of the Navigation Act in England, economists have used the tools of economic theory to understand and to evaluate the effects of laws and alternative legal arrangements on the workings of an economic system. Moreover, with the rapid growth of empirical methods in recent years, economists have produced a large number of studies that attempt to quantify the actual effects of the laws. However, both the theoretical and quantitative investigations have generally taken for granted the question of enforcement. Laws are assumed to be enforced, or incomplete enforcement is acknowledged but viewed as beyond the expertise of the economist. This failure to study enforcement has been a serious deficiency, because enforcement is an essential link in the relationship between a legal and an economic system.

The distinguishing and unifying feature of the essays in this volume is the systematic study of enforcement as an economic problem. The core of the economic approach to enforcement is the application of the principle of scarcity. Because enforcement of legal rules and regulations and the adaptation to them by individuals use scarce resources, choices must be made concerning the nature of the rules to be enforced, the methods to be used in detecting violations, the types of sanctions to be imposed on violators, and the procedures to be employed in adjudicating disputes on whether violations have occurred. Taking the fundamental notion of scarcity, combined with the specification of decision rules for governments and individuals, the economic theory of resource allocation can be used to analyze enforcement, to provide insights into the operation of the legal system, and to derive testable hypotheses for empirical analysis.

All the studies in this volume embody the essentials of the economic approach, although they differ in the emphasis placed on theoretical and empirical analysis. The studies cover a variety of subjects on enforcement, including the design of optimal rules for enforcing laws, quantitative estimates of the deterrent effect of law enforcement, the role of the bail and court system in the enforcement of laws, and the behavior of administrative agencies in enforcing violations. The following is a brief description of the material presented here.

In the first essay, Gary Becker utilizes the economic theory of resource allocation to develop optimal public and private policies to combat illegal activities. Optimal policies are defined as those that minimize the social loss from crime. That loss depends on the net damage to victims; the resource costs of discovering, apprehending, and convicting offenders; and the costs of punishment itself. These components of the loss, in turn, depend upon the number of criminal offenders, the probability of apprehending and convicting offenders, the size and form of punishments, the potential legal incomes of offenders, and several other variables. The optimal supply of criminal offenses — in essence, the optimal amount of crime — is then determined by selecting values for the probability of conviction, the penalty, and other variables determined by society that minimize the social loss from crime. Within this framework, theorems are derived that relate the optimal probability of conviction, the optimal punishments, and the optimal supply of criminal offenses to such factors as the size of the damages from various types of crimes, changes in the overall costs of apprehending and convicting offenders, and differences in the relative responsiveness of offenders to conviction probabilities and to penalties. The form of the punishment is analyzed as well, with particular reference to the choice between fines and other methods.

Optimal enforcement is also the subject of the second essay. Here, George Stigler considers (a) the effects on enforcement of cost limitations; (b) the appropriate definition of enforcement costs; (c) the optimal structure of penalties and probabilities of conviction for crimes of varying severity; and (d) the determinants of supply of offenses. He shows, among other things, that an optimal enforcement policy must incorporate the principle of marginal deterrence — the setting of higher penalties and conviction probabilities for more serious offenses — to account for the offender's ability to substitute more serious for less serious offenses. In the final part of his paper, Stigler develops a model for determining the optimum enforcement policy for agencies charged with economic regulation. He provides some evidence indicating that maximum statutory penalties for violations of economic regulations have little relationship to optimal penalties.

The third essay, by Isaac Ehrlich, develops in greater detail the supply function for criminal activities that is central to Becker's and Stigler's models of optimal law enforcement. In Ehrlich's model, legal and illegal activities both yield earnings, but the distinguishing feature of illegal activities is assumed to be their uncertain outcome due to possible punishment. Individuals may specialize in illegal or legal activities or participate in both, depending upon the alternative that maximizes their expected utility. Increases in punishments and probabilities of conviction, other things remaining constant, will lower the return from illegal activities and thereby reduce the incentive to participate in them. The main contribution of Ehrlich's study is his empirical analysis of deterrence. The continuing debate over whether punishments and conviction probabilities deter illegal behavior has been conducted with little evidence presented by either side. Using data from the 1940, 1950, and 1960 Uniform Crime Reports, and employing several statistical techniques, Ehrlich is able to measure across states, at different points in time, the response of specific felony rates to changes in variables reflecting deterrents and gains to crime. Ehrlich's results support the basic hypotheses of the economic model: crime rates appear to vary inversely with estimates of penalties, probabilities of conviction, and legal opportunities.

In the fourth essay, William Landes develops a model of an optimal bail system, using the same basic framework as Becker. Landes derives a social benefit function for the bail system that incorporates both the gains to defendants from being released on bail and the costs and gains to the rest of the community from the release of defendants. The optimal level of resource expenditures on the bail system and the optimal number of defendants to be released are determined by maximizing the social benefit. The main contribution of this essay, however, is the development of alternative methods for selecting defendants for release. Two basic methods and variations on them are analyzed. Both are consistent with the criterion of maximizing the social benefit function. The first, which corresponds to most existing bail systems, requires defendants to pay for their release. The second compensates defendants for their detention by means of monetary or other payment. There are several advantages to a system in which defendants are paid. The major advantage is a reduction in the punitive aspect of the bail system (since those detained are compensated for their losses from detention) that still allows the detention of persons in cases in which the potential damage to the community exceeds the gains from their release. Other advantages include reduced discrimination against low-income defendants and greater economic incentive for the state to improve pretrial detention facilities. The final part of Landes' paper considers the advantage of crediting a defendant's pretrial detention against his eventual sentence, the possibility of tort suits by detained defendants who are acquitted, and the role of bail bonds and bondsmen.

The development of a positive theory of legal decision-making as applied to enforcement decisions is the common theme of the remaining two essays. In Landes' study of the court system, a utility-maximization model is developed that explains the determinants of the choice between a trial and pretrial settlement in both criminal and civil cases, the terms of a settlement, and the outcome of a trial. For criminal cases, these decisions are shown to depend on such factors as estimates of the probability of conviction by trial, the severity of the crime, the availability and productivity of resources allocated to the resolution of legal disputes, trial versus settlement costs, and attitudes toward risk. The effects of the existing bail system and court delay are analyzed within the framework of the model, as well as the likely effects of a variety of proposals designed to improve the bail system and reduce court delay. Multiple regression techniques are used on data from both state and federal courts to test several hypotheses derived from the model. Considerable empirical evidence is adduced to support the hypothesis that the cost differential between a trial and settlement in criminal cases is a significant determinant of the choice between going to trial and settling. Cost differentials, which include the implicit value of time, were measured by court queues, pretrial detention, and the subsidization of legal fees. Landes also undertakes an empirical analysis of conviction rates in criminal cases, and of the trial versus settlement choice in civil cases.

Richard Posner's study of administrative agencies employs a model similar to the one used by Landes to analyze the court system. Posner assumes that an agency maximizes expected utility subject to a budget constraint. The agency's expected utility is defined to be a positive function of both the expected number of successful prosecutions and the public benefit from winning various types of cases. Posner's model is used to predict an agency's budgetary allocation across classes of cases, the agency's dismissal rate and successful prosecution rate for different types of cases, and the effects of assigning to a single agency both prosecution and adjudication functions. The major part of the empirical analysis is devoted to examining the thesis that an agency that both initiates and decides cases will bias adjudication in favor of the agency, as compared with an agency in which these functions are separated. In the context of the model, Posner derives numerous testable implications of the "bias" hypothesis. Using data from the National Labor Relations Board, which after 1947 no longer initiated complaints, and the Federal Trade Commission, Posner finds little evidence in support of the bias hypothesis.

The essays in this volume were written by members of the National Bureau's program of basic research in law and economics. This research program, begun in 1971, applies analytical and quantitative techniques of economics to the study of the deterrent effects of criminal sanctions, the functioning of the court and bail systems, the behavioral effects of legislation, and legal decision-making. These essays represent part of the research output of this project; each has been published over the past few years in one of several professional journals. We feel that the publication of the volume provides convincing evidence of the power of economic tools in analyzing the enforcement of law. We expect this to be the first of several volumes reporting the results of this program of research to National Bureau subscribers and to students of legal behavior and institutions. The law and economics research program is one of several housed within the National Bureau's new Center for Economic Analysis of Human Behavior and Social Institutions.

William M. Landes

ESSAYS IN THE ECONOMICS OF CRIME AND PUNISHMENT

Crime and Punishment:
An Economic Approach

Gary S. Becker

University of Chicago and National Bureau of Economic Research

I. INTRODUCTION

Since the turn of the century, legislation in Western countries has expanded rapidly to reverse the brief dominance of laissez faire during the nineteenth century. The state no longer merely protects against violations of person and property through murder, rape, or burglary but also restricts "discrimination" against certain minorities, collusive business arrangements, "jaywalking," travel, the materials used in construction, and thousands of other activities. The activities restricted not only are numerous but also range widely, affecting persons in very different pursuits and of diverse social backgrounds, education levels, ages, races, etc. Moreover, the likelihood that an offender will be discovered and con-

I would like to thank the Lilly Endowment for financing a very productive summer in 1965 at the University of California at Los Angeles. While there I received very helpful comments on an earlier draft from, among others, Armen Alchian, Roland McKean, Harold Demsetz, Jack Hirshliefer, William Meckling, Gordon Tullock, and Oliver Williamson. I have also benefited from comments received at seminars at the University of Chicago, Hebrew University, RAND Corporation, and several times at the Labor Workshop of Columbia; assistance and suggestions from Isaac Ehrlich and Robert Michael; and suggestions from the editor of the *Journal of Political Economy*, Robert A. Mundell.

victed and the nature and extent of punishments differ greatly from person to person and activity to activity. Yet, in spite of such diversity, some common properties are shared by practically all legislation, and these properties form the subject matter of this essay.

In the first place, obedience to law is not taken for granted, and public and private resources are generally spent in order both to prevent offenses and to apprehend offenders. In the second place, conviction is not generally considered sufficient punishment in itself; additional and sometimes severe punishments are meted out to those convicted. What determines the amount and type of resources and punishments used to enforce a piece of legislation? In particular, why does enforcement differ so greatly among different kinds of legislation?

The main purpose of this essay is to answer normative versions of these questions, namely, how many resources and how much punishment *should* be used to enforce different kinds of legislation? Put equivalently, although more strangely, how many offenses *should* be permitted and how many offenders *should* go unpunished? The method used formulates a measure of the social loss from offenses and finds those expenditures of resources and punishments that minimize this loss. The general criterion of social loss is shown to incorporate as special cases, valid under special assumptions, the criteria of vengeance, deterrence, compensation, and rehabilitation that historically have figured so prominently in practice and criminological literature.

The optimal amount of enforcement is shown to depend on, among other things, the cost of catching and convicting offenders, the nature of punishments — for example, whether they are fines or prison terms — and the responses of offenders to changes in enforcement. The discussion, therefore, inevitably enters into issues in penology and theories of criminal behavior. A second, although because of lack of space subsidiary, aim of this essay is to see what insights into these questions are provided by our "economic" approach. It is suggested, for example, that a useful theory of criminal behavior can dispense with special theories of anomie, psychological inadequacies, or inheritance of special traits and simply extend the economist's usual analysis of choice.

II. BASIC ANALYSIS

A. THE COST OF CRIME

Although the word "crime" is used in the title to minimize terminological innovations, the analysis is intended to be sufficiently general to cover

TABLE 1
ECONOMIC COSTS OF CRIMES

Type	Costs (Millions of Dollars)
Crimes against persons	815
Crimes against property	3,932
Illegal goods and services	8,075
Some other crimes	2,036
Total	14,858
Public expenditures on police, prosecution, and courts	3,178
Corrections	1,034
Some private costs of combating crime	1,910
Overall total	20,980

SOURCE. — President's Commission (1967*d*, p. 44).

all violations, not just felonies — like murder, robbery, and assault, which receive so much newspaper coverage — but also tax evasion, the so-called white-collar crimes, and traffic and other violations. Looked at this broadly, "crime" is an economically important activity or "industry," notwithstanding the almost total neglect by economists.[1] Some relevant evidence recently put together by the President's Commission on Law Enforcement and Administration of Justice (the "Crime Commission") is reproduced in Table 1. Public expenditures in 1965 at the federal, state, and local levels on police, criminal courts and counsel, and "corrections" amounted to over $4 billion, while private outlays on burglar alarms, guards, counsel, and some other forms of protection were about $2 billion. Unquestionably, public and especially private expenditures are significantly understated, since expenditures by many public agencies in the course of enforcing particular pieces of legislation, such as state fair-

---

1. This neglect probably resulted from an attitude that illegal activity is too immoral to merit any systematic scientific attention. The influence of moral attitudes on a scientific analysis is seen most clearly in a discussion by Alfred Marshall. After arguing that even fair gambling is an "economic blunder" because of diminishing marginal utility, he says, "It is true that this loss of probable happiness need not be greater than the pleasure derived from the excitement of gambling, and we are then thrown back upon the induction [*sic*] that pleasures of gambling are in Bentham's phrase 'impure'; since experience shows that they are likely to engender a restless, feverish character, unsuited for steady work as well as for the higher and more solid pleasures of life" (Marshall, 1961, Note X, Mathematical Appendix).

employment laws,[2] are not included, and a myriad of private precautions against crime, ranging from suburban living to taxis, are also excluded.

Table 1 also lists the Crime Commission's estimates of the direct costs of various crimes. The gross income from expenditures on various kinds of illegal consumption, including narcotics, prostitution, and mainly gambling, amounted to over $8 billion. The value of crimes against property, including fraud, vandalism, and theft, amounted to almost $4 billion,[3] while about $3 billion worth resulted from the loss of earnings due to homicide, assault, or other crimes. All the costs listed in the table total about $21 billion, which is almost 4 per cent of reported national income in 1965. If the sizable omissions were included, the percentage might be considerably higher.

Crime has probably become more important during the last forty years. The Crime Commission presents no evidence on trends in costs but does present evidence suggesting that the number of major felonies per capita has grown since the early thirties (President's Commission, 1967a, pp. 22–31). Moreover, with the large growth of tax and other legislation, tax evasion and other kinds of white-collar crime have presumably grown much more rapidly than felonies. One piece of indirect evidence on the growth of crime is the large increase in the amount of currency in circulation since 1929. For sixty years prior to that date, the ratio of currency either to all money or to consumer expenditures had declined very substantially. Since then, in spite of further urbanization and income growth and the spread of credit cards and other kinds of credit,[4] both ratios have increased sizably.[5] This reversal can be explained by an unusual increase in illegal activity, since currency has obvious advantages

---

2. Expenditures by the thirteen states with such legislation in 1959 totaled almost $2 million (see Landes, 1966).

3. Superficially, frauds, thefts, etc., do not involve true social costs but are simply transfers, with the loss to victims being compensated by equal gains to criminals. While these are transfers, their market value is, nevertheless, a first approximation to the direct social cost. If the theft or fraud industry is "competitive," the sum of the value of the criminals' time input—including the time of "fences" and prospective time in prison—plus the value of capital input, compensation for risk, etc., would approximately equal the market value of the loss to victims. Consequently, aside from the input of intermediate products, losses can be taken as a measure of the value of the labor and capital input into these crimes, which are true social costs.

4. For an analysis of the secular decline to 1929 that stresses urbanization and the growth in incomes, see Cagan (1965, chap. iv).

5. In 1965, the ratio of currency outstanding to consumer expenditures was 0.08, compared to only 0.05 in 1929. In 1965, currency outstanding per family was a whopping $738.

over checks in illegal transactions (the opposite is true for legal transactions) because no record of a transaction remains.[6]

B. THE MODEL

It is useful in determining how to combat crime in an optimal fashion to develop a model to incorporate the behavioral relations behind the costs listed in Table 1. These can be divided into five categories: the relations between (1) the number of crimes, called "offenses" in this essay, and the cost of offenses, (2) the number of offenses and the punishments meted out, (3) the number of offenses, arrests, and convictions and the public expenditures on police and courts, (4) the number of convictions and the costs of imprisonments or other kinds of punishments, and (5) the number of offenses and the private expenditures on protection and apprehension. The first four are discussed in turn, while the fifth is postponed until a later section.

1. DAMAGES

Usually a belief that other members of society are harmed is the motivation behind outlawing or otherwise restricting an activity. The amount of harm would tend to increase with the activity level, as in the relation

$$H_i = H_i(O_i),$$

with   (1)

$$H_i' = \frac{dH_i}{dO_i} > 0,$$

where H_i is the harm from the ith activity and O_i is the activity level.[7] The concept of harm and the function relating its amount to the activity level are familiar to economists from their many discussions of activities causing external diseconomies. From this perspective, criminal activities are an important subset of the class of activities that cause diseconomies, with the level of criminal activities measured by the number of offenses.

The social value of the gain to offenders presumably also tends to in-

---

6. Cagan (1965, chap. iv) attributes much of the increase in currency holdings between 1929 and 1960 to increased tax evasion resulting from the increase in tax rates.

7. The ith subscript will be suppressed whenever it is to be understood that only one activity is being discussed.

crease with the number of offenses, as in

$$G = G(O),$$

with   (2)

$$G' = \frac{dG}{dO} > 0.$$

The net cost or damage to society is simply the difference between the harm and gain and can be written as

$$D(O) = H(O) - G(O). \tag{3}$$

If, as seems plausible, offenders usually eventually receive diminishing marginal gains and cause increasing marginal harm from additional offenses, $G'' < 0$, $H'' > 0$, and

$$D'' = H'' - G'' > 0, \tag{4}$$

which is an important condition used later in the analysis of optimality positions (see, for example, the Mathematical Appendix). Since both H' and $G' > 0$, the sign of D' depends on their relative magnitudes. It follows from (4), however, that

$$D'(O) > 0 \text{ for all } O > O_a \text{ if } D'(O_a) \geqslant 0. \tag{5}$$

Until Section V the discussion is restricted to the region where $D' > 0$, the region providing the strongest justification for outlawing an activity. In that section the general problem of external diseconomies is reconsidered from our viewpoint, and there $D' < 0$ is also permitted.

The top part of Table 1 lists costs of various crimes, which have been interpreted by us as estimates of the value of resources used up in these crimes. These values are important components of, but are not identical to, the net damages to society. For example, the cost of murder is measured by the loss in earnings of victims and excludes, among other things, the value placed by society on life itself; the cost of gambling excludes both the utility to those gambling and the "external" disutility to some clergy and others; the cost of "transfers" like burglary and embezzlement excludes social attitudes toward forced wealth redistributions and also the effects on capital accumulation of the possibility of theft. Consequently, the $15 billion estimate for the cost of crime in Table 1 may be a significant understatement of the net damages to society, not only because the costs of many white-collar crimes are omitted, but also because much of the damage is omitted even for the crimes covered.

2. THE COST OF APPREHENSION AND CONVICTION

The more that is spent on policemen, court personnel, and specialized equipment, the easier it is to discover offenses and convict offenders. One can postulate a relation between the output of police and court "activity" and various inputs of manpower, materials, and capital, as in $A = f(m, r, c)$, where f is a production function summarizing the "state of the arts." Given f and input prices, increased "activity" would be more costly, as summarized by the relation

$$C = C(A)$$

and (6)

$$C' = \frac{dC}{dA} > 0.$$

It would be cheaper to achieve any given level of activity the cheaper were policemen,[8] judges, counsel, and juries and the more highly developed the state of the arts, as determined by technologies like fingerprinting, wiretapping, computer control, and lie-detecting.[9]

One approximation to an empirical measure of "activity" is the number of offenses cleared by conviction. It can be written as

$$A \cong pO,$$ (7)

where p, the ratio of offenses cleared by convictions to all offenses, is the overall probability that an offense is cleared by conviction. By substituting (7) into (6) and differentiating, one has

$$C_p = \frac{\partial C(pO)}{\partial p} = C'O > 0$$

and (8)

$$C_o = C'p > 0$$

if $pO \neq 0$. An increase in either the probability of conviction or the number of offenses would increase total costs. If the marginal cost of increased "activity" were rising, further implications would be that

---

8. According to the Crime Commission, 85–90 per cent of all police costs consist of wages and salaries (President's Commission, 1967a, p. 35).

9. A task-force report by the Crime Commission deals with suggestions for greater and more efficient usage of advanced technologies (President's Commission, 1967e).

$$C_{pp} = C''O^2 > 0,$$

$$C_{oo} = C''p^2 > 0, \tag{9}$$

and

$$C_{po} = C_{op} = C''pO + C' > 0.$$

A more sophisticated and realistic approach drops the implication of (7) that convictions alone measure "activity," or even that p and O have identical elasticities, and introduces the more general relation

$$A = h(p, O, a). \tag{10}$$

The variable a stands for arrests and other determinants of "activity," and there is no presumption that the elasticity of h with respect to p equals that with respect to O. Substitution yields the cost function $C = C(p, O, a)$. If, as is extremely likely, h_p, h_o, and h_a are all greater than zero, then clearly C_p, C_o, and C_a are all greater than zero.

In order to insure that optimality positions do not lie at "corners," it is necessary to place some restrictions on the second derivatives of the cost function. Combined with some other assumptions, it is *sufficient* that

$$C_{pp} \geqslant 0,$$

$$C_{oo} \geqslant 0, \tag{11}$$

and

$$C_{po} \cong 0$$

(see the Mathematical Appendix). The first two restrictions are rather plausible, the third much less so.[10]

Table 1 indicates that in 1965 public expenditures in the United States on police and courts totaled more than $3 billion, by no means a minor item. Separate estimates were prepared for each of seven major felonies.[11] Expenditures on them averaged about $500 per offense (reported) and about $2,000 per person arrested, with almost $1,000 being spent per murder (President's Commission, 1967a, pp. 264–65); $500 is an estimate of the average cost

$$AC = \frac{C(p, O, a)}{O}$$

---

10. Differentiating the cost function yields $C_{pp} = C''(h_p)^2 + C'h_{pp}$; $C_{oo} = C''(h_o)^2 + C'h_{oo}$; $C_{po} = C''h_oh_p + C'h_{po}$. If marginal costs were rising, C_{pp} or C_{oo} could be negative only if h_{pp} or h_{oo} were sufficiently negative, which is not very likely. However, C_{po} would be approximately zero only if h_{po} were sufficiently negative, which is also unlikely. Note that if "activity" is measured by convictions alone, $h_{pp} = h_{oo} = 0$, and $h_{po} > 0$.

11. They are willful homicide, forcible rape, robbery, aggravated assault, burglary, larceny, and auto theft.

of these felonies and would presumably be a larger figure if the number of either arrests or convictions were greater. Marginal costs (C_o) would be at least \$500 if condition (11), $C_{oo} \geq 0$, were assumed to hold throughout.

3. THE SUPPLY OF OFFENSES

Theories about the determinants of the number of offenses differ greatly, from emphasis on skull types and biological inheritance to family up-bringing and disenchantment with society. Practically all the diverse theories agree, however, that when other variables are held constant, an increase in a person's probability of conviction or punishment if convicted would generally decrease, perhaps substantially, perhaps negligibly, the number of offenses he commits. In addition, a common generalization by persons with judicial experience is that a change in the probability has a greater effect on the number of offenses than a change in the punishment,[12] although, as far as I can tell, none of the prominent theories shed any light on this relation.

The approach taken here follows the economists' usual analysis of choice and assumes that a person commits an offense if the expected utility to him exceeds the utility he could get by using his time and other resources at other activities. Some persons become "criminals," therefore, not because their basic motivation differs from that of other persons, but because their benefits and costs differ. I cannot pause to discuss the many general implications of this approach,[13] except to remark that criminal behavior becomes part of a much more general theory and does not require ad hoc concepts of differential association, anomie, and the like,[14] nor does it assume perfect knowledge, lightning-fast calculation, or any of the other caricatures of economic theory.

This approach implies that there is a function relating the number of offenses by any person to his probability of conviction, to his punishment if convicted, and to other variables, such as the income available to him in legal and other illegal activities, the frequency of nuisance arrests, and his willingness to commit an illegal act. This can be represented as

---

12. For example, Lord Shawness (1965) said, "Some judges preoccupy themselves with methods of punishment. This is their job. But in preventing crime it is of less significance than they like to think. Certainty of detection is far more important than severity of punishment." Also see the discussion of the ideas of C. B. Beccaria, an insightful eighteenth-century Italian economist and criminologist, in Radzinowicz (1948, I, p. 282).

13. See, however, the discussions in Smigel (1965) and Ehrlich (1967).

14. For a discussion of these concepts, see Sutherland (1960).

$$O_j = O_j(p_j, f_j, u_j), \tag{12}$$

where O_j is the number of offenses he would commit during a particular period, p_j his probability of conviction per offense, f_j his punishment per offense, and u_j a portmanteau variable representing all these other influences.[15]

Since only convicted offenders are punished, in effect there is "price discrimination" and uncertainty: if convicted, he pays f_j per convicted offense, while otherwise he does not. An increase in either p_j or f_j would reduce the utility expected from an offense and thus would tend to reduce the number of offenses because either the probability of "paying" the higher "price" or the "price" itself would increase.[16] That is,

$$O_{p_j} = \frac{\partial O_j}{\partial p_j} < 0$$

and   (13)

$$O_{f_j} = \frac{\partial O_j}{\partial f_j} < 0,$$

which are the generally accepted restrictions mentioned above. The effect of changes in some components of u_j could also be anticipated. For example, a rise in the income available in legal activities or an increase in law-abidingness due, say, to "education" would reduce the incentive to

---

15. Both p_j and f_j might be considered distributions that depend on the judge, jury, prosecutor, etc., that j happens to receive. Among other things, u_j depends on the p's and f's meted out for other competing offenses. For evidence indicating that offenders do substitute among offenses, see Smigel (1965).

16. The utility expected from committing an offense is defined as

$$EU_j = p_j U_j(Y_j - f_j) + (1 - p_j)U_j(Y_j),$$

where Y_j is his income, monetary plus psychic, from an offense; U_j is his utility function; and f_j is to be interpreted as the monetary equivalent of the punishment. Then

$$\frac{\partial EU_j}{\partial p_j} = U_j(Y_j - f_j) - U_j(Y_j) < 0$$

and

$$\frac{\partial EU_j}{\partial f_j} = - p_j U_j'(Y_j - f_j) < 0$$

as long as the marginal utility of income is positive. One could expand the analysis by incorporating the costs and probabilities of arrests, detentions, and trials that do not result in conviction.

enter illegal activities and thus would reduce the number of offenses. Or a shift in the form of the punishment, say, from a fine to imprisonment, would tend to reduce the number of offenses, at least temporarily, because they cannot be committed while in prison.

This approach also has an interesting interpretation of the presumed greater response to a change in the probability than in the punishment. An increase in p_j "compensated" by an equal percentage reduction in f_j would not change the expected income from an offense [17] but could change the expected utility, because the amount of risk would change. It is easily shown that an increase in p_j would reduce the expected utility, and thus the number of offenses, more than an equal percentage increase in f_j [18] if j has preference for risk; the increase in f_j would have the greater effect if he has aversion to risk; and they would have the same effect if he is risk neutral.[19] The widespread generalization that offenders are more deterred by the probability of conviction than by the punishment when convicted turns out to imply in the expected-utility approach that offenders are risk preferrers, at least in the relevant region of punishments.

The total number of offenses is the sum of all the O_j and would depend on the set of p_j, f_j, and u_j. Although these variables are likely to differ significantly between persons because of differences in intelligence, age, education, previous offense history, wealth, family upbringing, etc., for simplicity I now consider only their average values, p, f, and u,[20] and write

---

17. $EY_j = p_j(Y_j - f_j) + (1 - p_j)Y_j = Y_j - p_jf_j$.

18. This means that an increase in p_j "compensated" by a reduction in f_j would reduce utility and offenses.

19. From n. 16

$$\frac{-\partial EU_j}{\partial p_j}\frac{p_j}{U_j} = [U_j(Y_j) - U_j(Y_j - f_j)]\frac{p_j}{U_j} \gtreqless \frac{-\partial EU_j}{\partial f_j}\frac{f_j}{U_j} = p_jU_j'(Y_j - f_j)\frac{f_j}{U_j}$$

as

$$\frac{U_j(Y_j) - U_j(Y_j - f_j)}{f_j} \gtreqless U_j'(Y_j - f_j).$$

The term on the left is the average change in utility between $Y_j - f_j$ and Y_j. It would be greater than, equal to, or less than $U_j'(Y_j - f_j)$ as $U_j'' \gtreqless 0$. But risk preference is defined by $U_j'' > 0$, neutrality by $U_j'' = 0$, and aversion by $U_j'' < 0$.

20. p can be defined as a weighted average of the p_j, as

$$p = \sum_{j=1}^{n}\frac{O_jp_j}{\sum_{i=1}^{n}O_i},$$

and similar definitions hold for f and u.

the market offense function as

$$O = O(p, f, u). \tag{14}$$

This function is assumed to have the same kinds of properties as the individual functions, in particular, to be negatively related to p and f and to be more responsive to the former than the latter if, and only if, offenders on balance have risk preference. Smigel (1965) and Ehrlich (1967) estimate functions like (14) for seven felonies reported by the Federal Bureau of Investigation using state data as the basic unit of observation. They find that the relations are quite stable, as evidenced by high correlation coefficients; that there are significant negative effects on O of p and f; and that usually the effect of p exceeds that of f, indicating preference for risk in the region of observation.

A well-known result states that, in equilibrium, the real incomes of persons in risky activities are, at the margin, relatively high or low as persons are generally risk avoiders or preferrers. If offenders were risk preferrers, this implies that the real income of offenders would be lower, at the margin, than the incomes they could receive in less risky legal activities, and conversely if they were risk avoiders. Whether "crime pays" is then an implication of the attitudes offenders have toward risk and is not directly related to the efficiency of the police or the amount spent on combating crime. If, however, risk were preferred at some values of p and f and disliked at others, public policy could influence whether "crime pays" by its choice of p and f. Indeed, it is shown later that the social loss from illegal activities is usually minimized by selecting p and f in regions where risk is preferred, that is, in regions where "crime does not pay."

4. PUNISHMENTS

Mankind has invented a variety of ingenious punishments to inflict on convicted offenders: death, torture, branding, fines, imprisonment, banishment, restrictions on movement and occupation, and loss of citizenship are just the more common ones. In the United States, less serious offenses are punished primarily by fines, supplemented occasionally by probation, petty restrictions like temporary suspension of one's driver's license, and imprisonment. The more serious offenses are punished by a combination of probation, imprisonment, parole, fines, and various restrictions on choice of occupation. A recent survey estimated for an average day in 1965 the number of persons who were either on probation, parole, or institutionalized in a jail or juvenile home (President's Commission, 1967b). The total number of persons in one of these categories came to about 1,300,000, which is about 2 per cent of the labor force. About one-half were on probation, one-third were institutionalized, and the remaining one-sixth were on parole.

The cost of different punishments to an offender can be made comparable by converting them into their monetary equivalent or worth, which, of course, is directly measured only for fines. For example, the cost of an imprisonment is the discounted sum of the earnings foregone and the value placed on the restrictions in consumption and freedom. Since the earnings foregone and the value placed on prison restrictions vary from person to person, the cost even of a prison sentence of given duration is not a unique quantity but is generally greater, for example, to offenders who could earn more outside of prison.[21] The cost to each offender would be greater the longer the prison sentence, since both foregone earnings and foregone consumption are positively related to the length of sentences.

Punishments affect not only offenders but also other members of society. Aside from collection costs, fines paid by offenders are received as revenue by others. Most punishments, however, hurt other members as well as offenders: for example, imprisonment requires expenditures on guards, supervisory personnel, buildings, food, etc. Currently about $1 billion is being spent each year in the United States on probation, parole, and institutionalization alone, with the daily cost per case varying tremendously from a low of $0.38 for adults on probation to a high of $11.00 for juveniles in detention institutions (President's Commission, 1967b, pp. 193–94).

The total social cost of punishments is the cost to offenders plus the cost or minus the gain to others. Fines produce a gain to the latter that equals the cost to offenders, aside from collection costs, and so the social cost of fines is about zero, as befits a transfer payment. The social cost of probation, imprisonment, and other punishments, however, generally exceeds that to offenders, because others are also hurt. The derivation of optimality conditions in the next section is made more convenient if social costs are written in terms of offender costs as

$$f' \equiv bf, \tag{15}$$

where f' is the social cost and b is a coefficient that transforms f into f'. The size of b varies greatly between different kinds of punishments:

---

21. In this respect, imprisonment is a special case of "waiting time" pricing that is also exemplified by queueing (see Becker, 1965, esp. pp. 515–16, and Kleinman, 1967).

$b \cong 0$ for fines, while $b > 1$ for torture, probation, parole, imprisonment, and most other punishments. It is especially large for juveniles in detention homes or for adults in prisons and is rather close to unity for torture or for adults on parole.

III. OPTIMALITY CONDITIONS

The relevant parameters and behavioral functions have been introduced, and the stage is set for a discussion of social policy. If the aim simply were deterrence, the probability of conviction, p, could be raised close to 1, and punishments, f, could be made to exceed the gain: in this way the number of offenses, O, could be reduced almost at will. However, an increase in p increases the social cost of offenses through its effect on the cost of combating offenses, C, as does an increase in f if $b > 0$ through the effect on the cost of punishments, bf. At relatively modest values of p and f, these effects might outweigh the social gain from increased deterrence. Similarly, if the aim simply were to make "the punishment fit the crime," p could be set close to 1, and f could be equated to the harm imposed on the rest of society. Again, however, such a policy ignores the social cost of increases in p and f.

What is needed is a criterion that goes beyond catchy phrases and gives due weight to the damages from offenses, the costs of apprehending and convicting offenders, and the social cost of punishments. The social-welfare function of modern welfare economics is such a criterion, and one might assume that society has a function that measures the social loss from offenses. If

$$L = L(D, C, bf, O) \tag{16}$$

is the function measuring social loss, with presumably

$$\frac{\partial L}{\partial D} > 0, \quad \frac{\partial L}{\partial C} > 0, \quad \frac{\partial L}{\partial bf} > 0, \tag{17}$$

the aim would be to select values of f, C, and possibly b that minimize L.

It is more convenient and transparent, however, to develop the discussion at this point in terms of a less general formulation, namely, to assume that the loss function is identical with the total social loss in real income from offenses, convictions, and punishments, as in

$$L = D(O) + C(p, O) + bpfO. \tag{18}$$

The term $bpfO$ is the total social loss from punishments, since bf is the loss per offense punished and pO is the number of offenses punished (if there are a fairly large number of independent offenses). The variables directly subject to social control are the amounts spent in combating offenses, C; the punishment per offense for those convicted, f; and the form of punishments, summarized by b. Once chosen, these variables, via the D, C, and O functions, indirectly determine p, O, D, and ultimately the loss L.

Analytical convenience suggests that p rather than C be considered a decision variable. Also, the coefficient b is assumed in this section to be a given constant greater than zero. Then p and f are the only decision variables, and their optimal values are found by differentiating L to find the two first-order optimality conditions,[22]

$$\frac{\partial L}{\partial f} = D'O_f + C'O_f + bpfO_f + bpO = 0 \tag{19}$$

and

$$\frac{\partial L}{\partial p} = D'O_p + C'O_p + C_p + bpfO_p + bfO = 0. \tag{20}$$

If O_f and O_p are not equal to zero, one can divide through by them, and recombine terms, to get the more interesting expressions

$$D' + C' = -bpf\left(1 - \frac{1}{\epsilon_f}\right) \tag{21}$$

and

$$D' + C' + C_p\frac{1}{O_p} = -bpf\left(1 - \frac{1}{\epsilon_p}\right), \tag{22}$$

where

$$\epsilon_f = -\frac{f}{O}O_f$$

and $\tag{23}$

$$\epsilon_p = -\frac{p}{O}O_p.$$

The term on the left side of each equation gives the marginal cost of increasing the number of offenses, O: in equation (21) through a reduction in f and in (22) through a reduction in p. Since $C' > 0$ and O is assumed to be in a region where $D' > 0$, the marginal cost of increasing O through

---

22. The Mathematical Appendix discusses second-order conditions.

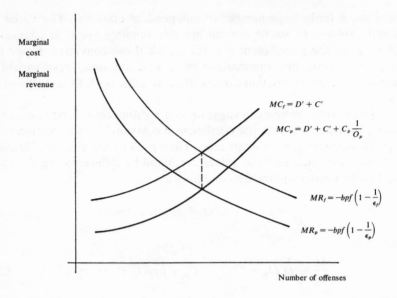

FIGURE 1

f must be positive. A reduction in p partly reduces the cost of combating offenses, and, therefore, the marginal cost of increasing O must be less when p rather than when f is reduced (see Figure 1); the former could even be negative if C_p were sufficiently large. Average "revenue," given by $-bpf$, is negative, but marginal revenue, given by the right-hand side of equations (21) and (22), is not necessarily negative and would be positive if the elasticities ϵ_p and ϵ_f were less than unity. Since the loss is minimized when marginal revenue equals marginal cost (see Figure 1), the optimal value of ϵ_f must be less than unity, and that of ϵ_p could only exceed unity if C_p were sufficiently large. This is a reversal of the usual equilibrium condition for an income-maximizing firm, which is that the elasticity of demand must exceed unity, because in the usual case average revenue is assumed to be positive.[23]

Since the marginal cost of changing O through a change in p is less than that of changing O through f, the equilibrium marginal revenue from p must also be less than that from f. But equations (21) and (22) indicate

---

23. Thus if $b < 0$, average revenue would be positive and the optimal value of ϵ_f would be greater than 1, and that of ϵ_p could be less than 1 only if C_p were sufficiently large.

that the marginal revenue from p can be less if, and only if, $\epsilon_p > \epsilon_f$. As pointed out earlier, however, this is precisely the condition indicating that offenders have preference for risk and thus that "crime does not pay." Consequently, the loss from offenses is minimized if p and f are selected from those regions where offenders are, on balance, risk preferrers. Although only the attitudes offenders have toward risk can directly determine whether "crime pays," rational public policy indirectly insures that "crime does not pay" through its choice of p and f.[24]

I indicated earlier that the actual p's and f's for major felonies in the United States generally seem to be in regions where the effect (measured by elasticity) of p on offenses exceeds that of f, that is, where offenders are risk preferrers and "crime does not pay" (Smigel, 1965; Ehrlich, 1967). Moreover, both elasticities are generally less than unity. In both respects, therefore, actual public policy is consistent with the implications of the optimality analysis.

If the supply of offenses depended only on pf—offenders were risk neutral—a reduction in p "compensated" by an equal percentage increase in f would leave unchanged pf, O, $D(O)$, and $bpfO$ but would reduce the loss, because the costs of apprehension and conviction would be lowered by the reduction in p. The loss would be minimized, therefore, by lowering p arbitrarily close to zero and raising f sufficiently high so that the product pf would induce the optimal number of offenses.[25] A fortiori, if offenders were risk avoiders, the loss would be minimized by setting p arbitrarily close to zero, for a "compensated" reduction in p reduces not only C but also O and thus D and $bpfO$.[26]

There was a tendency during the eighteenth and nineteenth centuries in Anglo-Saxon countries (and even today in many Communist and underdeveloped countries) to punish those convicted of criminal offenses rather severely, at the same time that the probability of capture and con-

---

24. If $b < 0$, the optimality condition is that $\epsilon_p < \epsilon_f$, or that offenders are risk avoiders. Optimal social policy would then be to select p and f in regions where "crime does pay."

25. Since $\epsilon_f = \epsilon_p = \epsilon$ if O depends only on pf, and $C = 0$ if $p = 0$, the two equilibrium conditions given by eqs. (21) and (22) reduce to the single condition

$$D' = -bpf\left(1 - \frac{1}{\epsilon}\right).$$

From this condition and the relation $O = O(pf)$, the equilibrium values of O and pf could be determined.

26. If $b < 0$, the optimal solution is p about zero and f arbitrarily high if offenders are either risk neutral or risk preferrers.

viction was set at rather low values.[27] A promising explanation of this tendency is that an increased probability of conviction obviously absorbs public and private resources in the form of more policemen, judges, juries, and so forth. Consequently, a "compensated" reduction in this probability obviously reduces expenditures on combating crime, and, since the expected punishment is unchanged, there is no "obvious" offsetting increase in either the amount of damages or the cost of punishments. The result can easily be continuous political pressure to keep police and other expenditures relatively low and to compensate by meting out strong punishments to those convicted.

Of course, if offenders are risk preferrers, the loss in income from offenses is generally minimized by selecting positive and finite values of p and f, even though there is no "obvious" offset to a compensated reduction in p. One possible offset already hinted at in footnote 27 is that judges or juries may be unwilling to convict offenders if punishments are set very high. Formally, this means that the cost of apprehension and conviction, C, would depend not only on p and O but also on f.[28] If C were more responsive to f than to p, at least in some regions,[29] the loss in income could be minimized at finite values of p and f even if offenders were risk avoiders. For then a compensated reduction in p could raise, rather than lower, C and thus contribute to an increase in the loss.

Risk avoidance might also be consistent with optimal behavior if the loss function were not simply equal to the reduction in income. For example, suppose that the loss were increased by an increase in the ex post "price discrimination" between offenses that are not and those that are cleared by punishment. Then a "compensated" reduction in p would increase the "price discrimination," and the increased loss from this could more than offset the reductions in C, D, and $bpfO$.[30]

---

27. For a discussion of English criminal law in the eighteenth and nineteenth centuries, see Radzinowicz (1948, Vol. I). Punishments were severe then, even though the death penalty, while legislated, was seldom implemented for less serious criminal offenses.

Recently South Vietnam executed a prominent businessman allegedly for "speculative" dealings in rice, while in recent years a number of persons in the Soviet Union have either been executed or given severe prison sentences for economic crimes.

28. I owe the emphasis on this point to Evsey Domar.

29. This is probably more likely for higher values of f and lower values of p.

30. If p is the probability that an offense would be cleared with the punishment f, then $1 - p$ is the probability of no punishment. The expected punishment would be $\mu = pf$, the variance $\sigma^2 = p(1 - p)f^2$, and the coefficient of variation

$$v = \frac{\sigma}{\mu} = \sqrt{\frac{1 - p}{p}};$$

IV. SHIFTS IN THE BEHAVIORAL RELATIONS

This section analyzes the effects of shifts in the basic behavioral relations—the damage, cost, and supply-of-offenses functions—on the optimal values of p and f. Since rigorous proofs can be found in the Mathematical Appendix, here the implications are stressed, and only intuitive
proofs are given. The results are used to explain, among other things,
why more damaging offenses are punished more severely and more impulsive offenders less severely.

An increase in the marginal damages from a given number of offenses,
D', increases the marginal cost of changing offenses by a change in either
p or f (see Figures 2a and b). The optimal number of offenses would
necessarily decrease, because the optimal values of both p and f would
increase. In this case (and, as shortly seen, in several others), the optimal
values of p and f move in the same, rather than in opposite, directions.[31]

An interesting application of these conclusions is to different kinds
of offenses. Although there are few objective measures of the damages
done by most offenses, it does not take much imagination to conclude
that offenses like murder or rape generally do more damage than petty
larceny or auto theft. If the other components of the loss in income were

---

v increases monotonically from a low of zero when $p = 1$ to an infinitely high value when
$p = 0$.

If the loss function equaled

$$L' = L + \psi(v), \qquad \psi' > 0,$$

the optimality conditions would become

$$D' + C' = -bpf\left(1 - \frac{1}{\epsilon_f}\right) \tag{21}$$

and

$$D' + C' + C_p \frac{1}{O_p} + \psi' \frac{dv}{dp} \frac{1}{O_p} = -bpf\left(1 - \frac{1}{\epsilon_p}\right). \tag{22}$$

Since the term $\psi'(dv/dp)(1/O_p)$ is positive, it could more than offset the negative term
$C_p(1/O_p)$.

31. I stress this primarily because of Bentham's famous and seemingly plausible dictum
that "the more deficient in certainty a punishment is, the severer it should be" (1931, chap.
ii of section entitled "Of Punishment," second rule). The dictum would be correct if p
(or f) were exogenously determined and if L were minimized with respect to f (or p) alone,
for then the optimal value of f (or p) would be inversely related to the given value of p (or f)
(see the Mathematical Appendix). If, however, L is minimized with respect to both, then
frequently they move in the same direction.

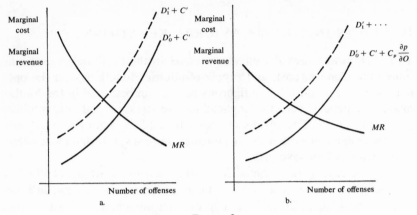

FIGURE 2

the same, the optimal probability of apprehension and conviction and the punishment when convicted would be greater for the more serious offenses.

Table 2 presents some evidence on the actual probabilities and punishments in the United States for seven felonies. The punishments are simply the average prison sentences served, while the probabilities are ratios of the estimated number of convictions to the estimated number of offenses and unquestionably contain a large error (see the discussions in Smigel, 1965, and Ehrlich, 1967). If other components of the loss function are ignored, and if actual and optimal probabilities and punishments are positively related, one should find that the more serious felonies have higher probabilities and longer prison terms. And one does: in the table, which lists the felonies in decreasing order of presumed seriousness, both the actual probabilities and the prison terms are positively related to seriousness.

Since an increase in the marginal cost of apprehension and conviction for a given number of offenses, C', has identical effects as an increase in marginal damages, it must also reduce the optimal number of offenses and increase the optimal values of p and f. On the other hand, an increase in the other component of the cost of apprehension and conviction, C_p, has no direct effect on the marginal cost of changing offenses with f and *reduces* the cost of changing offenses with p (see Figure 3). It therefore reduces the optimal value of p and only partially compensates with an increase in f, so that the optimal number of offenses increases. Accordingly, an increase in both C' and C_p must increase the optimal f but can either increase or decrease the optimal p and optimal number of offenses, depending on the relative importance of the changes in C' and C_p.

TABLE 2
PROBABILITY OF CONVICTION AND AVERAGE PRISON TERM FOR SEVERAL MAJOR FELONIES, 1960

	Murder and Non-negligent Man-slaughter	Forcible Rape	Robbery	Aggra-vated Assault	Burglary	Larceny	Auto Theft	All These Felonies Combined
1. Average time served (months) before first release:								
a) Federal civil institutions	111.0	63.6	56.1	27.1	26.2	16.2	20.6	18.8
b) State institutions	121.4	44.8	42.4	25.0	24.6	19.8	21.3	28.4
2. Probabilities of apprehension and conviction (per cent):								
a) Those found guilty of offenses known	57.9	37.7	25.1	27.3	13.0	10.7	13.7	15.1
b) Those found guilty of offenses charged	40.7	26.9	17.8	16.1	10.2	9.8	11.5	15.0
c) Those entering federal and state prisons (excludes many juveniles)	39.8	22.7	8.4	3.0	2.4	2.2	2.1	2.8

SOURCE. — 1, Bureau of Prisons (1960, Table 3); 2 (a) and (b), Federal Bureau of Investigation (1960, Table 10); 2 (c), Federal Bureau of Investigation (1961, Table 2), Bureau of Prisons (n.d., Table A1; 1961, Table 8).

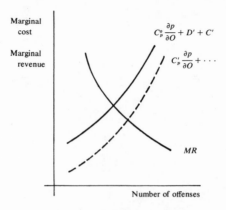

FIGURE 3

The cost of apprehending and convicting offenders is affected by a variety of forces. An increase in the salaries of policemen increases both C' and C_p, while improved police technology in the form of fingerprinting, ballistic techniques, computer control, and chemical analysis, or police and court "reform" with an emphasis on professionalism and merit, would tend to reduce both, not necessarily by the same extent. Our analysis implies, therefore, that although an improvement in technology and reform may or may not increase the optimal p and reduce the optimal number of offenses, it does reduce the optimal f and thus the need to rely on severe punishments for those convicted. Possibly this explains why the secular improvement in police technology and reform has gone hand in hand with a secular decline in punishments.

C_p, and to a lesser extent C', differ significantly between different kinds of offenses. It is easier, for example, to solve a rape or armed robbery than a burglary or auto theft, because the evidence of personal identification is often available in the former and not in the latter offenses.[32] This might tempt one to argue that the p's decline significantly as one moves across Table 2 (left to right) primarily because the C_p's are significantly lower for the "personal" felonies listed to the left than for the "impersonal" felonies listed to the right. But this implies that the f's would increase as one moved across the table, which is patently false. Consequently, the positive correlation between p, f, and the severity of

---

32. "If a suspect is neither known to the victim nor arrested at the scene of the crime, the chances of ever arresting him are very slim" (President's Commission, 1967e, p. 8). This conclusion is based on a study of crimes in parts of Los Angeles during January, 1966.

offenses observed in the table cannot be explained by a negative correlation between C_p (or C') and severity.

If $b > 0$, a reduction in the elasticity of offenses with respect to f increases the marginal revenue of changing offenses by changing f (see Figure 4a). The result is an increase in the optimal number of offenses and a decrease in the optimal f that is partially compensated by an increase in the optimal p. Similarly, a reduction in the elasticity of offenses with respect to p also increases the optimal number of offenses (see Figure 4b), decreases the optimal p, and partially compensates by an increase in f. An equal percentage reduction in both elasticities a fortiori increases the optimal number of offenses and also tends to reduce both p and f. If $b = 0$, both marginal revenue functions lie along the horizontal axis, and changes in these elasticities have no effect on the optimal values of p and f.

The income of a firm would usually be larger if it could separate, at little cost, its total market into submarkets that have substantially different elasticities of demand: higher prices would be charged in the submarkets having lower elasticities. Similarly, if the total "market" for offenses could be separated into submarkets that differ significantly in the elasticities of supply of offenses, the results above imply that if $b > 0$ the total loss would be reduced by "charging" *lower* "prices"—that is, lower p's and f's—in markets with *lower* elasticities.

Sometimes it is possible to separate persons committing the same offense into groups that have different responses to punishments. For example, unpremeditated murderers or robbers are supposed to act impulsively and, therefore, to be relatively unresponsive to the size of

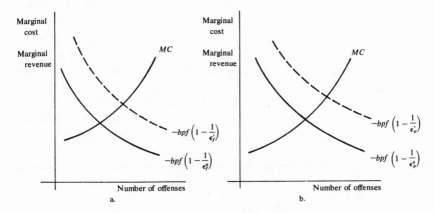

FIGURE 4

punishments; likewise, the insane or the young are probably less affected than other offenders by future consequences and, therefore,[33] probably less deterred by increases in the probability of conviction or in the punishment when convicted. The trend during the twentieth century toward relatively smaller prison terms and greater use of probation and therapy for such groups and, more generally, the trend away from the doctrine of "a given punishment for a given crime" is apparently at least broadly consistent with the implications of the optimality analysis.

An increase in b increases the marginal revenue from changing the number of offenses by changing p or f and thereby increases the optimal number of offenses, reduces the optimal value of f, and increases the optimal value of p. Some evidence presented in Section II indicates that b is especially large for juveniles in detention homes or adults in prison and is small for fines or adults on parole. The analysis implies, therefore, that other things the same, the optimal f's would be smaller and the optimal p's larger if punishment were by one of the former rather than one of the latter methods.

V. FINES

A. WELFARE THEOREMS AND TRANSFERABLE PRICING

The usual optimality conditions in welfare economics depend only on the levels and not on the slopes of marginal cost and average revenue functions, as in the well-known condition that marginal costs equal prices. The social loss from offenses was explicitly introduced as an application of the approach used in welfare economics, and yet slopes as incorporated into elasticities of supply do significantly affect the optimality conditions. Why this difference? The primary explanation would appear to be that it is almost always implicitly assumed that prices paid by consumers are fully transferred to firms and governments, so that there is no social loss from payment.

If there were no social loss from punishments, as with fines, b would equal zero, and the elasticity of supply would drop out of the optimality condition given by equation (21).[34] If $b > 0$, as with imprisonment, some

---

33. But see Becker (1962) for an analysis indicating that impulsive and other "irrational" persons may be as deterred from purchasing a commodity whose price has risen as more "rational" persons.

34. It remains in eq. (22), through the slope O_p, because ordinarily prices do not affect marginal costs, while they do here through the influence of p on C.

of the payment "by" offenders would not be received by the rest of society, and a net social loss would result. The elasticity of the supply of offenses then becomes an important determinant of the optimality conditions, because it determines the change in social costs caused by a change in punishments.

Although transferable monetary pricing is the most common kind today, the other is not unimportant, especially in underdeveloped and Communist countries. Examples in addition to imprisonment and many other punishments are the draft, payments in kind, and queues and other waiting-time forms of rationing that result from legal restrictions on pricing (see Becker, 1965) and from random variations in demand and supply conditions. It is interesting, and deserves further exploration, that the optimality conditions are so significantly affected by a change in the assumptions about the transferability of pricing.

B. OPTIMALITY CONDITIONS

If $b = 0$, say, because punishment was by fine, and if the cost of apprehending and convicting offenders were also zero, the two optimality conditions (21) and (22) would reduce to the same simple condition

$$D'(O) = 0. \qquad (24)$$

Economists generally conclude that activities causing "external" harm, such as factories that pollute the air or lumber operations that strip the land, should be taxed or otherwise restricted in level until the marginal external harm equaled the marginal private gain, that is, until marginal net damages equaled zero, which is what equation (24) says. If marginal harm always exceeded marginal gain, the optimum level would be presumed to be zero, and that would also be the implication of (24) when suitable inequality conditions were brought in. In other words, if the costs of apprehending, convicting, and punishing offenders were nil and if each offense caused more external harm than private gain, the social loss from offenses would be minimized by setting punishments high enough to eliminate all offenses. Minimizing the social loss would become identical with the criterion of minimizing crime by setting penalties sufficiently high.[35]

Equation (24) determines the optimal number of offenses, $\hat{O}$, and the fine and probability of conviction must be set at levels that induce

---

35. "The evil of the punishment must be made to exceed the advantage of the offense" (Bentham, 1931, first rule).

offenders to commit just $\hat{O}$ offenses. If the economists' usual theory of choice is applied to illegal activities (see Sec. II), the marginal value of these penalties has to equal the marginal private gain:

$$V = G'(\hat{O}), \tag{25}$$

where $G'(\hat{O})$ is the marginal private gain at $\hat{O}$ and V is the monetary value of the marginal penalties. Since by equations (3) and (24), $D'(\hat{O}) = H'(\hat{O}) - G'(\hat{O}) = 0$, one has by substitution in (25)

$$V = H'(\hat{O}). \tag{26}$$

The monetary value of the penalties would equal the marginal harm caused by offenses.

Since the cost of apprehension and conviction is assumed equal to zero, the probability of apprehension and conviction could be set equal to unity without cost. The monetary value of penalties would then simply equal the fines imposed, and equation (26) would become

$$f = H'(\hat{O}). \tag{27}$$

Since fines are paid by offenders to the rest of society, a fine determined by (27) would exactly compensate the latter for the marginal harm suffered, and the criterion of minimizing the social loss would be identical, at the margin, with the criterion of compensating "victims."[36] If the harm to victims always exceeded the gain to offenders, both criteria would reduce in turn to eliminating all offenses.

If the cost of apprehension and conviction were not zero, the optimality condition would have to incorporate marginal costs as well as marginal damages and would become, if the probability of conviction were still assumed to equal unity,

$$D'(\hat{O}) + C'(\hat{O}, 1) = 0. \tag{28}$$

Since $C' > 0$, (28) requires that $D' < 0$ or that the marginal private gain exceed the marginal external harm, which generally means a smaller number of offenses than when $D' = 0$.[37] It is easy to show that equation (28) would be satisfied if the fine equaled the sum of marginal harm and marginal costs:

---

36. By "victims" is meant the rest of society and not just the persons actually harmed.

37. This result can also be derived as a special case of the results in the Mathematical Appendix on the effects of increases in C'.

$$f = H'(\hat{O}) + C'(\hat{O}, 1).^{38} \qquad (29)$$

In other words, offenders have to compensate for the cost of catching them as well as for the harm they directly do, which is a natural generalization of the usual externality analysis.

The optimality condition

$$D'(\hat{O}) + C'(\hat{O}, \hat{p}) + C_p(\hat{O}, \hat{p}) \frac{1}{O_p} = 0 \qquad (30)$$

would replace equation (28) if the fine rather than the probability of conviction were fixed. Equation (30) would usually imply that $D'(\hat{O})$ > 0,[39] and thus that the number of offenses would exceed the optimal number when costs were zero. Whether costs of apprehension and conviction increase or decrease the optimal number of offenses largely depends, therefore, on whether penalties are changed by a change in the fine or in the probability of conviction. Of course, if both are subject to control, the optimal probability of conviction would be arbitrarily close to zero, unless the social loss function differed from equation (18) (see the discussion in Sec. III).

C. THE CASE FOR FINES

Just as the probability of conviction and the severity of punishment are subject to control by society, so too is the form of punishment: legislation usually specifies whether an offense is punishable by fines, probation, institutionalization, or some combination. Is it merely an accident, or

---

38. Since equilibrium requires that $f = G'(\hat{O})$, and since from (28)

$$D'(\hat{O}) = H'(\hat{O}) - G'(\hat{O}) = -C'(\hat{O}, 1),$$

then (29) follows directly by substitution.

39. That is, if, as seems plausible,

$$\frac{dC}{dp} = C' \frac{\partial O}{\partial p} + C_p > 0,$$

then

$$C' + C_p \frac{1}{\partial O/\partial p} < 0,$$

and

$$D'(\hat{O}) = -\left(C' + C_p \frac{1}{\partial O/\partial p}\right) > 0.$$

have optimality considerations determined that today, in most countries, fines are the predominant form of punishment, with institutionalization reserved for the more serious offenses? This section presents several arguments which imply that social welfare is increased if fines are used *whenever feasible*.

In the first place, probation and institutionalization use up social resources, and fines do not, since the latter are basically just transfer payments, while the former use resources in the form of guards, supervisory personnel, probation officers, and the offenders' own time.[40] Table 1 indicates that the cost is not minor either: in the United States in 1965, about $1 billion was spent on "correction," and this estimate excludes, of course, the value of the loss in offenders' time.[41]

Moreover, the determination of the optimal number of offenses and severity of punishments is somewhat simplified by the use of fines. A wise use of fines requires knowledge of marginal gains and harm and of marginal apprehension and conviction costs; admittedly, such knowledge is not easily acquired. A wise user of imprisonment and other punishments must know this too, however; and, in addition, must know about the elasticities of response of offenses to changes in punishments. As the bitter controversies over the abolition of capital punishment suggest, it has been difficult to learn about these elasticities.

I suggested earlier that premeditation, sanity, and age can enter into the determination of punishments as proxies for the elasticities of response. These characteristics may not have to be considered in levying fines, because the optimal fines, as determined, say, by equations (27) or (29), do not depend on elasticities. Perhaps this partly explains why economists discussing externalities almost never mention motivation or intent, while sociologists and lawyers discussing criminal behavior invariably do. The former assume that punishment is by a monetary tax or fine, while the latter assume that nonmonetary punishments are used.

Fines provide compensation to victims, and optimal fines at the margin fully compensate victims and restore the status quo ante, so that

---

40. Several early writers on criminology recognized this advantage of fines. For example, "Pecuniary punishments are highly economical, since all the evil felt by him who pays turns into an advantage for him who receives" (Bentham, 1931, chap. vi), and "Imprisonment would have been regarded in these old times [*ca.* tenth century] as a useless punishment; it does not satisfy revenge, it keeps the criminal idle, and do what we may, *it is costly*" (Pollock and Maitland, 1952, p. 516; my italics).

41. On the other hand, some transfer payments in the form of food, clothing, and shelter are included.

they are no worse off than if offenses were not committed.[42] Not only do other punishments fail to compensate, but they also require "victims" to spend additional resources in carrying out the punishment. It is not surprising, therefore, that the anger and fear felt toward ex-convicts who in fact have *not* "paid their debt to society" have resulted in additional punishments,[43] including legal restrictions on their political and economic opportunities [44] and informal restrictions on their social acceptance. Moreover, the absence of compensation encourages efforts to change and otherwise "rehabilitate" offenders through psychiatric counseling, therapy, and other programs. Since fines do compensate and do not create much additional cost, anger toward and fear of appropriately fined persons do not easily develop. As a result, additional punishments are not usually levied against "ex-finees," nor are strong efforts made to "rehabilitate" them.

One argument made against fines is that they are immoral because, in effect, they permit offenses to be bought for a price in the same way that bread or other goods are bought for a price.[45] A fine *can* be considered the price of an offense, but so too can any other form of punishment; for example, the "price" of stealing a car might be six months in jail. The only difference is in the units of measurement: fines are prices measured in monetary units, imprisonments are prices measured in time units, etc. If anything, monetary units are to be preferred here as they are generally preferred in pricing and accounting.

Optimal fines determined from equation (29) depend only on the marginal harm and cost and not at all on the economic positions of offenders. This has been criticized as unfair, and fines proportional to the in-

---

42. Bentham recognized this and said, "To furnish an indemnity to the injured party is another useful quality in a punishment. It is a means of accomplishing two objects at once – punishing an offense and repairing it: removing the evil of the first order, and putting a stop to alarm. This is a characteristic advantage of pecuniary punishments" (1931, chap. vi).

43. In the same way, the guilt felt by society in using the draft, a forced transfer *to* society, has led to additional payments to veterans in the form of education benefits, bonuses, hospitalization rights, etc.

44. See Sutherland (1960, pp. 267–68) for a list of some of these.

45. The very early English law relied heavily on monetary fines, even for murder, and it has been said that "every kind of blow or wound given to every kind of person had its price, and much of the jurisprudence of the time must have consisted of a knowledge of these preappointed prices" (Pollock and Maitland, 1952, p. 451).

The same idea was put amusingly in a recent *Mutt and Jeff* cartoon which showed a police car carrying a sign that read: "Speed limit 30 M per H – $5 fine every mile over speed limit – pick out speed you can afford."

comes of offenders have been suggested.[46] If the goal is to minimize the social loss in income from offenses, and not to take vengeance or to inflict harm on offenders, then fines should depend on the total harm done by offenders, and not directly on their income, race, sex, etc. In the same way, the monetary value of optimal prison sentences and other punishments depends on the harm, costs, and elasticities of response, but not directly on an offender's income. Indeed, if the monetary value of the punishment by, say, imprisonment were independent of income, the length of the sentence would be *inversely* related to income, because the value placed on a given sentence is positively related to income.

We might detour briefly to point out some interesting implications for the probability of conviction of the fact that the monetary value of a given fine is obviously the same for all offenders, while the monetary equivalent or "value" of a given prison sentence or probation period is generally positively related to an offender's income. The discussion in Section II suggested that actual probabilities of conviction are not fixed to all offenders but usually vary with their age, sex, race, and, in particular, income. Offenders with higher earnings have an incentive to spend more on planning their offenses, on good lawyers, on legal appeals, and even on bribery to reduce the probability of apprehension and conviction for offenses punishable by, say, a given prison term, because the cost to them of conviction is relatively large compared to the cost of these expenditures. Similarly, however, poorer offenders have an incentive to use more of their time in planning their offenses, in court appearances, and the like, to reduce the probability of conviction for offenses punishable by a given fine, because the cost to them of conviction is relatively large compared to the value of their time.[47] The implication is that the probability of conviction would be systematically related to the earnings of offenders: negatively for offenses punishable by imprisonment and positively for those punishable by fines. Although a negative relation for

---

46. For example, Bentham said, "A pecuniary punishment, if the sum is fixed, is in the highest degree unequal. . . . Fines have been determined without regard to the profit of the offense, to its evil, or to the wealth of the offender. . . . Pecuniary punishments should always be regulated by the fortune of the offender. The relative amount of the fine should be fixed, not its absolute amount; for such an offense, such a part of the offender's fortune" (1931, chap. ix). Note that optimal fines, as determined by eq. (29), do depend on "the profit of the offense" and on "its evil."

47. Note that the incentive to use time to reduce the probability of a given prison sentence is unrelated to earnings, because the punishment is fixed in time, not monetary, units; likewise, the incentive to use money to reduce the probability of a given fine is also unrelated to earnings, because the punishment is fixed in monetary, not time, units.

felonies and other offenses punishable by imprisonment has been frequently observed and deplored (see President's Commission, 1967c, pp. 139–53), I do not know of any studies of the relation for fines or of any recognition that the observed negative relation may be more a consequence of the nature of the punishment than of the influence of wealth.

Another argument made against fines is that certain crimes, like murder or rape, are so heinous that no amount of money could compensate for the harm inflicted. This argument has obvious merit and is a special case of the more general principle that fines cannot be relied on exclusively whenever the harm exceeds the resources of offenders. For then victims could not be fully compensated by offenders, and fines would have to be supplemented with prison terms or other punishments in order to discourage offenses optimally. This explains why imprisonments, probation, and parole are major punishments for the more serious felonies; considerable harm is inflicted, and felonious offenders lack sufficient resources to compensate. Since fines are preferable, it also suggests the need for a flexible system of instalment fines to enable offenders to pay fines more readily and thus avoid other punishments.

This analysis implies that if some offenders could pay the fine for a given offense and others could not,[48] the former should be punished solely by fine and the latter partly by other methods. In essence, therefore, these methods become a vehicle for punishing "debtors" to society. Before the cry is raised that the system is unfair, especially to poor offenders, consider the following.

Those punished would be debtors in "transactions" that were never agreed to by their "creditors," not in voluntary transactions, such as loans,[49] for which suitable precautions could be taken in advance by creditors. Moreover, punishment in any economic system based on voluntary market transactions inevitably must distinguish between such "debtors" and others. If a rich man purchases a car and a poor man steals one, the former is congratulated, while the latter is often sent to prison when apprehended. Yet the rich man's purchase is equivalent to a "theft" subsequently compensated by a "fine" equal to the price of the car, while the poor man, in effect, goes to prison because he cannot pay this "fine."

Whether a punishment like imprisonment in lieu of a full fine for offenders lacking sufficient resources is "fair" depends, of course, on the

---

48. In one study, about half of those convicted of misdemeanors could not pay the fines (see President's Commission, 1967c, p. 148).

49. The "debtor prisons" of earlier centuries generally housed persons who could not repay loans.

length of the prison term compared to the fine.[50] For example, a prison term of one week in lieu of a $10,000 fine would, if anything, be "unfair" to wealthy offenders paying the fine. Since imprisonment is a more costly punishment to society than fines, the loss from offenses would be reduced by a policy of leniency toward persons who are imprisoned because they cannot pay fines. Consequently, optimal prison terms for "debtors" would not be "unfair" to them in the sense that the monetary equivalent to them of the prison terms would be less than the value of optimal fines, which in turn would equal the harm caused or the "debt." [51]

It appears, however, that "debtors" are often imprisoned at rates of exchange with fines that place a low value on time in prison. Although I have not seen systematic evidence on the different punishments actually offered convicted offenders, and the choices they made, many statutes in the United States do permit fines and imprisonment that place a low value on time in prison. For example, in New York State, Class A Misdemeanors can be punished by a prison term as long as one year or a fine no

---

50. Yet without any discussion of the actual alternatives offered, the statement is made that "the money judgment assessed the punitive damages defendant hardly seems comparable in effect to the criminal sanctions of death, imprisonment, and stigmatization" ("Criminal Safeguards . . . ," 1967).

51. A formal proof is straightforward if for simplicity the probability of conviction is taken as equal to unity. For then the sole optimality condition is

$$D' + C' = -bf\left(1 - \frac{1}{\epsilon_f}\right). \qquad (1')$$

Since $D' = H' - G'$, by substitution one has

$$G' = H' + C' + bf\left(1 - \frac{1}{\epsilon_f}\right), \qquad (2')$$

and since equilibrium requires that $G' = f$,

$$f = H' + C' + bf\left(1 - \frac{1}{\epsilon_f}\right), \qquad (3')$$

or

$$f = \frac{H' + C'}{1 - b(1 - 1/\epsilon_f)}. \qquad (4')$$

If $b > 0$, $\epsilon_f < 1$ (see Sec. III), and hence by eq. (4'),

$$f < H' + C', \qquad (5')$$

where the term on the right is the full marginal harm. If p as well as f is free to vary, the analysis becomes more complicated, but the conclusion about the relative monetary values of optimal imprisonments and fines remains the same (see the Mathematical Appendix).

larger than $1,000 and Class B Misdemeanors, by a term as long as three months or a fine no larger than $500 (*Laws of New York*, 1965, chap. 1030, Arts. 70 and 80).[52] According to my analysis, these statutes permit excessive prison sentences relative to the fines, which may explain why imprisonment in lieu of fines is considered unfair to poor offenders, who often must "choose" the prison alternative.

D. COMPENSATION AND THE CRIMINAL LAW

Actual criminal proceedings in the United States appear to seek a mixture of deterrence, compensation, and vengeance. I have already indicated that these goals are somewhat contradictory and cannot generally be simultaneously achieved; for example, if punishment were by fine, minimizing the social loss from offenses would be equivalent to compensating "victims" fully, and deterrence or vengeance could only be partially pursued. Therefore, if the case for fines were accepted, and punishment by optimal fines became the norm, the traditional approach to criminal law would have to be significantly modified.

First and foremost, the primary aim of all legal proceedings would become the same: not punishment or deterrence, but simply the assessment of the "harm" done by defendants. Much of traditional criminal law would become a branch of the law of torts,[53] say "social torts," in which the public would collectively sue for "public" harm. A "criminal" action would be defined fundamentally not by the nature of the action [54] but by the inability of a person to compensate for the "harm" that he caused. Thus an action would be "criminal" precisely because it results in uncompensated "harm" to others. Criminal law would cover all such actions, while tort law would cover all other (civil) actions.

As a practical example of the fundamental changes that would be wrought, consider the antitrust field. Inspired in part by the economist's classic demonstration that monopolies distort the allocation of resources and reduce economic welfare, the United States has outlawed con-

---

52. "Violations," however, can only be punished by prison terms as long as fifteen days or fines no larger than $250. Since these are maximum punishments, the actual ones imposed by the courts can, and often are, considerably less. Note, too, that the courts can punish by imprisonment, by fine, or by *both* (*Laws of New York*, 1965, chap. 1030, Art. 60).

53. "The cardinal principle of damages in Anglo-American law [of torts] is that of *compensation* for the injury caused to plaintiff by defendant's breach of duty" (Harper and James, 1956, p. 1299).

54. Of course, many traditional criminal actions like murder or rape would still usually be criminal under this approach too.

spiracies and other constraints of trade. In practice, defendants are often simply required to cease the objectionable activity, although sometimes they are also fined, become subject to damage suits, or are jailed.

If compensation were stressed, the main purpose of legal proceedings would be to levy fines equal to [55] the harm inflicted on society by constraints of trade. There would be no point to cease and desist orders, imprisonment, ridicule, or dissolution of companies. If the economist's theory about monopoly is correct, and if optimal fines were levied, firms would automatically cease any constraints of trade, because the gain to them would be less than the harm they cause and thus less than the fines expected. On the other hand, if Schumpeter and other critics are correct, and certain constraints of trade raise the level of economic welfare, fines could fully compensate society for the harm done, and yet some constraints would not cease, because the gain to participants would exceed the harm to others.[56]

One unexpected advantage, therefore, from stressing compensation and fines rather than punishment and deterrence is that the validity of the classical position need not be judged a priori. If valid, compensating fines would discourage all constraints of trade and would achieve the classical aims. If not, such fines would permit the socially desirable constraints to continue and, at the same time, would compensate society for the harm done.

Of course, as participants in triple-damage suits are well aware, the harm done is not easily measured, and serious mistakes would be inevitable. However, it is also extremely difficult to measure the harm in many civil suits,[57] yet these continue to function, probably reasonably well on the whole. Moreover, as experience accumulated, the margin of error would decline, and rules of thumb would develop. Finally, one must

---

55. Actually, fines should exceed the harm done if the probability of conviction were less than unity. The possibility of avoiding conviction is the intellectual justification for punitive, such as triple, damages against those convicted.

56. The classical view is that $D'(M)$ always is greater than zero, where M measures the different constraints of trade and D' measures the marginal damage; the critic's view is that for some M, $D'(M) < 0$. It has been shown above that if D' always is greater than zero, compensating fines would discourage all offenses, in this case constraints of trade, while if D' sometimes is less than zero, some offenses would remain (unless $C'[M]$, the marginal cost of detecting and convicting offenders, were sufficiently large relative to D').

57. Harper and James said, "Sometimes [compensation] can be accomplished with a fair degree of accuracy. But obviously it cannot be done in anything but a figurative and essentially speculative way for many of the consequences of personal injury. Yet it is the aim of the law to attain at least a rough correspondence between the amount awarded as damages and the extent of the suffering" (1956, p. 1301).

realize that difficult judgments are also required by the present antitrust policy, such as deciding that certain industries are "workably" competitive or that certain mergers reduce competition. An emphasis on fines and compensation would at least help avoid irrelevant issues by focusing attention on the information most needed for intelligent social policy.

VI. PRIVATE EXPENDITURES AGAINST CRIME

A variety of private as well as public actions also attempt to reduce the number and incidence of crimes: guards, doormen, and accountants are employed, locks and alarms installed, insurance coverage extended, parks and neighborhoods avoided, taxis used in place of walking or subways, and so on. Table 1 lists close to $2 billion of such expenditures in 1965, and this undoubtedly is a gross underestimate of the total. The need for private action is especially great in highly interdependent modern economies, where frequently a person must trust his resources, including his person, to the "care" of employees, employers, customers, or sellers.

If each person tries to minimize his expected loss in income from crimes, optimal private decisions can be easily derived from the previous discussion of optimal public ones. For each person there is a loss function similar to that given by equation (18):

$$L_j = H_j(O_j) + C_j(p_j, O_j, C, C_k) + b_j p_j f_j O_j. \tag{31}$$

The term H_j represents the harm to j from the O_j offenses committed against j, while C_j represents his cost of achieving a probability of conviction of p_j for offenses committed against him. Note that C_j not only is positively related to O_j but also is negatively related to C, public expenditures on crime, and to C_k, the set of private expenditures by other persons.[58]

The term $b_j p_j f_j O_j$ measures the expected [59] loss to j from punishment of offenders committing any of the O_j. Whereas most punishments result in a net loss to society as a whole, they often produce a gain for the actual victims. For example, punishment by fines given to the actual victims is just a transfer payment for society but is a clear gain to victims; similarly,

---

58. An increase in $C_k - O_j$ and C held constant—presumably helps solve offenses against j, because more of those against k would be solved.

59. The expected private loss, unlike the expected social loss, is apt to have considerable variance because of the small number of independent offenses committed against any single person. If j were not risk neutral, therefore, L would have to be modified to include a term that depended on the distribution of $b_j p_j f_j O_j$.

punishment by imprisonment is a net loss to society but is a negligible loss to victims, since they usually pay a negligible part of imprisonment costs. This is why b_j is often less than or equal to zero, at the same time that b, the coefficient of social loss, is greater than or equal to zero.

Since b_j and f_j are determined primarily by public policy on punishments, the main decision variable directly controlled by j is p_j. If he chooses a p_j that minimizes L_j, the optimality condition analogous to equation (22) is

$$H'_j + C'_j + C_{jp_j} \frac{\partial p_j}{\partial O_j} = -b_j p_j f_j \left(1 - \frac{1}{\epsilon_{jp_j}}\right).^{60} \tag{32}$$

The elasticity ϵ_{jp_j} measures the effect of a change in p_j on the number of offenses committed against j. If $b_j < 0$, and if the left-hand side of equation (32), the marginal cost of changing O_j, were greater than zero, then (32) implies that $\epsilon_{jp_j} > 1$. Since offenders can substitute among victims, ϵ_{jp_j} is probably much larger than ϵ_p, the response of the total number of offenses to a change in the average probability, p. There is no inconsistency, therefore, between a requirement from the optimality condition given by (22) that $\epsilon_p < 1$ and a requirement from (32) that $\epsilon_{jp_j} > 1$.

VII. SOME APPLICATIONS

A. OPTIMAL BENEFITS

Our analysis of crime is a generalization of the economist's analysis of external harm or diseconomies. Analytically, the generalization consists in introducing costs of apprehension and conviction, which make the

---

60. I have assumed that

$$\frac{\partial C}{\partial p_j} = \frac{\partial C_k}{\partial p_j} = 0,$$

in other words, that j is too "unimportant" to influence other expenditures. Although usually reasonable, this does suggest a modification to the optimality conditions given by eqs. (21) and (22). Since the effects of public expenditures depend on the level of private ones, and since the public is sufficiently "important" to influence private actions, eq. (22) has to be modified to

$$D' + C' + C_p \frac{\partial p}{\partial O} + \sum_{i=1}^{n} \frac{dC}{dC_i} \frac{dC_i}{dp} \frac{\partial p}{\partial O} = -bpf \left(1 + \frac{1}{\epsilon_p}\right), \tag{22'}$$

and similarly for eq. (21). "The" probability p is, of course, a weighted average of the p_j. Eq. (22') incorporates the presumption that an increase in public expenditures would be partially thwarted by an induced decrease in private ones.

probability of apprehension and conviction an important decision variable, and in treating punishment by imprisonment and other methods as well as by monetary payments. A crime is apparently not so different analytically from any other activity that produces external harm and when crimes are punishable by fines, the analytical differences virtually vanish.

Discussions of external economies or advantages are usually perfectly symmetrical to those of diseconomies, yet one searches in vain for analogues to the law of torts and criminality. Generally, compensation cannot be collected for the external advantages as opposed to harm caused, and no public officials comparable to policemen and district attorneys apprehend and "convict" benefactors rather than offenders. Of course, there is public interest in benefactors: medals, prizes, titles, and other privileges have been awarded to military heroes, government officials, scientists, scholars, artists, and businessmen by public and private bodies. Among the most famous are Nobel Prizes, Lenin Prizes, the Congressional Medal of Honor, knighthood, and patent rights. But these are piecemeal efforts that touch a tiny fraction of the population and lack the guidance of any body of law that codifies and analyzes different kinds of advantages.

Possibly the explanation for this lacuna is that criminal and tort law developed at the time when external harm was more common than advantages, or possibly the latter have been difficult to measure and thus considered too prone to favoritism. In any case, it is clear that the asymmetry in the law does not result from any analytical asymmetry, for a formal analysis of advantages, benefits, and benefactors can be developed that is quite symmetrical to the analysis of damages, offenses, and offenders. A function $A(B)$, for example, can give the net social advantages from B benefits in the same way that $D(O)$ gives the net damages from O offenses. Likewise, $K(B, p_1)$ can give the cost of apprehending and rewarding benefactors, where p_1 is the probability of so doing, with K' and $K_p > 0$; $B(p_1, a, v)$ can give the supply of benefits, where a is the award per benefit and v represents other determinants, with $\partial B/\partial p_1$ and $\partial B/\partial a > 0$; and b_1 can be the fraction of a that is a net loss to society. Instead of a loss function showing the decrease in social income from offenses, there can be a profit function showing the increase in income from benefits:

$$\Pi = A(B) - K(B, p_1) - b_1 p_1 aB. \tag{33}$$

If Π is maximized by choosing appropriate values of p_1 and a, the optimality conditions analogous to equations (21) and (22) are

$$A' - K' = b_1 p_1 a \left(1 + \frac{1}{e_a}\right) \tag{34}$$

and

$$A' - K' - K_p \frac{\partial p_1}{\partial B} = b_1 p_1 a \left(1 + \frac{1}{e_p}\right), \tag{35}$$

where

$$e_a = \frac{\partial B}{\partial a} \frac{a}{B}$$

and

$$e_p = \frac{\partial B}{\partial p_1} \frac{p_1}{B}$$

are both greater than zero. The implications of these equations are related to and yet differ in some important respects from those discussed earlier for (21) and (22).

For example, if $b_1 > 0$, which means that a is not a pure transfer but costs society resources, clearly (34) and (35) imply that $e_p > e_a$, since both $K_p > 0$ and $\partial p_1 / \partial B > 0$. This is analogous to the implication of (21) and (22) that $\epsilon_p > \epsilon_f$, but, while the latter implies that, at the margin, offenders are risk *preferrers*, the former implies that, at the margin, benefactors are risk *avoiders*.[61] Thus, while the optimal values of p and f would be in a region where "crime does not pay" — in the sense that the

---

61. The relation $e_p > e_a$ holds if, and only if,

$$\frac{\partial EU}{\partial p_1} \frac{p_1}{U} > \frac{\partial EU}{\partial a} \frac{a}{U}, \tag{1'}$$

where

$$EU = p_1 U(Y + a) + (1 - p_1)U(Y) \tag{2'}$$

(see the discussion on pp. 177–78). By differentiating eq. (2'), one can write (1') as

$$p_1[U(Y + a) - U(Y)] > p_1 a U'(Y + a), \tag{3'}$$

or

$$\frac{U(Y + a) - U(Y)}{a} > U'(Y + a). \tag{4'}$$

But (4') holds if everywhere $U'' < 0$ and does not hold if everywhere $U'' \geq 0$, which was to be proved.

marginal income of criminals would be less than that available to them in less risky legal activities – the optimal values of p_1 and a would be where "benefits do pay" – in the same sense that the marginal income of benefactors would exceed that available to them in less risky activities. In this sense it "pays" to do "good" and does not "pay" to do "bad."

As an illustration of the analysis, consider the problem of rewarding inventors for their inventions. The function $A(B)$ gives the total social value of B inventions, and A' gives the marginal value of an additional one. The function $K(B, p_1)$ gives the cost of finding and rewarding inventors; if a patent system is used, it measures the cost of a patent office, of preparing applications, and of the lawyers, judges, and others involved in patent litigation.[62] The elasticities e_p and e_a measure the response of inventors to changes in the probability and magnitude of awards, while b_1 measures the social cost of the method used to award inventors. With a patent system, the cost consists in a less extensive use of an invention than would otherwise occur, and in any monopoly power so created.

Equations (34) and (35) imply that with any system having $b_1 > 0$, the smaller the elasticities of response of inventors, the smaller should be the probability and magnitude of awards. (The value of a patent can be changed, for example, by changing its life.) This shows the relevance of the controversy between those who maintain that most inventions stem from a basic desire "to know" and those who maintain that most stem from the prospects of financial awards, especially today with the emphasis on systematic investment in research and development. The former quite consistently usually advocate a weak patent system, while the latter equally consistently advocate its strengthening.

Even if A', the marginal value of an invention, were "sizable," the optimal decision would be to abolish property rights in an invention, that is, to set $p_1 = 0$, if b_1 and K [63] were sufficiently large and/or the elasticities e_p and e_a sufficiently small. Indeed, practically all arguments to eliminate or greatly alter the patent system have been based either on its alleged costliness, large K or b_1, or lack of effectiveness, low e_p or e_a (see, for example, Plant, 1934, or Arrow, 1962).

If a patent system were replaced by a system of cash prizes, the elasticities of response would become irrelevant for the determination of

---

62. These costs are not entirely trivial: for example, in 1966 the U.S. Patent Office alone spent $34 million (see Bureau of the Budget, 1967), and much more was probably spent in preparing applications and in litigation.

63. Presumably one reason patents are not permitted on basic research is the difficulty (that is, cost) of discovering the ownership of new concepts and theorems.

optimal policies, because b_1 would then be approximately zero.[64] A system of prizes would, moreover, have many of the same other advantages that fines have in punishing offenders (see the discussion in Sec. V). One significant advantage of a patent system, however, is that it automatically "meters" A', that is, provides an award that is automatically positively related to A', while a system of prizes (or of fines and imprisonment) has to estimate A' (or D') independently and often somewhat arbitrarily.

B. THE EFFECTIVENESS OF PUBLIC POLICY

The anticipation of conviction and punishment reduces the loss from offenses and thus increases social welfare by discouraging some offenders. What determines the increase in welfare, that is "effectiveness," of public efforts to discourage offenses? The model developed in Section III can be used to answer this question if social welfare is measured by income and if "effectiveness" is defined as a ratio of the maximum feasible increase in income to the increase if all offenses causing net damages were abolished by fiat. The maximum feasible increase is achieved by choosing optimal values of the probability of apprehension and conviction, p, and the size of punishments, f (assuming that the coefficient of social loss from punishment, b, is given).[65]

Effectiveness so defined can vary between zero and unity and depends essentially on two behavioral relations: the costs of apprehension and conviction and the elasticities of response of offenses to changes in p and f. The smaller these costs or the greater these elasticities, the smaller the cost of achieving any given reduction in offenses and thus the greater

---

64. The right side of both (34) and (35) would vanish, and the optimality conditions would be

$$A' - K' = 0 \tag{34'}$$

and

$$A' - K' - K_p \frac{\partial p_1}{\partial B} = 0. \tag{35'}$$

Since these equations are not satisfied by any finite values of p_1 and a, there is a difficulty in allocating the incentives between p_1 and a (see the similar discussion for fines in Sec. V).

65. In symbols, effectiveness is defined as

$$E = \frac{D(O_1) - [D(\hat{O}) + C(\hat{p}, \hat{O}) + b\hat{p}\hat{f}\hat{O}]}{D(O_1) - D(O_2)},$$

where $\hat{p}$, $\hat{f}$, and $\hat{O}$ are optimal values, O_1 offenses would occur if $p = f = 0$, and O_2 is the value of O that minimizes D.

the effectiveness. The elasticities may well differ considerably among different kinds of offenses. For example, crimes of passion, like murder or rape, or crimes of youth, like auto theft, are often said to be less responsive to changes in p and f than are more calculating crimes by adults, like embezzlement, antitrust violation, or bank robbery. The elasticities estimated by Smigel (1965) and Ehrlich (1967) for seven major felonies do differ considerably but are not clearly smaller for murder, rape, auto theft, and assault than for robbery, burglary, and larceny.[66]

Probably effectiveness differs among offenses more because of differences in the costs of apprehension and conviction than in the elasticities of response. An important determinant of these costs, and one that varies greatly, is the time between commission and detection of an offense.[67] For the earlier an offense is detected, the earlier the police can be brought in and the more likely that the victim is able personally to identify the offender. This suggests that effectiveness is greater for robbery than for a related felony like burglary, or for minimum-wage and fair-employment legislation than for other white-collar legislation like antitrust and public-utility regulation.[68]

C. A THEORY OF COLLUSION

The theory developed in this essay can be applied to any effort to preclude certain kinds of behavior, regardless of whether the behavior is "unlawful." As an example, consider efforts by competing firms to collude in order to obtain monopoly profits. Economists lack a satisfactory theory of the determinants of price and output policies by firms in an industry, a theory that could predict under what conditions perfectly competitive, monopolistic, or various intermediate kinds of behavior would emerge. One by-product of our approach to crime and punishment is a theory of collusion that appears to fill a good part of this lacuna.[69]

The gain to firms from colluding is positively related to the elasticity of their marginal cost curves and is inversely related to the elasticity of

---

66. A theoretical argument that also casts doubt on the assertion that less "calculating" offenders are less responsive to changes in p and f can be found in Becker (1962).

67. A study of crimes in parts of Los Angeles during January, 1966, found that "more than half the arrests were made within 8 hours of the crime, and almost two-thirds were made within the first week" (President's Commission 1967e, p. 8).

68. Evidence relating to the effectiveness of actual, which are not necessarily optimal, penalties for these white-collar crimes can be found in Stigler (1962, 1966), Landes (1966), and Johnson (1967).

69. Jacob Mincer first suggested this application to me.

their collective demand curve. A firm that violates a collusive arrangement by pricing below or producing more than is specified can be said to commit an "offense" against the collusion. The resulting harm to the collusion would depend on the number of violations and on the elasticities of demand and marginal cost curves, since the gain from colluding depends on these elasticities.

If violations could be eliminated without cost, the optimal solution would obviously be to eliminate all of them and to engage in pure monopoly pricing. In general, however, as with other kinds of offenses, there are two costs of eliminating violations. There is first of all the cost of discovering violations and of "apprehending" violators. This cost is greater, the greater the desired probability of detection and the greater the number of violations. Other things the same, the latter is usually positively related to the number of firms in an industry, which partly explains why economists typically relate monopoly power to concentration. The cost of achieving a given probability of detection also depends on the number of firms, on the number of customers, on the stability of customer buying patterns, and on government policies toward collusive arrangements (see Stigler, 1964).

Second, there is the cost to the collusion of punishing violators. The most favorable situation is one in which fines could be levied against violators and collected by the collusion. If fines and other legal recourse are ruled out, methods like predatory price-cutting or violence have to be used, and they hurt the collusion as well as violators.

Firms in a collusion are assumed to choose probabilities of detection, punishments to violators, and prices and outputs that minimize their loss from violations, which would at the same time maximize their gain from colluding. Optimal prices and outputs would be closer to the competitive position the more elastic demand curves were, the greater the number of sellers and buyers, the less transferable punishments were, and the more hostile to collusion governments were. Note that misallocation of resources could not be measured simply by the deviation of actual from competitive outputs but would depend also on the cost of enforcing collusions. Note further, and more importantly, that this theory, unlike most theories of pricing, provides for continuous variation from purely competitive through intermediate situations to purely monopolistic pricing. These situations differ primarily because of differences in the "optimal" number of violations, which in turn are related to differences in the elasticities, concentrations, legislation, etc., already mentioned.

These ideas appear to be helpful in understanding the relative success of collusions in illegal industries themselves! Just as firms in legal industries have an incentive to collude to raise prices and profits, so too do firms producing illegal products, such as narcotics, gambling, prostitution, and abortion. The "syndicate" is an example of a presumably highly successful collusion that covers several illegal products.[70] In a country like the United States that prohibits collusions, those in illegal industries would seem to have an advantage, because force and other illegal methods could be used against violators without the latter having much legal recourse. On the other hand, in countries like prewar Germany that legalized collusions, those in legal industries would have an advantage, because violators could often be legally prosecuted. One would predict, therefore, from this consideration alone, relatively more successful collusions in illegal industries in the United States, and in legal ones in prewar Germany.

VIII. SUMMARY AND CONCLUDING REMARKS

This essay uses economic analysis to develop optimal public and private policies to combat illegal behavior. The public's decision variables are its expenditures on police, courts, etc., which help determine the probability (p) that an offense is discovered and the offender apprehended and convicted, the size of the punishment for those convicted (f), and the form of the punishment: imprisonment, probation, fine, etc. Optimal values of these variables can be chosen subject to, among other things, the constraints imposed by three behavioral relations. One shows the damages caused by a given number of illegal actions, called offenses (O), another the cost of achieving a given p, and the third the effect of changes in p and f on O.

"Optimal" decisions are interpreted to mean decisions that minimize the social loss in income from offenses. This loss is the sum of damages, costs of apprehension and conviction, and costs of carrying out the punishments imposed, and can be minimized simultaneously with respect to p, f, and the form of f unless one or more of these variables is constrained by "outside" considerations. The optimality conditions derived from the minimization have numerous interesting implications that can be illustrated by a few examples.

If carrying out the punishment were costly, as it is with probation, imprisonment, or parole, the elasticity of response of offenses with respect to a change in p would generally, in equilibrium, have to exceed its

---

70. An interpretation of the syndicate along these lines is also found in Schilling (1967).

response to a change in f. This implies, if entry into illegal activities can be explained by the same model of choice that economists use to explain entry into legal activities, that offenders are (at the margin) "risk preferrers." Consequently, illegal activities "would not pay" (at the margin) in the sense that the real income received would be less than what could be received in less risky legal activities. The conclusion that "crime would not pay" is an optimality condition and not an implication about the efficiency of the police or courts; indeed, it holds for any level of efficiency, as long as optimal values of p and f appropriate to each level are chosen.

If costs were the same, the optimal values of both p and f would be greater, the greater the damage caused by an offense. Therefore, offenses like murder and rape should be solved more frequently and punished more severely than milder offenses like auto theft and petty larceny. Evidence on actual probabilities and punishments in the United States is strongly consistent with this implication of the optimality analysis.

Fines have several advantages over other punishments: for example, they conserve resources, compensate society as well as punish offenders, and simplify the determination of optimal p's and f's. Not surprisingly, fines are the most common punishment and have grown in importance over time. Offenders who cannot pay fines have to be punished in other ways, but the optimality analysis implies that the monetary value to them of these punishments should generally be less than the fines.

Vengeance, deterrence, safety, rehabilitation, and compensation are perhaps the most important of the many desiderata proposed throughout history. Next to these, minimizing the social loss in income may seem narrow, bland, and even quaint. Unquestionably, the income criterion can be usefully generalized in several directions, and a few have already been suggested in the essay. Yet one should not lose sight of the fact that it is more general and powerful than it may seem and actually includes more dramatic desiderata as special cases. For example, if punishment were by an optimal fine, minimizing the loss in income would be equivalent to compensating "victims" fully and would eliminate the "alarm" that so worried Bentham; or it would be equivalent to deterring all offenses causing great damage if the cost of apprehending, convicting, and punishing these offenders were relatively small. Since the same could also be demonstrated for vengeance or rehabilitation, the moral should be clear: minimizing the loss in income is actually very general and thus is *more useful* than these catchy and dramatic but inflexible desiderata.

This essay concentrates almost entirely on determining optimal policies to combat illegal behavior and pays little attention to actual policies. The small amount of evidence on actual policies that I have examined certainly suggests a positive correspondence with optimal policies. For example, it is found for seven major felonies in the United States that more damaging ones are penalized more severely, that the elasticity of response of offenses to changes in p exceeds the response to f, and that both are usually less than unity, all as predicted by the optimality analysis. There are, however, some discrepancies too: for example, the actual tradeoff between imprisonment and fines in different statutes is frequently less, rather than the predicted more, favorable to those imprisoned. Although many more studies of actual policies are needed, they are seriously hampered on the empirical side by grave limitations in the quantity and quality of data on offenses, convictions, costs, etc., and on the analytical side by the absence of a reliable theory of political decision-making.

Reasonable men will often differ on the amount of damages or benefits caused by different activities. To some, any wage rates set by competitive labor markets are permissible, while to others, rates below a certain minimum are violations of basic rights; to some, gambling, prostitution, and even abortion should be freely available to anyone willing to pay the market price, while to others, gambling is sinful and abortion is murder. These differences are basic to the development and implementation of public policy but have been excluded from my inquiry. I assume consensus on damages and benefits and simply try to work out rules for an optimal implementation of this consensus.

The main contribution of this essay, as I see it, is to demonstrate that optimal policies to combat illegal behavior are part of an optimal allocation of resources. Since economics has been developed to handle resource allocation, an "economic" framework becomes applicable to, and helps enrich, the analysis of illegal behavior. At the same time, certain unique aspects of the latter enrich economic analysis: some punishments, such as imprisonments, are necessarily nonmonetary and are a cost to society as well as to offenders; the degree of uncertainty is a decision variable that enters both the revenue and cost functions; etc.

Lest the reader be repelled by the apparent novelty of an "economic" framework for illegal behavior, let him recall that two important contributors to criminology during the eighteenth and nineteenth centuries, Beccaria and Bentham, explicitly applied an economic calculus. Unfortunately, such an approach has lost favor during the last hundred years, and my efforts can be viewed as a resurrection, modernization, and thereby I hope improvement, of these much earlier pioneering studies.

MATHEMATICAL APPENDIX

This Appendix derives the effects of changes in various parameters on the optimal values of p and f. It is assumed throughout that $b > 0$ and that equilibrium occurs where

$$\frac{\partial D}{\partial O} + \frac{\partial C}{\partial O} + \frac{\partial C}{\partial p}\frac{\partial p}{\partial O} = D' + C' + C_p\frac{\partial p}{\partial O} > 0;$$

the analysis could easily be extended to cover negative values of b and of this marginal cost term. The conclusion in the text (Sec. II) that $D'' + C'' > 0$ is relied on here. I take it to be a reasonable first approximation that the elasticities of O with respect to p or f are constant. At several places a sufficient condition for the conclusions reached is that

$$C_{pO} = C_{Op} = \frac{\partial^2 C}{\partial p\partial O} = \frac{\partial^2 C}{\partial O\partial p}$$

is "small" relative to some other terms. This condition is utilized in the form of a strong assumption that $C_{pO} = 0$, although I cannot claim any supporting intuitive or other evidence.

The social loss in income from offenses has been defined as

$$L = D(O) + C(O, p) + bpfO. \tag{A1}$$

If b and p were fixed, the value of f that minimized L would be found from the necessary condition

$$\frac{\partial L}{\partial f} = 0 = (D' + C')\frac{\partial O}{\partial f} + bpf(1 - E_f)\frac{\partial O}{\partial f}, \tag{A2}$$

or

$$0 = D' + C' + bpf(1 - E_f), \tag{A3}$$

if

$$\frac{\partial O}{\partial f} = O_f \neq 0,$$

where

$$E_f = \frac{-\partial f}{\partial O}\frac{O}{f}.$$

The sufficient condition would be that $\partial^2 L/\partial f^2 > 0$; using $\partial L/\partial f = 0$ and E_f is constant, this condition becomes

$$\frac{\partial^2 L}{\partial f^2} = (D'' + C'')O_f^2 + bp(1 - E_f)O_f > 0, \tag{A4}$$

or

$$\Delta \equiv D'' + C'' + bp(1 - E_f)\frac{1}{O_f} > 0. \tag{A5}$$

Since $D' + C' > 0$, and b is not less than zero, equation (A3) implies that $E_f > 1$. Therefore Δ would be greater than zero, since we are assuming that $D'' + C'' > 0$; and $\hat{f}$, the value of f satisfying (A3), would minimize (locally) the loss L.

Suppose that D' is positively related to an exogenous variable α. The effect of a change in α on $\hat{f}$ can be found by differentiating equation (A3):

$$D'_\alpha + (D'' + C'')O_f\frac{d\hat{f}}{d\alpha} + bp(1 - E_f)\frac{d\hat{f}}{d\alpha} = 0,$$

or

$$\frac{d\hat{f}}{d\alpha} = \frac{-D'_\alpha(1/O_f)}{\Delta}. \tag{A6}$$

Since $\Delta > 0$, $O_f < 0$, and by assumption $D'_\alpha > 0$, then

$$\frac{d\hat{f}}{d\alpha} = \frac{+}{+} > 0. \tag{A7}$$

In a similar way it can be shown that, if C' is positively related to an exogenous variable β,

$$\frac{d\hat{f}}{d\beta} = \frac{-C'_\beta(1/O_f)}{\Delta} = \frac{+}{+} > 0. \tag{A8}$$

If b is positively related to γ, then

$$(D'' + C'')O_f\frac{d\hat{f}}{d\gamma} + bp(1 - E_f)\frac{d\hat{f}}{d\gamma} + pf(1 - E_f)b\gamma = 0,$$

or

$$\frac{d\hat{f}}{d\gamma} = \frac{-b_\gamma pf(1 - E_f)(1/O_f)}{\Delta}. \tag{A9}$$

Since $1 - E_f < 0$, and by assumption $b_\gamma > 0$,

$$\frac{d\hat{f}}{d\gamma} = \frac{-}{+} < 0. \tag{A10}$$

Note that since $1/E_f < 1$,

$$\frac{d(p\hat{f}O)}{d\gamma} < 0. \tag{A11}$$

If E_f is positively related to δ, then

$$\frac{d\hat{f}}{d\delta} = \frac{E_{f\delta}bpf(1/O_f)}{\Delta} = \frac{-}{+} < 0. \tag{A12}$$

Since the elasticity of O with respect to f equals

$$\epsilon_f = -O_f \frac{f}{O} = \frac{1}{E_f},$$

by (A12), a reduction in ϵ_f would reduce $\hat{f}$.

Suppose that p is related to the exogenous variable r. Then the effect of a shift in r on $\hat{f}$ can be found from

$$(D'' + C'')O_f \frac{d\hat{f}}{dr} + (D'' + C'')O_p p_r + C_{pO} p_r + bp(1 - E_f) \frac{\partial \hat{f}}{\partial r} + bf(1 - E_f)p_r = 0,$$

or

$$\frac{d\hat{f}}{dr} = \frac{-(D'' + C'')O_p(1/O_f)p_r - bf(1 - E_f)p_r(1/O_f)}{\Delta}, \tag{A13}$$

since by assumption $C_{pO} = 0$. Since $O_p < 0$, and $(D'' + C'') > 0$,

$$\frac{d\hat{f}}{dr} = \frac{(-) + (-)}{+} = \frac{-}{+} < 0. \tag{A14}$$

If f rather than p were fixed, the value of p that minimizes L, $\hat{p}$, could be found from

$$\frac{\partial L}{\partial p} = [D' + C' + C_p \frac{1}{O_p} + bpf(1 - E_p)]O_p = 0, \tag{A15}$$

as long as

$$\frac{\partial^2 L}{\partial p^2} = [(D'' + C'')O_p + C_p' + C_{pp} \frac{1}{O_p} + C_{pO} + C_p \frac{\partial^2 p}{\partial O \partial p}$$

$$+ bf(1 - E_p)]O_p > 0. \tag{A16}$$

Since $C_p' = C_{pO} = 0$, (A16) would hold if

$$\Delta' \equiv D'' + C'' + C_{pp} \frac{1}{O_p^2} + C_p \frac{1}{O_p} \frac{\partial^2 p}{\partial O \partial p} + bf(1 - E_p) \frac{1}{O_p} > 0. \tag{A17}$$

It is suggested in Section II that C_{pp} is generally greater than zero. If, as assumed,

$$D' + C' + C_p \frac{1}{O_p} > 0,$$

equation (A15) implies that $E_p > 1$ and thus that

$$bf(1 - E_p) \frac{1}{O_p} > 0.$$

If E_p were constant, $\partial^2 p/\partial O \partial p$ would be negative,[71] and, therefore, $C_p(1/O_p)$ $(\partial^2 p/\partial O \partial p)$ would be positive. Hence, none of the terms of (A17) are negative, and a value of p satisfying equation (A15) would be a local minimum.

The effects of changes in different parameters on $\hat{p}$ are similar to those already derived for $\hat{f}$ and can be written without comment:

$$\frac{d\hat{p}}{d\alpha} = \frac{-D'_a(1/O_p)}{\Delta'} > 0, \tag{A18}$$

$$\frac{d\hat{p}}{d\beta} = \frac{-C'_\beta(1/O_p)}{\Delta'} > 0, \tag{A19}$$

and

$$\frac{d\hat{p}}{d\gamma} = \frac{-b_\gamma pf(1 - E_p)(1/O_p)}{\Delta'} < 0. \tag{A20}$$

If E_p is positively related to δ',

$$\frac{d\hat{p}}{d\delta'} = \frac{E_{p\delta'}bpf(1/O_p)}{\Delta'} < 0. \tag{A21}$$

If C_p were positively related to the parameter s, the effect of a change in s on $\hat{p}$ would equal

$$\frac{d\hat{p}}{ds} = \frac{-C_{ps}(1/O_p^2)}{\Delta'} < 0. \tag{A22}$$

If f were related to the exogenous parameter t, the effect of a change in t on $\hat{p}$ would be given by

$$\frac{d\hat{p}}{dt} = \frac{-(D'' + C'')O_p f_t(1/O_p) - bf(1 - E_p)f_t(1/O_p) - C_p(\partial^2 p/\partial O \partial f)f_t(1/O_p)}{\Delta'} < 0 \tag{A23}$$

(with $C_{po} = 0$), since all the terms in the numerator are negative.

If both p and f were subject to control, L would be minimized by choosing

---

71. If E_p and E_f are constants, $O = kp^{-a}f^{-b}$, where $a = 1/E_p$ and $b = 1/E_f$.

Then

$$\frac{\partial p}{\partial O} = -\frac{1}{ka} p^{a+1}f^b,$$

and

$$\frac{\partial^2 p}{\partial O \partial p} = \frac{-(a + 1)}{ka} p^a f^b < 0.$$

optimal values of both variables simultaneously. These would be given by the solutions to the two first-order conditions, equations (A2) and (A15), assuming that certain more general second-order conditions were satisfied. The effects of changes in various parameters on these optimal values can be found by differentiating both first-order conditions and incorporating the restrictions of the second-order conditions.

The values of p and f satisfying (A2) and (A15), $\hat{p}$ and $\hat{f}$, minimize L if

$$L_{pp} > 0, \quad L_{ff} > 0, \tag{A24}$$

and

$$L_{pp}L_{ff} > L_{fp}^2 = L_{pf}^2. \tag{A25}$$

But $L_{pp} = O_p^2\Delta'$, and $L_{ff} = O_f^2\Delta$, and since both Δ' and Δ have been shown to be greater than zero, (A24) is proved already, and only (A25) remains. By differentiating L_f with respect to p and utilizing the first-order condition that $L_f = 0$, one has

$$L_{fp} = O_f O_p[D'' + C'' + bf(1 - E_f)p_0] = O_f O_p\Sigma, \tag{A26}$$

where Σ equals the term in brackets. Clearly $\Sigma > 0$.

By substitution, (A25) becomes

$$\Delta\Delta' > \Sigma^2, \tag{A27}$$

and (A27) holds if Δ and Δ' are both greater than Σ. $\Delta > \Sigma$ means that

$$D'' + C'' + bp(1 - E_f)f_0 > D'' + C'' + bf(1 - E_f)p_0, \tag{A28}$$

or

$$\frac{bfp}{O}(1 - E_f)E_f < \frac{bpf}{O}(1 - E_f)E_p. \tag{A29}$$

Since $1 - E_f < 0$, (A29) implies that

$$E_f > E_p, \tag{A30}$$

which necessarily holds given the assumption that $b > 0$; prove this by combining the two first-order conditions (A2) and (A15). $\Delta' > \Sigma$ means that

$$D'' + C'' + C_{pp}p_0^2 + C_p p_0 p_{0p} + bf(1 - E_p)p_0 > D'' + C'' + bf(1 - E_f)p_0. \tag{A31}$$

Since $C_{pp}p_0^2 > 0$, and $p_0 < 0$, this necessarily holds if

$$C_p p p_{0p} + bpf(1 - E_p) < bpf(1 - E_f). \tag{A32}$$

By eliminating $D' + C'$ from the first-order conditions (A2) and (A15) and by combining terms, one has

$$C_p p_0 - bpf(E_p - E_f) = 0. \tag{A33}$$

By combining (A32) and (A33), one gets the condition

$$C_p p p_{Op} < C_p p_O,$$ (A34)

or

$$E_{pO,p} = \frac{p}{p_O} \frac{\partial p_O}{\partial p} > 1.$$ (A35)

It can be shown that

$$E_{pO,p} = 1 + \frac{1}{E_p} > 1,$$ (A36)

and, therefore, (A35) is proven.

It has now been proved that the values of p and f that satisfy the first-order conditions (A2) and (A15) do indeed minimize (locally) L. Changes in different parameters change these optimal values, and the direction and magnitude can be found from the two linear equations

$$O_f \Delta \frac{\partial \tilde{f}}{\partial z} + O_p \Sigma \frac{\partial \tilde{p}}{\partial z} = C_1$$

and (A37)

$$O_f \Sigma \frac{\partial \tilde{f}}{\partial z} + O_p \Delta' \frac{\partial \tilde{p}}{\partial z} = C_2$$

By Cramer's rule,

$$\frac{\partial \tilde{f}}{\partial z} = \frac{C_1 O_p \Delta' - C_2 O_p \Sigma}{O_p O_f (\Delta \Delta' - \Sigma^2)} = \frac{O_p (C_1 \Delta' - C_2 \Sigma)}{+},$$ (A38)

$$\frac{\partial \tilde{p}}{\partial z} = \frac{C_2 O_f \Delta - C_1 O_f \Sigma}{O_p O_f (\Delta \Delta' - \Sigma^2)} = \frac{O_f (C_2 \Delta - C_1 \Sigma)}{+},$$ (A39)

and the signs of both derivatives are the same as the signs of the numerators.

Consider the effect of a change in D' resulting from a change in the parameter α. It is apparent that $C_1 = C_2 = -D'_\alpha$, and by substitution

$$\frac{\partial \tilde{f}}{\partial \alpha} = \frac{-O_p D'_\alpha (\Delta' - \Sigma)}{+} = \frac{+}{+} > 0$$ (A40)

and

$$\frac{\partial \tilde{p}}{\partial \alpha} = \frac{-O_p D'_\alpha (\Delta - \Sigma)}{+} = \frac{+}{+} > 0,$$ (A41)

since O_f and $O_p < 0$, $D'_\alpha > 0$, and Δ and $\Delta' > \Sigma$.

Similarly, if C' is changed by a change in β, $C_1 = C_2 = -C'_\beta$,

$$\frac{\partial \tilde{f}}{\partial \beta} = \frac{-O_p C'_\beta (\Delta' - \Sigma)}{+} = \frac{+}{+} > 0,$$ (A42)

and

$$\frac{\partial \bar{p}}{\partial \beta} = \frac{-O_f C_\beta'(\Delta - \Sigma)}{+} = \frac{+}{+} > 0.$$ (A43)

If E_f is changed by a change in δ, $C_1 = E_{f\delta}bpf$, $C_2 = 0$,

$$\frac{\partial \tilde{f}}{\partial \delta} = \frac{O_p E_f bpf \Delta'}{+} = \frac{-}{+} < 0,$$ (A44)

and

$$\frac{\partial \bar{p}}{\partial \delta} = \frac{-O_f E_f bpf \Sigma}{+} = \frac{+}{+} > 0.$$ (A45)

Similarly, if E_p is changed by a change in δ', $C_1 = 0$, $C_2 = E_{p\delta'}bpf$,

$$\frac{\partial \tilde{f}}{\partial \delta'} = -\frac{O_p E_{p\delta'} bpf \Sigma}{+} = \frac{+}{+} > 0,$$ (A46)

and

$$\frac{\partial \bar{p}}{\partial \delta'} = \frac{O_f E_{p\delta'} bpf \Delta}{+} = \frac{-}{+} < 0.$$ (A47)

If b is changed by a change in γ, $C_1 = -b_\gamma pf(1 - E_f)$, $C_2 = -b_\gamma pf(1 - E_p)$, and

$$\frac{\partial \tilde{f}}{\partial \gamma} = \frac{-O_p b_\gamma pf[(1 - E_f)\Delta' - (1 - E_p)\Sigma]}{+} = \frac{-}{+} < 0,$$ (A48)

since $E_f > E_p > 1$ and $\Delta' > \Sigma$; also,

$$\frac{\partial \bar{p}}{\partial \gamma} = \frac{-O_f b_\gamma pf[(1 - E_p)\Delta - (1 - E_f)\Sigma]}{+} = \frac{+}{+} > 0,$$ (A49)

for it can be shown that $(1 - E_p)\Delta > (1 - E_f)\Sigma$.[72] Note that when f is held constant the optimal value of p is decreased, not increased, by an increase in γ.

---

72. The term $(1 - E_p)\Delta$ would be greater than $(1 - E_f)\Sigma$ if

$$(D'' + C'')(1 - E_p) + bp(1 - E_f)(1 - E_p)f_0 > (D'' + C'')(1 - E_f) + bf(1 - E_f)^2 p_0,$$

or

$$(D'' + C'')(E_f - E_p) > -\frac{bpf}{O}(1 - E_f)\left[(1 - E_p)\frac{f_0 O}{f} - (1 - E_f)\frac{p_0 O}{p}\right],$$

$$(D'' + C'')(E_f - E_p) > -\frac{bpf}{O}(1 - E_f)[(1 - E_p)(E_f) - (1 - E_f)E_p],$$

$$(D'' + C'')(E_f - E_p) > -\frac{bpf}{O}(1 - E_f)(E_f - E_p).$$

Since the left-hand side is greater than zero, and the right-hand side is less than zero, the inequality must hold.

If C_p is changed by a change in s, $C_2 = -p_0 C_{ps}$, $C_1 = 0$,

$$\frac{\partial \tilde{f}}{\partial s} = \frac{O_p p_0 C_{ps} \Sigma}{+} = \frac{C_{ps} \Sigma}{+} = \frac{+}{+} > 0,$$ (A50)

and

$$\frac{\partial \tilde{p}}{\partial s} = \frac{-O_f p_0 C_{ps} \Delta}{+} = \frac{-}{+} < 0.$$ (A51)

REFERENCES

Arrow, Kenneth J. "Economic Welfare and Allocation of Resources for Invention," in National Bureau Committee for Economic Research. *The Rate and Direction of Inventive Activity: Economic and Social Factors.* Princeton, N.J.: Princeton Univ. Press (for the Nat. Bureau of Econ. Res.), 1962.

Becker, Gary S. "Irrational Behavior and Economic Theory." *Journal of Political Economy* 70 (February 1962).

———. "A Theory of the Allocation of Time." *Economic Journal* 75 (September 1965).

Bentham, Jeremy. *Theory of Legislation.* New York: Harcourt Brace Co., 1931.

Bureau of the Budget. *The Budget of United States Government, 1968, Appendix.* Washington: U.S. Government Printing Office, 1967.

Bureau of Prisons. *Prisoners Released from State and Federal Institutions.* ("National Prisoner Statistics.") Washington: U.S. Dept. of Justice, 1960.

———. *Characteristics of State Prisoners, 1960.* ("National Prisoner Statistics.") U.S. Dept. of Justice, n.d.

———. *Federal Prisons, 1960.* Washington: U.S. Dept. of Justice, 1961.

Cagan, Phillip. *Determinants and Effects of Changes in the Stock of Money, 1875-1960.* New York: Columbia Univ. Press (for the Nat. Bureau of Econ. Res.), 1965.

"Criminal Safeguards and the Punitive Damages Defendant." *University of Chicago Law Review* 34 (Winter 1967).

Ehrlich, Isaac. "The Supply of Illegitimate Activities." Unpublished manuscript, Columbia Univ., New York, 1967.

Federal Bureau of Investigation. *Uniform Crime Reports for the United States.* Washington: U.S. Dept. of Justice, 1960.

———. *Ibid.,* 1961.

Harper, F. V., and James, F. *The Law of Torts.* Vol. II. Boston: Little-Brown & Co., 1956.

Johnson, Thomas. "The Effects of the Minimum Wage Law." Ph.D. dissertation, Columbia Univ., New York, 1967.

Kleinman, E. "The Choice between Two 'Bads' – Some Economic Aspects of Criminal Sentencing." Unpublished manuscript, Hebrew Univ., Jerusalem, 1967.

Landes, William. "The Effect of State Fair Employment Legislation on the Economic Position of Nonwhite Males." Ph.D. dissertation, Columbia Univ., New York, 1966.

Laws of New York. Vol. II (1965).

Marshall, Alfred. *Principles of Economics.* 8th ed. New York: Macmillan Co., 1961.

Plant, A. "The Economic Theory concerning Patents for Inventions." *Economica* 1 (February 1934).

Pollock, F., and Maitland, F. W. *The History of English Law.* Vol. II. 2d ed. Cambridge: Cambridge Univ. Press, 1952.

President's Commission on Law Enforcement and Administration of Justice. *The Challenge of Crime in a Free Society.* Washington: U.S. Government Printing Office, 1967(*a*).

————. *Corrections.* ("Task Force Reports.") Washington: U.S. Government Printing Office, 1967(*b*).

————. *The Courts.* ("Task Force Reports.") Washington: U.S. Government Printing Office, 1967(*c*).

————. *Crime and Its Impact—an Assessment.* ("Task Force Reports.") Washington: U.S. Government Printing Office, 1967(*d*).

————. *Science and Technology.* ("Task Force Reports.") Washington: U.S. Government Printing Office, 1967(*e*).

Radzinowicz, L. *A History of English Criminal Law and Its Administration from 1750.* Vol. I. London: Stevens & Sons, 1948.

Schilling, T. C. "Economic Analysis of Organized Crime," in President's Commission on Law Enforcement and Administration of Justice. *Organized Crime.* ("Task Force Reports.") Washington: U.S. Government Printing Office, 1967.

Shawness, Lord. "Crime *Does* Pay because We Do Not Back Up the Police." *New York Times Magazine,* June 13, 1965.

Smigel, Arleen. "Does Crime Pay? An Economic Analysis." M.A. thesis, Columbia Univ., New York, 1965.

Stigler, George J. "What Can Regulators Regulate? The Case of Electricity." *Journal of Law and Economics* 5 (October 1962).

————. "A Theory of Oligopoly." *Journal of Political Economy* 72 (February 1964).

————. "The Economic Effects of the Antitrust Laws." *Journal of Law and Economics* 9 (October 1966).

Sutherland, E. H. *Principles of Criminology.* 6th ed. Philadelphia: J. B. Lippincott Co., 1960.

The Optimum Enforcement of Laws

George J. Stigler

University of Chicago and National Bureau of Economic Research

All prescriptions of behavior for individuals require enforcement. Usually the obligation to behave in a prescribed way is entered into voluntarily by explicit or implicit contract. For example, I promise to teach certain classes with designated frequency and to discuss matters which I, and possibly others, believe are relevant to the course titles. By negotiation, and in the event of its failure, by legal action, I and my employer seek to enforce the contract of employment against large departures from the promised behavior. Performance of some kinds of behavior is difficult or impossible to enforce — such as promises to be creative, noble, or steadfast in crisis — and as a result such contractual promises are either not made or enforced only when there is an uncontroversially flagrant violation. The influence upon contract, and upon economic organization generally, of the costs of enforcing various kinds of contracts has received virtually no study by economists, despite its immense potential explanatory power.

When the prescribed behavior is fixed unilaterally rather than by individual agreement, we have the regulation or law, and enforcement of these unilateral rules is the subject of the present essay. Departures of actual from prescribed behavior are crimes or violations, although one could wish for a less formidable description than "criminal" to describe many of the trifling offenses or the offenses against unjust laws. My primary purpose is to construct a theory of rational enforcement, a theory which owes much to Gary Becker's major article on the subject (1968). In the conclusion the problem of explanation, as distinguished from prescription, will be commented upon.

I. THE GOAL OF ENFORCEMENT

The goal of enforcement, let us assume, is to achieve that degree of compliance with the rule of prescribed (or proscribed) behavior that the society believes it can afford. There is one decisive reason why the society must forego "complete" enforcement of the rule: enforcement is costly.

The extent of enforcement of laws depends upon the amount of resources devoted to the task. With enough policemen, almost every speeding automobile could be identified. The success of tenacious pursuit of the guilty in celebrated crimes (such as the great English train robbery and the assassination of Martin King) suggests that few crimes of sane men could escape detection. We could make certain that crime does not pay by paying enough to apprehend most criminals. Such a level of enforcement would of course be enormously expensive, and only in crimes of enormous importance will such expenditures be approached. The society will normally give to the enforcement agencies a budget which dictates a much lower level of enforcement.

The cost limitation upon the enforcement of laws would prevent the society from forestalling, detecting, and punishing all offenders, but it would appear that punishments which would be meted out to the guilty could often be increased without using additional resources. The offender is deterred by the expected punishment, which is (as a first approximation) the probability of punishment times the punishment—$100 if the probability of conviction is 1/10 and the fine $1,000. Hence, increasing the punishment would seem always to increase the deterrence. Capital punishment is cheaper than long term imprisonment; and seizure of all the offender's property may not be much more expensive than collecting a more moderate fine.

To escape from this conclusion, Becker introduces as a different limitation on punishment the "social value of the gain to offenders" from the offense. The determination of this social value is not explained, and one is entitled to doubt its usefulness as an explanatory concept: what evidence is there that society sets a positive value upon the utility derived from a murder, rape, or arson? In fact the society has branded the utility derived from such activities as illicit. It may be that in a few offenses some gain to the offender is viewed as a gain to society,[1] but such social gains seem too infrequent, small, and capricious to put an effective limitation upon the size of punishments.

Instead we take account of another source of limitation of punishment, which arises out of the nature of the supply of offenses. It is no doubt true that the larger the punishment, the smaller will be the expected net utility to the prospective offender from the commission of a given offense. But marginal decisions are made here as in the remainder of life, and the marginal deterrence of heavy punishments could be very small or even negative. If the offender will be executed for a minor assault and for a murder, there is no marginal deterrence to murder. If the thief has his hand cut off for taking five dollars, he had just as well take $5,000. Marginal costs are necessary to marginal deterrence.[2] The marginal deterrence to committing small crimes is also distorted if an otherwise appropriate schedule of penalties is doubled or halved.

One special aspect of this cost limitation upon enforcement is the need to avoid overenforcement. The enforcement agency could easily apprehend most guilty people if we placed no limits upon the charging and frequent conviction of innocent people. In any real enforcement system, there will in fact be conviction and punishment of some innocent parties, and these miscarriages of justice impose costs of both resources and loss of confidence in the enforcement machinery. The costs of defense of innocent parties, whether borne by themselves or by the state, are part of the costs of enforcement from the social viewpoint. The conviction of innocent persons encourages the crime because it reduces the marginal deterrence to its commission.

The significance of an offense to society – the quantity of resources that will be used to "prevent" the offense – will in general increase with the gravity of the offense. The increase in resources, however, will not manifest itself only in an increase in punishments. The state will pursue more tenaciously the offender who commits a larger crime (or repeti-

---

1. For example, the thief reduces the welfare expenditures of the state, or the arsonist warms the neighboring houses.

2. Becker writes the expected utility from an offense as $EU = pU(Y-f) + (1-p)U(Y)$, where Y is the money value of the gain, p the probability of detection and conviction, and f the fine. (The income, Y, and fine, f, must be interpreted as average annual flows; for a single offense Y must be less than f.) If this expression is differentiated partially with respect to Y, $\delta EU/\delta Y = pU'(Y-f) + (1-p)U'(Y) \simeq U'(Y) - pfU''(Y)$, which is positive for all Y. Of course p and f will increase with Y to prevent this incitement to larger crime.

tive crimes) and thus increase also the probability of apprehending him.

There is a division of labor between the state and the citizen in the prevention of virtually every offense. The owner of large properties is required to do much of his direct policing: there are surely more watchmen and guards than policemen in a typical city. The larger accumulations of wealth, moreover, are to be guarded by the owner through devices such as nonnegotiability and custody of funds by specialists. Accordingly, the *public* punishments for crimes against property do not increase in proportion to the value of the property. In the protection of people, as distinguished from their property, the individual is required to protect himself from minor offenses or at least to detect their occurrence and assume a large part of the burden of prosecution (for example, shoplifting, insults, simple trespass), but he is allowed less discretion in prosecution for major assaults.

The relationship of duration and nature of penalties to age and sex of offender, frequency of previous offenses, and so forth is also explicable in terms of cost of enforcement. The first-time offender may have committed the offense almost accidentally and (given any punishment) with negligible probability of repetition, so heavy penalties (which have substantial costs to the state) are unnecessary. The probability of a repetition of an offense by a seasoned offender is also zero during his imprisonment, so the probability of repetition of an offense is relevant to the penalty also in his case.

Indeed, the problem of determining the efficient penalty may be viewed as one in statistical inference: to estimate the individual's average, durable propensity to offend (the population value) on the basis of a sample of his observed behavior and how this propensity responds to changes in penalties. As in other sequential sampling problems, one can estimate this propensity more accurately, the longer the individual's behavior is observed.

The society will be more concerned (because each individual is more concerned) with major than minor offenses in the following sense: there is increasing marginal disutility of offenses, so a theft of $1,000 is more than twice as harmful as a theft of $500. In the area of offenses to property, this result is implied by diminishing marginal utility of income. In the area of offenses to persons, it is more difficult to measure damage in any direct way, but a similar rule probably holds.

So much for prevention and punishment; let us turn to the offenses.

II. THE SUPPLY OF OFFENSES

The commission of offenses will be an act of production for income or an act of consumption. A consumption offense would be illustrated by speeding in an automobile used for recreation or assaulting a courtship rival (when the girl is poor). A production offense would be illustrated by theft, smuggling, and the violation of economic regulations. In the realm of offenses to property, income objectives are of course paramount, and we may recall Adam Smith's emphasis upon the economic nature of crime:

The affluence of the rich excites the indignation of the poor, who are often both driven by want, and prompted by envy, to invade his possessions. It is only under the shelter of the civil magistrate that the owner of that valuable property, which is acquired by the labour of many years, or perhaps of many successive generations, can sleep a single night in security. He is at all times surrounded by unknown enemies, whom, though he never provoked, he can never appease, and from whose injustice he can be protected only by the powerful arm of the civil magistrate continually held up to chastise it. The acquisition of valuable and extensive property, therefore, necessarily requires the establishment of civil government. Where there is no property, or at least none that exceeds the value of two or three days labour, civil government is not so necessary (Smith, 1937, p. 670).

The professional criminal seeks income, and for him the usual rules of occupational choice will hold. He will reckon the present value of the expected returns and costs of the criminal activity and compare their difference with the net returns from other criminal activities and from legitimate activities. The costs of failure in the execution of the crime correspond to the costs of failure in other occupations. The costs of injuries to a professional athlete are comparable to the costs to the offender of apprehension, defense, and conviction, but normally legal occupations have only monetary costs of failure.

The details of occupational choice in illegal activity are not different from those encountered in the legitimate occupations. One must choose the locality of maximum income expectation (and perhaps, like a salesman, move from area to area). One must choose between large, relatively infrequent crimes and smaller, more frequent crimes. One must reckon in periods of (involuntary) unemployment due to imprisonment. Earnings can be expected to rise for a time with experience.

The probability of apprehension (and therefore of conviction) is an increasing function of the frequency of commission of offenses. If the probability of detection is p for one offense, it is $1 - (1 - p)^n$ for at least one conviction in n offenses, and this expression approaches unity as n becomes large. In fact, the probability of detection (p) rises after each apprehension because the enforcement agency is also learning the offender's habits. On this score alone, there is a strong incentive to the criminal to make very infrequent attempts to obtain very large sums of money. The probability of success is also affected by the precautions of the prospective victim: Fort Knox is more difficult to enter than a liquor store. The efforts of detection will also increase with the size of the offense.

We may postulate, in summary, a supply of offenses which in equilibrium has the following properties:

1. Net returns are equalized, allowance being made for risk and costs of special equipment required for various activities.
2. The determinants of supply which are subject to the control of society are: (a) the structure of penalties by offense; (b) the probability of detection for each offense; (c) certain costs of the conduct of the offending activity; for example, the cost of making successful counterfeit money can be increased by complicating the genuine money.
3. The penalties and chances of detection and punishment must be increasing functions of the enormity of the offense.

Although it smacks of paradox, it may be useful to reinterpret the offending activity as providing a variety of products (offenses). These offenses are in a sense demanded by the society: my wallet is an invitation to the footpad, my office funds to the embezzler. The costs of production of the offenses are the ordinary outlays of offenders plus the penalties imposed by the society. The industry will operate at a scale and composition of output set by the competition of offenders and the cost of producing offenses.

The structure of rational enforcement activities will have these properties:

1. Expected penalties increase with expected gains so there is no marginal net gain from larger offenses. Let the criminal commit in a year S crimes of size Q, where Q is the monetary value to the criminal of the successful completion of the crime. The fraction

(p) of crimes completed successfully (or the probability of successful completion of one crime) is a decreasing function of the amount of expenditure (E) undertaken by society to prevent and punish the crime. (Punishment is used for deterrence, and is only a special form of prevention.) Hence $p = p(E, Q)$, or possibly $p = p(E, Q, S)$. The expected punishment is the fraction of crimes apprehended (and punished) times the punishment, F. The condition for marginal deterrence is, for all Q, $d(pSQ)/dQ \leq d(1 - p)SF/dQ$.

2. The expenditures on prevention and enforcement should yield a diminution in offenses, at the margin, equal to the return upon these resources in other areas. An increment of expenditures yields a return in reduced offenses,

$$\sum_{Q'} d(pSQ')/dE = \text{marginal return on expenditures elsewhere,}$$

where Q' is the monetary value of the offense to society.[3]

I do not include foregone lawful services of the criminal in the cost of his activity to society (= noncriminals) since he, not others, would receive the return (taxes aside!) if he shifted from crime to a lawful occupation.

III. THE ENFORCEMENT AGENCY: A NORMATIVE APPROACH

A law is enforced, not by "society," but by an agency instructed to that task. That agency must be given more than a mandate (an elegant admonition) to enforce the statute with vigor and wisdom: it must have incentives to enforce the law efficiently. There are at least two deficiencies in the methods by which most agencies are induced to enforce the laws properly.

The first deficiency is that the enforcement agency does not take into account, at least explicitly and fully, the costs it imposes upon the activity or persons regulated. In the area of ordinary criminal offenses, the society will, if anything, wish to increase (at no expense to itself) the costs of defense for guilty persons, but it should not impose costs (and certainly not unnecessary costs) upon innocent parties. In fact, the administration of criminal justice should in principle include as a cost the reimbursement

---

3. Currency has the same value to the criminal as to society, so $Q' = Q$. But for any commodity which does not have a market price independent of ownership, $Q < Q'$.

of the expenses of defense of people charged and acquitted. The compensation actually paid will not exactly compensate injured persons, because of the administrative costs of ascertaining exact compensation, but the taking of an innocent person's personal wealth, including foregone income, differs in no respect from the taking of some of his real estate (for which under eminent domain it is necessary to compensate him fully).[4]

In the area of economic regulation, guilt is often an inappropriate notion, and when it is inappropriate all costs of compliance must be reckoned into the social costs of enforcement. The utility's costs in preparing a rate case or Texas Gulf Sulfur's costs in defending itself against the Securities and Exchange Commission are social costs of the regulatory process. Reimbursement is now achieved by charging the consumers of the products and the owners of specialized resources of these industries: they bear the private costs of the regulatory process. This is at least an accidental allocation of costs, and when the regulation seeks to aid the poorer consumers or resource owners, a perverse allocation.

The second deficiency in the design of enforcement is the use of inappropriate methods of determining the extent of enforcement. The annual report of an enforcement agency is in effect the justification of its previous expenditures and the plea for enlarged appropriations. The Federal Trade Commission will tell us, for example, that in fiscal 1966 as part of its duty to get truthful labeling of furs and textiles, it inspected 12,625 plants and settled 213 "cases" for $1,272,000 plus overhead. The agency may recite scandals corrected or others still unrepressed, but it neither offers nor possesses a criterion by which to determine the correct scale of its activities.

A rational measure of enforcement procedure could in principle be established in almost any area. Consider the fraudulent labeling of textiles. We could proceed as follows:

1. The damage to the consumer from the purchase of a mislabeled textile could be estimated, and will obviously vary with the mislabeling (assuming that the legal standards are sensible!). The difference between market value of the true and alleged grades is one component of the damage. A second and more elusive component is the additional cost of deception (earlier replacement, skin irritation, and so forth): the consumer who would not have purchased the inferior quality at a competitive price had he known its

---

4. It is an interesting aspect of our attitudes in this area that many people believe that acquitted persons are probably guilty.

inferiority has suffered additional damage. Thus the measure of damage is the amount a consumer would pay to avoid the deception, that is, the value of the *insured* correct quality minus the value of the actual quality.

2. As a matter of deterrence, the penalties on the individual mislabeler should be equal to a properly taken sum of the following items: (a) The damage per yard times the number of yards, say per year. Let this be H. (b) The costs of the enforcement agency, say E, per year. This sum should include reimbursement of the costs of those charged and acquitted. (c) The costs of defense (if detected) for the mislabeler, D. Where guilt is an appropriate notion, as presumably in the case of mislabeling, the society may wish to ignore these costs, which is to say, resources devoted to this end deserve no return. Where guilt is inappropriate, these costs should be reckoned in. The sum of these penalties must be multiplied by $1/p$, where p is the probability of detection of the offense within the year. This probability is a function of E and H.

3. The enforcement agency should minimize the sum of damages plus enforcement costs, $(\Sigma h + E)$ or $(\Sigma H + \Sigma D + E)$.[5]

This goal will serve two functions. The first is to set the scale of enforcement, namely where marginal return equals marginal cost. If the scale of enforcement is correct, society is not spending two dollars to save itself one dollar of damage, or failing to spend one dollar where it will save more than that amount of damage. The second function is to guide the selection of cases: the agency will not (as often now) seek numerous, easy cases to dress up its record, but will pursue the frequent violator and the violator who does much damage.

This sort of criterion of enforcement is readily available in certain areas. The secret service, for example, reports that in fiscal 1967 the loss to the public from counterfeit money was $1,658,100.75 (an excellent instance of counterfeit accuracy). Perhaps half of the $17 million spent by this agency was devoted to the suppression of counterfeiting, and to this one must add the costs of legal actions, imprisonment, and so forth. The secret service should be asking whether the amount of counterfeit money passed would fall by a dollar if a dollar more were spent on enforcement costs minus the corresponding fines collected.

---

5. The fines will be $\Sigma H/p$, but the fines per se are transfers rather than social costs; see Becker (1958), pp. 180–81.

The penalty structure should incorporate the social appraisal of the importance of the suppression of the offenses. The law does not in general provide this scale of values, as can be shown by the list of maximum penalties for the violations of economic regulations listed in Table 1.

The use of criminal sanctions is erratic, and the implicit equivalence of fines and imprisonment varies from $1,000 per year to $10,000 per

TABLE 1
PUBLIC PENALTIES FOR VIOLATION OF ECONOMIC STATUTES

Offense	Enforcement Agency	Maximum Penalty	Statute
Restraint of trade	Antitrust Division	$50,000 + 1 year (+ triple damages and costs)	Sherman (1890, 1955)
Unfair methods of competition	FTC	Cease and desist order	FTC (1914)
Refusal to testify, or testify falsely, under same	FTC	$1,000–$5,000 + 1 year	Same
Price discrimination	FTC	Cease and desist (+ triple damages and costs)	Clayton (1914)
False advertisements of foods, drugs, or cosmetics	FTC	$5,000 + 6 months	Wheeler-Lea (1938)
Adulteration or misbranding of food	Secretary of Health, Education, and Welfare	$1,000 + 1 year, first offense; $10,000 + 3 years, later offense	Copeland Act (1938)
Exporting apples and pears without certificate of quality	Dept. of Agriculture	Denial of certificate for 10 days; $100–$1,000 for knowing violation	Apples and Pears for Export (1933)
Exporting apples in improper barrels	Dept. of Agriculture	$1 barrel	Standard Barrels and Standard Grades of Apples Act (1912)

TABLE 1 (Concluded)
PUBLIC PENALTIES FOR VIOLATION OF ECONOMIC STATUTES

Offense	Enforcement Agency	Maximum Penalty	Statute
Exporting other fruit or vegetables in improper barrels	Dept. of Agriculture	$500 or 6 months if willful	Standard Barrels . . . for Fruits, Vegetables and Other Dry Commodities (1915)
Exporting grapes in improper baskets	Dept. of Agriculture	$25	Standard Baskets Act (1916)
Giving rebates in freight charges (trucks)	ICC	$200–$500 first offense; $250–$5,000 repeated offense	Motor Carrier Act (1935)
Same, water carriers	ICC	$5,000 if willful	Transportation Act (1940)
Failure to disclose interest charges	FRB	Twice finance charge, within $100–$1,000; $5,000 and/or 1 year if willful	Consumer Credit Protection Act (1968)
Falsely certify a check	FBI	$5,000 and/or 5 years	62 Stat. 749 (June 25, 1948)
Failure to deliver gold or certificates to FR Bank when ordered	FRB	Twice the number of dollars	Federal Reserve Act (1913)
Evasion of excise taxes	Treasury	$10,000 and/or 5 years if willful; forfeiture of goods and conveyance	Revenue Act (1954)
Securities Act violation	SEC	$5,000 and/or 5 years	Securities Act (1934)
Misbrand hazardous substances	Secretary of Health, Education, and Welfare	$500 and 90 days; $3,000 or 1 year if willful or repeated	Hazardous Substances Act (1960)

year. Many of the penalties are not even stated in the statutes: the penalty for drinking (industrial) alcohol which has not paid its beverage tax is sometimes blindness or death. The penalties for the essentially similar offense (if such it must be called) of reducing freight rates can be ten times as much for a barge operator as for a trucker. Of course these maximum penalties are not actual penalties, but one is not entitled to hope for much more rationality or uniformity in the fixing of penalties for specific offenses. (The lawyers have apparently not studied in adequate detail the actual sanctions for economic offenses.)

One may conjecture that two features of punishment of traditional criminal law have been carried over to economic regulation: the attribution of a substantial cost to the act of conviction itself, and the related belief that moral guilt does not vary closely with the size of the offense. Whatever the source, the penalty structure is not well designed for either deterrence or guidance of enforcement.

IV. CONCLUSION

The widespread failure to adopt rational criteria of enforcement of laws has been due often and perhaps usually to a simple lack of understanding of the need for and nature of rational enforcement. The clarification of the logic of rational enforcement, and the demonstration that large gains would be obtained by shifting to a rational enforcement scheme, are presumably the necessary (and hopefully sufficient) conditions for improving public understanding of enforcement problems.[6]

There is, however, a second and wholly different reason for the use of what appear to be inappropriate sanctions and inappropriate appropriations to enforcement bodies: the desire of the public *not* to enforce the laws. The appropriations to the enforcement agency and the verdicts of juries are the instruments by which the community may constantly review public policy. If the society decides that drinking alcoholic beverages or speeding in automobiles is not a serious offense in its ordinary form, they may curtail resources for enforcement and so compel the enforcement agency to deal only with a smaller number of offenses (perhaps offenses of larger magnitude, such as chronic drunkenness or driving at extremely high speeds). There is considerable inertia in the legislative

---

6. The peculiarities of the structure of sanctions in economic regulation are partially due also to the response of the regulated businesses. They may effectively lobby to limit appropriations to the regulatory body, but they can also impose costly activities upon the regulatory body which force it to curtail other controls.

process — inertia that serves highly useful functions — and it is much easier to make continuous marginal adjustments in a policy through the appropriations committee by varying the resources for its enforcement than it is to modify the statute. Variation in enforcement provides desirable flexibility in public policy.

REFERENCES

Becker, Gary. "Crime and Punishment: An Economic Approach." *Journal of Political Economy* 76 (March–April 1968). Included in this volume.

Smith, Adam. *The Wealth of Nations*. New York: Modern Library, 1937.

Participation in Illegitimate Activities: An Economic Analysis

Isaac Ehrlich

University of Chicago and National Bureau of Economic Research

INTRODUCTION

Much of the search in the criminological literature for a theory explaining participation in illegitimate activities seems to have been guided by the predisposition that since crime is a deviant behavior, its causes must be sought in deviant factors and circumstances determining behavior. Criminal behavior has traditionally been linked to the offender's presumed unique motivation which, in turn, has been traced to his allegedly unique inner structure, to the impact of exceptional social or family circumstances, or to both (for an overview of the literature see, e.g., Taft and England, 1964).

Reliance on a motivation unique to the offender as a major explana-

I would like to thank Gary S. Becker, Jacob Mincer, Lawrence Fisher, Arnold Zellner, H. Gregg Lewis, Christopher Sims, and Hans Zeisel for helpful suggestions and criticism on earlier drafts. I have also benefited from competent assistance and suggestions from Uri Ben-Zion and later from Walter Vandaell. This study has been supported by a grant for the study of law and economics from the National Science Foundation to the National Bureau of Economic Research. This essay contains, essentially, my 1973 article in the *Journal of Political Economy* entitled "Participation in Illegitimate Activities: A Theoretical and Empirical Investigation," supplemented by some relevant appendixes included in my doctoral dissertation (Ehrlich, 1970).

tion of actual crime does not, in general, render possible predictions regarding the outcome of objective circumstances. We are also unaware of any persuasive empirical evidence reported in the literature in support of theories using this approach. Our alternative point of reference, although not necessarily incompatible, is that even if those who violate certain laws differ systematically in various respects from those who abide by the same laws, the former, like the latter, do respond to incentives. Rather than resort to hypotheses regarding unique personal characteristics and social conditions affecting respect for the law, penchant for violence, preference for risk, or in general preference for crime, one may separate the latter from measurable opportunities and see to what extent illegal behavior can be explained by the effect of opportunities, given preferences.

In recent years a few studies attempted to investigate the relation between crime and various measurable opportunities. For example, Fleisher (1966) studied the relation between juvenile delinquency and variations in income and unemployment conditions via a regression analysis, using inter- and intracity data relating to the United States in 1960. Smigel-Leibowitz (1965) and Ehrlich (1967) used several regression methods to study the effect of the probability and severity of punishment on the rate of crime across states in the United States in 1960. In his significant theoretical contribution to the study of crime in economic terms, Becker (1968) has developed a formal model of the decision to commit offenses which emphasizes the relation between crime and punishment. Stigler (1970) also approaches the determinants of the supply of offenses in similar terms. Following these studies, and particularly my 1970 study, an attempt is made in this paper to formulate a more comprehensive model of the decision to engage in unlawful activities and to test it against some available empirical evidence. My analysis goes beyond that of Becker and other previous contributions in several ways. First, it incorporates in the concept of opportunities both punishment and reward — costs and gains from legitimate and illegitimate pursuits — rather than the cost of punishment alone, and attempts to identify and to test the effect of their empirical counterparts. Specifically, it predicts and verifies empirically a systematic association between the rate of specific crimes on the one hand, and income inequality as well as law enforcement activity on the other. Second, it links formally the theory of participation in illegitimate activities with the general theory of occupational choice by presenting the offender's decision problem as an optimal allocation of resources under uncertainty to competing activities both inside and outside the market sector, rather than as a choice between mutually exclusive activities. The model developed can be used to predict not only the *direction*, but also the relative *magnitude* of the response of specific offenders to changes in various observable opportunities. In addition, the analysis distinguishes between the deterrent and preventive effects of punishment by imprisonment on the rate of crime (by the latter is meant the reduction in criminal activity due to the temporary separation of imprisoned offenders from potential victims) and permits an empirical verification of the former effect alone. Finally, in the context of the empirical implementation, I analyze the interaction between offense and defense — between crime and (collective) law-enforcement activity through police and courts — and employ a simultaneous-equation econometric model in estimating supply-of-offenses functions and a production function of law-enforcement activity. The results of the empirical investigation are then used to provide some tentative estimates of the effectiveness of law enforcement in deterring crime and reducing the social loss from crime.

The plan of the paper is as follows: In Section I, I develop a model of participation in illegitimate activities and derive some behavioral implications. In Section II those implications are applied in developing supply-of-offenses functions. Section III is devoted to an econometric specification of a simultaneous-equation model of crime and law enforcement, and in Section IV, I present and discuss the results of the empirical investigation.

I. THE CRIMINAL PROSPECT

In spite of the diversity of activities defined as illegal, all such activities share some common properties which form the subject matter of our analytical and empirical investigation. Any violation of the law can be conceived of as yielding a potential increase in the offender's pecuniary wealth, his psychic well-being, or both. In violating the law, one also risks a reduction in one's wealth and well-being, for conviction entails paying a penalty (a monetary fine, probation, the discounted value of time spent in prison and related psychic disadvantages, net of any direct benefits received), acquiring a criminal record (and thus reducing earning opportunities in legitimate activities), and other disadvantages. As an alternative to violating the law one may engage in a legal wealth- or consumption-generating activity, which may also be subject to specific risks. The net gain in both activities is thus subject to uncertainty.

A simple model of choice between legal and illegal activity can be formulated within the framework of the usual economic theory of choice under uncertainty. A central hypothesis of this theory is that if, in a given period, the two activities were mutually exclusive, one would choose between them by comparing the expected utility associated with each alone.[1] The problem may be formulated within a more general context, however, for the decision to engage in illegal activity is not inherently an either/or choice: offenders are free to combine a number of legitimate and illegitimate activities or to switch from one to another during any period throughout their lifetime.[2] The relevant object of choice to an offender may thus be defined more properly as his optimal activity mix: the optimal allocation of his time and other resources to competing legal and illegal activities.[3] Allowing explicitly for varying degrees of participation in illegitimate activity, we then develop behavioral implications concerning entry into, and optimal participation in, such activity.

A. OPTIMAL PARTICIPATION IN ILLEGITIMATE MARKET ACTIVITIES: A ONE-PERIOD UNCERTAINTY MODEL

For the sake of a simple yet general illustration, assume that an individual can participate in two market activities: i, an illegal activity, and l, a legal one, and must make a choice regarding his optimal participation in each at the beginning of a given period. No training or other entry costs are required in either activity, neither are there costs of movement between the two. The returns in both activities are monotonically increasing functions of working time. Activity l is safe in the sense that its net returns are given with certainty by the function $W_l(t_l)$, where t denotes the time input. Activity i is risky, however, in the sense that its net returns are

---

1. Such formulation is used in Ehrlich (1967) and Becker (1968), included in this volume.

2. The standard literature on occupational choices usually assumes specialization in a single activity, rather than multiple-job holding. An important incentive for such specialization arises from time dependencies generated by specific training, for wages in activities involving training stand in some positive relation to the total amount of time previously spent there training or learning by doing. Multiple-job holding also entails various costs of movement between jobs that may offset potential gains due, say, to the increased returns on time spent in each. Specialization in a single market activity may thus be optimal, at least during periods of intensive training. Nevertheless, in the case of market activities involving a large measure of risk, there may be an incentive for diversifying resources among several competing activities. We propose that such an incentive exists in the case of illegitimate activities, especially those that do not require specific training.

3. In addition, an offender's probability of being apprehended and convicted of a specific charge is not determined by society's actions alone, but is modifiable through his deliberate actions (self-protection). For an analysis of an offender's simultaneous decision to allocate resources to illegal and legal activities as well as to self-protection, see Appendix 2 to this section.

conditional upon, say, two states of the world: a, apprehension and punishment at the end of the period, with (subjective) probability p_i, and b, escaping apprehension, with probability $1 - p_i$. If successful, the offender reaps the entire value (pecuniary and nonpecuniary) of the output of his illegitimate activity, net of the costs of purchased inputs (accomplices' and accessories' services), $W_i(t_i)$.[4] If apprehended and punished, his returns are reduced by an amount $F_i(t_i)$: the discounted (pecuniary and nonpecuniary) value of the penalty for his entire illegitimate activity and other related losses, including the possible loss of his loot. It is assumed that the probability of apprehension and punishment is independent of the amount of time spent in i and l,[5] and that time is proportionally related to any other direct inputs employed in the production of market returns.

The individual is assumed to behave as if he were interested in maximizing the expected utility of a one-period consumption prospect.[6] For analytical convenience, let the utility in any given state of the world s, be given by the function

$$U_s = U(X_s, t_c), \qquad (1.1)$$

where X_s denotes the stock of a composite market good (including assets, earnings within the period, and the real wealth equivalent of nonpecuniary returns from legitimate and illegitimate activity), the command over which is contingent upon the occurrence of state s; t_c is the amount of time devoted to consumption or nonmarket activity; and U is an indirect

---

4. In large measure, the pecuniary returns from crime are positively related to the amount of transferable goods and assets and other wealth possessed by potential victims. More important, these returns may be subject to uncertainty due in large measure to varying degrees of self-protection provided by potential victims. (For a theoretical analysis of private self-protection, see Ehrlich and Becker, 1972.) For analytical simplicity, and in view of the limited data available for an empirical estimation of illegitimate returns (see Sect. III, B), we here treat W_i as a single-valued function of t_i.

5. This assumption is relaxed in Appendix 2 to this section, where we have allowed p_i to be a positive function of t_i (or the number of offenses committed), and a negative function of the degree of self-protection provided by the offender, which, in turn, is expected to be positively related to t_i. The behavioral implications of the more simple model are shown to hold in this more general case, as well.

6. This may be compatible with the assumption that the individual wishes to maximize the expected utility of his lifetime consumption, since it is possible, in general, to represent his decision problem at any given period in terms of maximizing a derived one-period utility function, which is explicitly a function of current variables, but which also summarizes realized past consumption and the results of optimal decisions at relevant subsequent periods for all possible future events. For an elaborate discussion of this proposition, see Fama (1970).

utility function that also converts X_s and t_c into consumption flows. Denoting all earnings within the period in real terms, that is, in terms of the composite good X, there exist under the foregoing assumptions regarding the earning functions in i and l only two states of the world with respect to X. Either

$$X_b = W' + W_i(t_i) + W_l(t_l) \tag{1.2}$$

is obtained with probability $1 - p_i$, or

$$X_a = W' + W_i(t_i) - F_i(t_i) + W_l(t_l) \tag{1.3}$$

is obtained with probability p_i, where W' denotes the real value of the individual's assets (net of current earnings), including his borrowing opportunities against earnings in future periods, and is assumed to be known with certainty, given the state of the world in the beginning of each period. The expected utility which is generally given by

$$EU(X_s, t_c) = \sum_{s=a}^{n} \pi_s U(X_s, t_c) \tag{1.4}$$

where π_s denotes the probability of state s, reduces in this case to

$$EU(X_s, t_c) = (1 - p_i)U(X_b, t_c) + p_i U(X_a, t_c). \tag{1.4a}$$

The problem thus becomes that of maximizing equation (1.4a) with respect to the choice variables t_i, t_l, and t_c, subject to the wealth constraints given by equations (1.2) and (1.3), a time constraint,

$$t_0 = t_i + t_l + t_c, \tag{1.5}$$

and nonnegativity requirements,

$$t_i \geq 0; \quad t_l \geq 0; \quad t_c \geq 0. \tag{1.6}$$

Substituting equations (1.2) and (1.3) in equation (1.4a), the Kuhn-Tucker first-order optimality conditions can be stated as follows:

$$\frac{\partial EU}{\partial t} - \lambda \leq 0,$$

$$\left(\frac{\partial EU}{\partial t} - \lambda \right) t = 0, \tag{1.7}$$

$$t \geq 0,$$

where t stands for the optimal values of each of t_i, t_l, and t_c, and λ is the marginal utility of time spent in consumption. It can easily be shown that

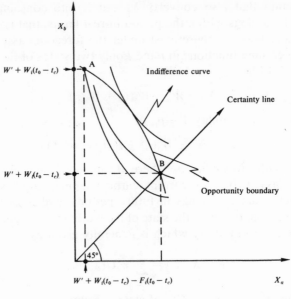

Figure 1

given the amount of time allocated to consumption t_c, the optimal allocation of working time between i and l, in case of an interior solution, must satisfy the first-order condition,

$$-\frac{w_i - w_l}{w_i - f_i - w_l} = \frac{p_i U'(X_a)}{(1 - p_i)U'(X_b)},\qquad (1.8)$$

where $w_i = (dW_i/dt_i)$, $f_i = (dF_i/dt_i)$, and $w_l = (dW_l/dt_l)$. The term on the left-hand side of equation (1.8) is the slope of an opportunity boundary, the production transformation curve of the composite good X between the two states of the world considered in this example (by condition [1.6] it is defined only between points A and B in Figure 1), and the term on the right is the slope of an indifference curve (defined along $dU^* = 0$). In an equilibrium position involving participation in both i and l, they must be the same. Clearly, a necessary prerequisite for equation (1.8) is that the potential marginal penalty, f_i, exceed the differential marginal return from illegitimate activity, $w_i - w_l$, for otherwise the marginal opportunities in i would always dominate those in l.[7] The imposition of concurrent

---

7. This paraphrases and modifies a well-known argument that "the evil of punishment must be made to exceed the advantage of the offense" (see Bentham, 1931, p. 325).

imprisonment terms for several offenses committed by the same offender is thus shown to create an incentive for offenders to specialize in illegitimate activity. Equation (1.8) would be necessary and sufficient for a strict global maximum involving participation in both i and l if the indifference curve is strictly convex to the origin (which implies diminishing marginal utility of real wealth) and the opportunity boundary is linear or strictly concave (which is consistent with, say, diminishing marginal wages and constant or increasing marginal penalties).[8]

Figure 1 and equation (1.7) can be used to analyze the range of possible combinations of illegitimate and (safe) legitimate activities. A *sufficient* condition for entry into i—regardless of attitudes toward risk—is that the absolute slope of the opportunity boundary exceed the absolute slope of the indifference curve at the position where the total working time is spent in legitimate activity (point B on the certainty line) or $-(w_i - w_l)/(w_i - f_i - w_l) > p_i/(1 - p_i)$. This requires, in turn, that the marginal expected return in i exceed that in l. For risk avoiders or risk-neutral persons, this is also a necessary condition for entry into i, and its converse would imply their specialization in l.

If the opportunity boundary were concave to the origin, as in Figure 1 (or if the probability of apprehension and punishment were a positive function of t_i), participation in both legitimate and illegitimate activity may be consistent with constant or increasing marginal utility of wealth. Assuming that the opportunities available to offenders were independent of their attitudes toward risk, it can then be shown that a risk-neutral offender will spend more time in illegitimate activity relative to a risk avoider, and a risk preferrer will spend more time there relative to both.[9] Moreover, if the opportunity boundary were linear (and p_i were constant),

---

8. The second-order condition for a (strict) local maximum in this case is

$$\Delta = (1 - p_i)U''(X_b)(w_i - w_l)^2 + p_iU''(X_a)(w_i - f_i - w_l)^2$$

$$+ (1 - p_i)U'(X_b)\left(\frac{dw_i}{dt_i} + \frac{dw_l}{dt_l}\right)$$

$$+ pU'(X_a)\left(\frac{dw_i}{dt_i} - \frac{df_i}{dt_i} + \frac{dw_l}{dt_l}\right) < 0. \qquad (1.8a)$$

9. By equation (1.8) in an equilibrium position, $-(1 - p_i)(w_i - w_l)/p_i(w_i - f_i - w_l) \gtrless 1$; that is, $E(w_i) = (1 - p_i)w_i + p_i(w_i - f_i) \gtrless w_l$, as $U'' \gtrless 0$. Since the opportunity boundary is concave to the origin, the equilibrium position of a risk preferrer must be to the left of that of a risk neutral, and even further to the left of that of a risk avoider (i.e., closer to the X_b axis).

offenders who are risk preferrers would necessarily specialize in illegitimate activity, since the optimality conditions imply a corner solution in this case. In contrast, offenders who are risk avoiders are likely to combine a relatively safe legitimate activity with their illegitimate activity to hedge against the relatively greater risk involved in a full-time pursuit of the latter. Whether offenders are likely to specialize in illegitimate acitvity thus becomes an aspect of their attitudes toward risk, as well as their relative opportunities in alternative legitimate and illegitimate activities [10] (the latter including, by definition, nonpecuniary costs and returns). Also, whether in equilibrium crime pays in terms of expected (real) marginal returns is simply a derivative of an offender's attitude toward risk, since in equilibrium the expected marginal returns from crime would exceed, be equal to, or fall short of the marginal returns from legitimate activity, depending on whether the offender were a risk avoider, risk neutral, or a risk preferrer, respectively.[11]

Although our model has been illustrated for two states of the world, the analysis generally applies to n states — various combinations of contingencies in legitimate and illegitimate activities. For example, if returns in i and l are (each) subject to a single trial binomial probability distribution due to success or failure in i and employment or unemployment in l throughout a given period, the necessary condition for an interior solution with respect to the allocation of working time between i and l that maximizes equation (1.4) becomes

$$(1 - p_i)(1 - u_l)U_a'(w_i - w_l) + (1 - p_i)u_l U_b' w_i$$
$$+ p_i(1 - u_l)U_c'(w_i - f_i - w_l) + p_i u_l U_d'(w_i - f_i) = 0, \quad (1.9)$$

where u_l is the probability of unemployment in l and a, b, c, and d are the four relevant states of the world.[12] The basic implications of the

---

10. At present, no reliable statistics exist which indicate to what extent crimes are committed by full-time criminals. Studies of prisoners in federal, state, and local correctional institutions in the United States show that a majority of these offenders did have legitimate occupational experience — mainly in unskilled occupations — prior to their apprehension, and that only a small fraction never worked. Other available data indicate that professional criminals are responsible for a large proportion of major thefts (see PCL, 1967 (b), p. 47).

11. A proof is given in n. 9. Some evidence as to whether crime pays in the monetary sense alone is discussed in Appendix 2 to Section IV.

12. In deriving eq. (1.9), we have implicitly assumed that legitimate wage rates in case of unemployment are zero. Note that losses from unemployment may be insured via market insurance, whereas no such insurance is available against punishment for crime. This is one reason for expecting l to be a safer activity relative to i.

preceding analysis hold with some modifications in this more general case as well (see Appendix 1 to this section).

The model developed in this section can be used to explain why many offenders, even those convicted and punished, tend to repeat their crimes. Given the offender's opportunities and preferences, it may be optimal for him to commit several offenses in any given period. Moreover, even if there were no systematic variations in preferences for crime from one period to another (these may in fact intensify), an offender is likely to repeat his illegitimate activity if the opportunities available to him remain unchanged. Indeed, legitimate earning opportunities of convicted offenders may become much more scarce relative to their illegitimate opportunities because of the criminal record effect and the effect of long imprisonment terms on legitimate skills and employment opportunities. Recidivism is thus not necessarily the result of an offender's myopia, erratic behavior, or lack of self-control, but may rather be the result of choice dictated by opportunities.

B. SOME BEHAVIORAL IMPLICATIONS

Equation (1.7), and, more specifically, equation (1.8) or (1.9), identify the basic factors determining entry into and optimal participation in illegitimate activities. We now turn to derive some comparative statics implications associated with these factors and start by considering their effects on the allocation of working time $(t_0 - t_c)$ between competing legitimate and illegitimate activities in the market sector.

An increase in either p_i or f_i with no change in the other variables entering equation (1.8) or (1.9) reduces the incentive to enter and participate in illegitimate activity because it increases the expected marginal cost of punishment, $p_i f_i$. If an offender had a neutral attitude toward risk, and thus were interested only in the expected value of his wealth prospect, the magnitude of his response to a 1 per cent increase in either p_i or f_i would be the same, for equal percentage changes in each of these variables have the same effect on $p_i f_i$. Equal percentage changes in p_i and f_i may have quite different effects on the expected utility from crime, however, if one has nonneutral attitudes toward risk. The deterrent effect of a 1 per cent increase in the marginal or average penalty per offense can be shown to exceed or fall short of that of a similar increase in the probability of apprehension and punishment if the offender is a risk avoider or a risk preferrer, respectively. Moreover, if the offender was a risk preferrer and yet partly engaged in legitimate activity, an increase in the average penalty per offense might not deter his participation in crime. Such participation might even increase.[13] This result is not inconsistent with an assertion often made by writers on criminal behavior regarding the low, or even positive effect of punishment on the criminal propensities of *some* offenders. Such behavior is here found to be consistent with preference for risk and need not be interpreted as evidence of an offender's lack of response to incentives.

Similarly, an increase in the marginal or average differential return from illegal activity, $w_i - w_l$, resulting from an increase in (real) illegitimate payoffs or a decrease in (real) legitimate wages with no change in the other variables entering equation (1.8) or (1.9), can be shown generally to increase the incentive to enter into or allocate more time to illegitimate activity: since the opportunity boundary in Figure 1 becomes steeper about point B, some persons who initially specialized in legitimate activity would now find it optimal to allocate some time to an illegitimate activity (more general proofs are given in Ehrlich, 1970, under some restrictive assumptions regarding absolute risk aversion). However, an increase in the *probability* of unemployment, u_l (if unemployment is viewed as an uncertain event in the beginning of a given period), has a more ambiguous effect on the incentive to assume the greater risk involved in additional illegitimate activity if offenders are risk avoiders.[14]

---

13. The effect of a 1 per cent increase in p_i on the optimal fraction of working time allocated to i, $t_i^* - W'$, w_i, w_l, f_i, and t_c held constant—can be found, for example, by differentiating eq. (1.8) with respect to ln p_i: $(\partial t_i^*/\partial p_i)p_i = (1/\Delta)[-U_a'(w_i - f_i - w_l)p_i + U_b'(w_i - w_l)p_i] = (+)/(-) < 0$, where Δ is defined in eq. (1.8a) in n. 8. Similarly, the partial effect of a 1 per cent increase in all the penalty rates, f_i, hence in the average rate, $f = (F/t_i)$, would be given by $(\partial t_i^*/\partial f)f = (1/\Delta)[U_a'p_i f_i + U_a''(w_i - f_i - w_l)p_i f t_i^*]$. If $U'' \leq 0$, the preceding equation would always be negative. The result would be ambiguous, however, if $U'' > 0$, and would depend on opposite wealth and substitution effects. Moreover, it can easily be verified that

$$-\frac{\partial t_i^*}{\partial p_i} p_i \gtrless -\frac{\partial t_i^*}{\partial f} f, \text{ as } U'' \gtrless 0, \qquad (1.10)$$

where the right-hand side of eq. (1.10) represents the effect of a 1 per cent change in either the marginal or the average penalty for crime. This result can also be shown to apply under some restrictive assumptions to the relative effects of probability and severity of punishment on the *absolute* amount of time allocated to i. Moreover, it holds unambiguously for the relative effects of these variables on the incentive to enter (or exit from) illegal activity (proofs are given in Appendix 1 to this section).

14. The reason is that the increase in the probability of the least desirable state of the world (unemployment in l and failure in i) increases the demand for wealth in this state and might decrease the incentive to participate in i since the latter decreases the potential wealth in this state (see Appendix 1 to this section). However, the partial effect of an increase in u_l on entry into i is unambiguously positive and symmetrical to that of an increase in p_i.

A pure wealth effect may be defined as the effect of an equal proportional increase in wealth in every state of the world with no change in the probability distribution of states. Such may be the case when legitimate and illegitimate returns increase by the same proportion, and punishment for crime is by imprisonment (an empirical implementation of this case is considered below in Sec. III, B). Whether the optimal allocation of working time between i and l changes would then depend on whether an offender has increasing or decreasing relative risk aversion.[15] Increasing relative risk aversion thus implies that the rich have a lesser incentive to participate in crimes punishable by imprisonment relative to the poor.

Note, finally, that a decrease in the amount of time allocated to non-market activities (including schooling), due to a change in factors other than those considered in the preceding analysis, is likely to generate a positive scale effect on participation in i and l: since more time is spent in market activities, more time would be spent in both legal and illegal market activities, provided that the reduction in t_c did not affect one's relative allocation of working time between the latter activities.

We have so far considered the effects of changes in various indicators of the opportunities available in legitimate and illegitimate activities on the fraction of working time allocated to these activities. The behavioral implications of the preceding analysis would strictly apply to the absolute level of participation in i and l if changes in market opportunities did not affect the demand for time in nonmarket activities due, say, to offsetting wealth and substitution effects. This may not be true in general. For example, wealth-compensated changes in legitimate and illegitimate opportunities generate a pure substitution effect on the demand for consumption time. A partial increase in w_i is then expected to increase both the fraction of working time devoted to i as well as its absolute level, due to a complementary scale effect on working time. In contrast, a partial increase in w_l would lead to a decrease in the absolute level of participation in i only if the resulting substitution effect within the market sector exceeds an opposite scale effect on working time. This analysis shows that the effect of compensated and even uncompensated changes in legitimate market wages on the extent of participation in i may be lower than that of changes in illegitimate payoffs. A further implication is that the effect of uncompensated changes in various legitimate and illegitimate opportunities on the extent of participation in illegitimate activities is generally

---

15. For an elaborate discussion of this result, see Ehrlich and Becker (1972).

expected to be greater on offenders who participate in such activities on a part-time basis than on those who specialize in such activities. To illustrate, if an offender specializes in i—a boundary solution obtains—his objective opportunities will not be affected at all by small changes in legitimate employment opportunities, and he may not respond even to changes in illegitimate opportunities if such uncompensated changes have no effect on the demand for consumption time.[16] Thus, the extent of (initial) participation in illegitimate activity may be an important determinant of the *magnitude* of the response of specific offenders to changes in various market opportunities. Full-time or hard-core offenders may be less deterred in absolute magnitude by, say, an increase in law-enforcement activity, relative to part-time or occasional offenders, simply because of their greater involvement in illegitimate activity.

C. Market Opportunities and Crimes Against the Person

Unlike crimes involving material gains that may be motivated largely by the offender's desire for self-enrichment, crimes against the person may be motivated primarily by hate or passion: phenomena involving interdependencies in utilities among individuals whereby the utility of one is systematically affected by specific characteristics of another.[17] It may thus be appropriate to consider crimes against the person nonmarket activities, that is, activities that directly meet needs, as distinct from market or wealth-generating activities.

Since those who hate need not respond to incentives any differently from those who love or are indifferent to the well-being of others, the analysis of the preceding sections would apply, with some modifications,

---

16. More generally, let the total time spent in illegitimate activity be given by the identity $i \equiv t_0 - c - l$, where i, c, and l denote the number of hours an offender spends in i, c, and l, respectively. Let the subscripts p and f distinguish between relatively part-time and full-time offenders. By assumption, then, $i_f > i_p$ and $l_p > l_f \geq 0$. If α is a parameter that improves the relative opportunities in i, the effect of an uncompensated increase in α on i_p and i_f will be denoted by $E_{pa} = (\partial i_p/\partial \alpha)(\alpha/i_p)$ and by $E_{fa} = (\partial i_f/\partial \alpha)(\alpha/i_f)$, respectively. Assuming, now, that the partial elasticities of l and c with respect to α, $\sigma_{la} = -(\partial l/\partial \alpha)(\alpha/l)$ and $\sigma_{ca} = -(\partial c/\partial \alpha)(\alpha/c)$, are the same for both groups of offenders, then it can easily be shown that $D \equiv E_{pa} - E_{fa} = \sigma_{la}(l_p/i_p - l_f/i_f) + \sigma_{ca}(c_p/i_p - c_f/i_f)$ is necessarily positive if $\sigma_{la} \geq \sigma_{ca} \geq 0$.

17. Indeed, the empirical evidence lends support to such a proposition, for it shows that crimes against the person, unlike crimes against property, occur most frequently among people known to exercise close and frequent social contact and whose utilities are likely to be interdependent. For a more elaborate discussion, see Ehrlich (1970).

to crimes against the person as well as to crime involving material gains. Specifically, an increase in the probability and severity of punishment would deter crimes against the person for the same reasons it was expected to deter participation in crimes against property. Moreover, independent changes in legitimate market opportunities may also have a systematic effect on participation in crimes against the person. For example, given the total time spent in nonmarket activities, t_c, an increase in w_l that was fully compensated by a reduction in other income would reduce the demand for time-intensive consumption activities (for this concept, see Becker, 1965) because of the increase in their relative costs; some crimes against the person might fit into this category.[18] In contrast to crimes against property, however, a decrease in t_c due to specific exogenous factors is likely to produce a negative scale effect on participation in crimes against the person simply because less time could then be spent on all nonmarket activities, legitimate, as well as illegitimate. Accordingly, an improvement in legitimate earning opportunities that increases the total amount of time spent at work may reduce participation in crimes against the person even if it did not increase the cost of such crimes relative to other nonmarket activities. Some empirical evidence pertaining to these implications is discussed in Sec. IV, B.

II. THE SUPPLY OF OFFENSES

A. THE BEHAVIORAL FUNCTION

Given the validity of our analysis and the behavioral implications developed in the preceding section, we may now specify a behavioral function relating a person's actual participation in illegal activity in a given period to its basic determinants. Because in many illegal activities crime is comprised of discrete actions, or offenses, the dependent variable could be generally specified in terms of the directly observable number of offenses one commits, q_{ij}, rather than as the amount of time and other resources one devotes to such activities, assuming that all these variables are monotonically related:

$$q_{ij} = \psi_{ij}(p_{ij}, f_{ij}, w_{ij}, w_{lj}, u_{lj}, \pi_j). \tag{2.1}$$

---

18. This is likely particularly in view of the prospect of imprisonment associated with these crimes. If the length of incarceration, rather than the full cost of imprisonment, f_i, is held constant, as in the empirical implementation of our model, an increase in w_l is likely to increase the cost of crimes against persons relative to legitimate consumption activities.

The argument π_j is introduced in equation (2.1) to denote other variables that may affect the frequency of offenses committed by a specific individual, j, in addition to those discussed in the preceding section. These include his personal or family level of wealth, his efficiency at self-protection, the amount of private insurance provided by his family (or a criminal organization), and other factors that may affect the demand for time spent in nonmarket activities. In addition, the variable π includes costs and gains in other specific illegal activities which are close substitutes or complements to the illegal activity, (i).[19] Finally, π accounts for the form of the penalty: imprisonment, a fine, or a combination of the two. The importance of this latter distinction is discussed below in Sec. II, C.

B. The Aggregate Function

If all individuals were identical, the behavioral function (2.1), except for change in scale, could also be regarded as an aggregate supply function in a given period of time. In general, however, none of the variables entering (2.1) is a unique quantity, since people differ in their legitimate and illegitimate earning opportunities and hence in their opportunity costs of imprisonment (if punishment assumes such form). Therefore, the behavioral implications derived in Section I apply here for independent changes in the level of the entire distributions of these variables, or for changes in the mean variables within specific communities, holding all other parameters of the distributions constant:

$$Q_i = \Psi_i(P_i, F_i, Y_i, Y_l, U_l, \Pi_i), \tag{2.2}$$

where P_i, F_i, etc., denote the mean values of p_{ij}, f_{ij}, etc., and Π includes, in addition to environmental variables, all the moments of the distributions of p, f, etc., other than their means.

Our general expectations concerning the effect of exogenous shifts in various opportunities on the number of offenses committed may hold with fewer qualifications in the aggregate than in the case of individual offenders. The aggregate supply curve of offenses can be conceived of as the cumulative distribution of a density function showing variations across persons with respect to the minimum expected net gain that is sufficient to induce them to enter an illegal activity (their entry payoffs)

---

19. In Section I we considered the choice between single legitimate and illegitimate activities, but the analysis could easily be extended and applied to a choice among several competing legitimate and illegitimate activities. Participation in i might, in general, be affected by the opportunities available in some related illegal activities, as well as in l.

as well as the extent of response of active offenders to changes in net gains. Variations in entry payoffs across persons reflect different attitudes toward risk (as well as different psychic net benefits if the net gain is defined to include monetary elements only). People with preference for risk or a penchant for violence may enter crime even when their expected monetary gains are negative. Others, risk averters or law abiders, may enter crime only when the expected monetary gains are very high. A positive elasticity of the aggregate supply of offenses with respect to an increase in net gains from an offense may thus be expected, even if all individual supply curves were infinitely elastic—that is, if all offenders specialized in illegitimate activity and did not respond to such change at all—because the higher net gains would induce the entry of new offenders into illegitimate activity.

C. The Preventive Effect of Imprisonment

The set of hypotheses spelled out in Sections I, B and I, C regarding the effect of various opportunities on individuals', and hence the aggregate, supply of offenses, follows from our basic thesis that offenders respond to incentives. However, an increase in the probability and severity of punishment by imprisonment might reduce the total number of offenses even in the absence of any deterrent effect on offenders, because at least those imprisoned are temporarily prevented from committing further crimes. While both deterrence and prevention may serve equally well the basic purpose of law enforcement, which is to reduce total crime, they involve different costs. Moreover, the preventive effect of imprisonment may be partly offset by the enhanced incentive for recidivism generated through the possible adverse effect of imprisonment on legitimate relative to illegitimate skills and employment opportunities. It is therefore important (and challenging) to establish the existence of an independent deterrent effect of imprisonment on crime, both to verify the validity of our theory and to determine the effectiveness of penal modes that may have a deterrent effect only.

An estimation of the preventive effect of imprisonment can be derived through the following reasoning. Suppose that offenders constituted a noncompeting group that does not respond to incentives, the constant proportion of which $\bar{S} = S/N$, is determined by nature, and let punishment be imposed solely in the form of imprisonment. In this model, where no deterrent effect of imprisonment (or other factors) is assumed, the rate (per capita) of flow of offenses in any given period,

$k = Q/N$, would be a positive function of the rate of offenders at large (those free to commit offenses), $\bar{\theta} = \theta/N$, or

$$k_t = \zeta\bar{\theta}_t, \tag{2.3}$$

where ζ is the number of offenses committed by an average offender in a given period and is assumed to be constant. The rate of offenders at large in the population is in turn identically equal to the rate of the offenders' subpopulation net of the rate of those in jail, or

$$\bar{\theta}_t = \bar{S}_t - \bar{J}_t. \tag{2.4}$$

Let the fraction of offenders apprehended and imprisoned in any period (the probability that an offender is apprehended and jailed in t) be P, and let the average duration of time spent in jail by each convict be T periods. It can then be shown that in a steady state the rate of offenders in jail would be

$$\bar{J} = \frac{\bar{S}P \sum_{\tau=1}^{T} (1 + g)^{-\tau}}{1 + P \sum_{\tau=1}^{T} (1 + g)^{-\tau}}, \text{ for } P < 1,^{20} \tag{2.5}$$

where g is a constant rate of growth (per period) of both the total population and the offender subpopulation. Substituting equations (2.5) and (2.4) in (2.3) yields

$$k = \frac{\zeta\bar{S}}{1 + p \sum_{\tau=1}^{T} (1 + g)^{-\tau}} \approx \frac{\zeta\bar{S}}{1 + PT} \text{ for } g \approx 0. \tag{2.6}$$

Since ζ, g, and $\bar{S}$ are assumed given constants, the rate of offenses committed in a steady state would be a negative function of PT, the expected

---

20. The number of offenders jailed in the beginning of each period is identically equal to the total number of offenders apprehended and jailed in the preceding T periods, or

$$J_t \equiv \sum_{\tau=1}^{T} P(S_{t-\tau} - J_{t-\tau}).$$

Given that $S_t = S_0(1 + g)^t$ and $N_t = N_0(1 + g)^t$, the identity above can be expressed as a linear difference equation of the Tth degree,

$$\bar{J}_t + P(1 + g)^{-1}\bar{J}_{t-1} + \cdots + P(1 + g)^{-T}\bar{J}_{t-T} = P\bar{S} \sum_{\tau=1}^{T} (1 + g)^{-\tau}. \tag{2.5a}$$

Equation (2.5) is the particular integral of eq. (2.5a). The condition $P < 1$ (if $g \geq 0$) can be shown to be a sufficient condition for the general solution of (2.5a) to converge toward the equilibrium value of its particular integral.

length of imprisonment for an offender. In particular, the absolute value of the elasticity of the rate of offenses per period with respect to changes in probability and severity of imprisonment would be approximately the same: [21]

$$\sigma_{kP} \approx \sigma_{kT} \approx \frac{PT}{1 + PT} \text{ for } g \approx 0. \tag{2.7}$$

Clearly, σ is independent of the value of ζ and is positively related to PT.[22] Therefore, the preventive effect of imprisonment may be relatively small for less serious crimes. Equation (2.7) establishes the important point that the preventive effect of P and T is in principle distinguishable from the deterrent effect: not only is the latter compatible with, say, $\sigma_{kT} \geq 1$, it is also compatible with $\sigma_{kT} \gtrless \sigma_{kP}$.[23] The existence of a deterrent effect can thus be inferred from empirical estimates of the absolute and relative values of σ_{kP} and σ_{kT}.

III. AN ECONOMETRIC SPECIFICATION OF THE MODEL

A. THE SUPPLY-OF-OFFENSES EQUATION

The variables entering the behavioral function (2.1) have been generally defined in terms of the real wealth equivalent of both monetary and psychic elements. Since psychic elements cannot be accounted for explicitly in an empirical investigation, it will be useful to modify equations (2.1) and (2.2) by separating quantifiable from nonquantifiable variables. A simple form of a mean (group) supply-of-offense function

---

21. An increase in P may have a greater preventive effect than an equal proportional increase in T in the short run, however, because the latter does not have any immediate impact on the number of offenders at large, whereas an increase in P does. Indeed, that may have led some criminologists to believe the probability of punishment to be of greater importance than severity of punishment in preventing crime (see Becker, 1968, included in this volume, p. 9, n. 12). A comparison of the exact values of σ_{kP} and σ_{kT} in eq. (2.7) shows that a relatively greater effect of P may persist, to a limited extent, even in a steady state, if $g > 0$ and $T > 1$.

22. This implies a potential variation across states in the coefficients (elasticities) b_1 and b_2 of the regression eq. (3.2), for states with relatively higher values of PT might have higher elasticities of offenses with respect to P and T. However, the variation in PT of specific crimes across states is found to be quite small in practice.

23. In terms of our model (see eq. [1.10] in n. 13), $\sigma_{kT} > \sigma_{kP}$ indicates risk aversion on the part of the average offender. Since $\sigma_{kT} \leq \sigma_{kF}$ (see Appendix 1 to Section III, item 3), this conclusion may be strengthened if $\sigma_{kT} > \sigma_{kP}$.

which is consistent with this modification is

$$\left(\frac{Q}{N}\right)_i = P_i^{b_{1i}}F_i^{b_{2i}}Y_i^{c_{1i}}Y_l^{c_{2i}}U_i^{d_i}V^{c_i}Z_i, \tag{3.1}$$

where $(Q/N)_i$ denotes the number of offenses of crime category i committed by the average person in a community (crime rate); F_i, Y_i, and Y_l are arithmetic means of the monetary components of f_{ij}, w_{ij}, and w_{lj} in eq. (2.1); V is a vector of environmental variables; and Z summarizes the effect of psychic and other nonquantifiable variables on the crime rate.[24]

To the extent that individuals' taste for crime was either proportional to some of the quantifiable variables affecting crime, or uncorrelated in the natural logarithms with all the explanatory variables, it is possible to specify a stochastic function of the form

$$\left(\frac{Q}{N}\right)_i = AP_i^{b_{1i}}F_i^{b_{2i}}Y_i^{c_{1i}}Y_l^{c_{2i}}U_i^{d_i}V^{e_i} \exp{(\mu_i)}, \tag{3.2}$$

where A is a constant, and μ_i stands for random errors of measurement and other stochastic effects and is assumed to have a normal distribution. In this paper we apply equation (3.2) in a cross-state regression analysis.[25]

---

24. The mean supply-of-offenses function given by eq. (3.1) can be derived by integrating individual supply-of-offenses functions of the same form if the individual elasticities b_{1ij}, b_{2ij}, etc., are the same for all. The variables entering eq. (3.1) would then be the geometric means of the corresponding variables entering eq. (2.1). However, if the density function of, say, $p_{ij} - g(p_{ij}P_i)$ — were equal across states and homogeneous of degree minus one in p_{ij} and P_i (the arithmetic mean), and similarly for all the explanatory variables entering eq. (2.1) then eq. (3.1) could be specified in terms of arithmetic rather than geometric means, with an appropriate modification of the constant term Z (for proofs see Tobin, 1950, or Chow, 1957). Note, however, that to the extent that the variation in the rate of crime across communities is due to changes in the average offender's participation in crime, and not only to entry and exit of offenders, the coefficients of eq. (3.2) may vary systematically with Q/N, as our discussion in the last paragraph of Sec. I, B indicates; the regression equation may not, then, be strictly linear in the parameters. This problem is ignored in our analysis.

25. The cross-state regression analysis does not control spillovers or displacement effects due to a possible migration of individuals from one state to another in response to differences in opportunities across states. To the extent that such effects exist, the estimated coefficients associated with P_i, F_i, and Y_i would be overstated, while those associated with Y_l and U would be understated, relative to their values in closed communities. We implicitly assume, however, that there is no perfect mobility of resources across states because of considerable costs of migration. Different states can thus be viewed essentially as different markets.

B. Crime, Income Inequality, and Affluence

In Section I, B it was shown that the extent of individual participation in crime, and hence the crime rate in each state, is a positive function of the absolute differential returns from crime $(Y_i - Y_l)$.[26] Information concerning such monetary differential returns is at present unavailable on a statewide basis, and alternative income opportunities cannot be estimated unless one is able to identify a control group representing potential offenders and study its alternative income prospects. The difficulty may be met, in part, by making some plausible assumptions regarding the occupational characteristics of activities such as robbery, burglary, and theft, which are actually investigated in our empirical analysis. We postulate that payoffs on such crimes depend, primarily, on the level of transferable assets in the community, that is, on opportunities provided by potential victims of crime, and to a much lesser extent on the offender's education and legitimate training. The relative variation in the average potential illegal payoff, Y_i, may be approximated by the relative variation in, say, the median value of transferable goods and assets or family income across states which we denote W.[27] The preceding postulate also implies that those in a state with legitimate returns well below the median have greater differential returns from property crimes and, hence, a greater incentive to participate in such crimes, relative to those with income well above the median. The variation in the mean legitimate opportunities available to potential offenders across states, Y_l, may therefore be approximated by that of the mean income level of those below the state's median. Partly because of statistical considerations, we have chosen to compute the latter somewhat indirectly as the

---

26. The *elasticity* of offenses with respect to Y_i need not be equal to that with respect to Y_l (see the final paragraph in Sec. I, B). We have therefore introduced both variables in eq. (3.2) (rather than the difference $Y_i - Y_l$), allowing for their coefficients c_1 and c_2 to be different.

27. More precisely, the assumption is that, given the relative distribution of family income in a state, variations in average potential payoffs on property crimes can be approximated by the variation in the level of the *entire* distribution. If the income distribution were of the log-normal variety, it can be shown that variation in its level would be reflected by an equal proportional variation in its *median* value. Note that the relative variation in *potential* payoffs on property crimes may be an unbiased estimator of the relative variation in the realized gross payoffs if self-protection (of property) by potential victims were proportionally related to their wealth.

percentage of families below one-half of the median income in a state, which we denote X (income inequality).[28]

Since X is a measure of the *relative* distance between legitimate and illegitimate opportunities, changes in W, X held constant, would amount to equal percentage changes in the absolute wage differential, $Y_i - Y_l$. Given the probability and severity of punishment, an increase in W might have a positive effect on the rate of property crimes similar to that of X. In our empirical implementation, the severity of punishment, F, is measured by the effective incarceration period of offenders, T. If punishment were solely by imprisonment, an increase in W, with X and T constant, might increase $Y_i - Y_l$ and F (the opportunity cost of imprisonment) by the same proportion, and its net effect could be nil (see our discussion of pure-wealth effects in Sec. I, B). In contrast, an increase in X would imply in this case a decrease in both Y_l and F. In practice, however, a major proportion of offenders is punished by means other than imprisonment (see Ehrlich, 1970, Table 1). Consequently, we may expect the median income level (affluence) as well as income inequality to be positively related to the incidence of property crimes. Note that an advantage of introducing W and X in equation (3.2) in lieu of $Y_i - Y_l$ is that the former can be treated as exogenous variables, whereas the actual differential gain from crime may be a function of both the crime rate and private expenditure on self-protection (see our discussion in footnotes 4 and 29).

---

28. Let the average legitimate income of those with income below and above the average be w_p and w_r, respectively. Our measure of income inequality X (originally used by Fuchs, 1967, as an index of poverty) can be regarded as inversely related to w_p/W. If median income, W, were held constant, the effect of an increase in X on the rate of property crimes $k = Q/N$ would be given by $\sigma_X = -d \ln k/d \ln (w_p/W) = \eta_p + \eta_r \, d \ln w_r/d \ln w_p$, where $\eta_p = -\partial \ln k/\partial \ln (w_p/W)$ and $\eta_r = -\partial \ln k/\partial \ln (w_r/W)$. By our assumptions η_r is much smaller than η_p. A 1 per cent increase in X might therefore have approximately the same effect as a 1 per cent decrease in legitimate opportunities available to potential offenders, or $\sigma_X \approx \eta_p$. In contrast, if the income effect on the supply of malice and acts of hate were the same for rich and poor alike, $\eta_p = \eta_r = \eta$, then an increase in income inequality—mean and median income held constant—can be shown to have a positive effect on the incidence of crimes against the person only if the income effect were negative ($\eta > 0$), for then $\sigma_X = \eta[1 - (w_p/w_r)] > 0$. Precisely the same result applies in reference to the impact of an increase in X on crime through its opposing effects on self-protection by potential victims. One reason for employing X rather than w_p in the regression analysis is that its correlation with W is relatively lower.

C. CRIME AND LAW ENFORCEMENT: A SIMULTANEOUS-EQUATION MODEL

Equation (3.2) defines the rate of a specific crime category $(Q/N)_i$ as a function of a set of explanatory variables, including the probability and severity of punishment. In general, both P and F may not be exogenous variables, since they are determined by the public's allocation of resources to law-enforcement activity and, as will be argued below, by the level of crime itself. The expenditure on law enforcement, in turn, is likely to be affected by the rate of crime and the resulting social loss. In order to insure consistent estimates of equation (3.2), it is desirable to construct a simultaneous-equation model of crime and law enforcement.[29]

To simplify matters, we assume that the severity of punishment is in practice largely unaffected by the joint determination of Q/N and P.[30] Our model consists of a supply-of-offenses function, as discussed above, a production function of direct law-enforcement activity by police and courts, and a (public) demand function for such activity.

An increase in expenditure on police and courts, E/N, can be expected to result in a greater proportion of offenders apprehended and convicted of crime. However, the productivity of these resources is likely to be lower at higher levels of criminal activity because more offenders must then be apprehended, charged, and tried in court in order to achieve a given level of P. Thus, with a given level of expenditure devoted to law-enforcement activity, the rate of crime and the probability of appre-

29. Simultaneous relations may also exist between the rate of crime, the average payoff from crime, Y_i, and *private* self-protection against crime that can be expected to have an adverse effect on both (see our discussion in n. 4). We do not elaborate on these relations here because in our empirical investigation we use indirect estimates of Y_i (see Sec. III, B above) that can be considered largely exogenous to our system of equations and because of the lack of reliable data on private self-protection.

30. Bureau of Prisons statistics from 1940, 1951, 1960, and 1964 show little variation in the median time served in state prisons by felony offenders over the past few decades. For example, the median time served for burglary (T_b) in the United States in 1940 and 1964 was virtually identical: 20.6 and 20.1 months, respectively, even though the national burglary rates in those 2 years (based on unpublished FBI data) were 285.6 and 630.3 per 100,000 civilian population, respectively, and the number of prisoners received from court in federal and state institutions for the crime of burglary (based on unpublished Bureau of Prisons data) rose from 7,434 in 1942 to 21,600 in 1962. Furthermore, there had been relatively little change in the distribution of T_b across states: in 35 out of 44 states in our sample, changes in T_b between 1940 and 1964 were in the order of magnitude of ± 6 months, with the number of increases approximately matching the number of declines.

hension and punishment for crime might be negatively related, with the causality running in an opposite direction from that predicted by our analysis: for example, in a riot, the probability of apprehension for individual rioters, as well as for offenders committing other crimes, falls considerably below its normal level due to the excessive load on local police units. (This is a source of external economies in criminal activity.) Population size and density may also be negatively related to P because of the relative ease with which an offender could elude the police in densely populated areas. A natural way to summarize these relations is via a production function of the Cobb-Douglas variety:

$$P = B \left(\frac{E}{N}\right)^{\beta_1} \left(\frac{Q}{N}\right)^{\beta_2} Z^\delta \exp{(\xi)} \tag{3.3}$$

with $\beta_1 > 0$ and $\beta_2 < 0$,[31] where B is a constant, Z is a vector of environmental variables (productivity indicators), and ξ is a random variable.[32]

The demand for law-enforcement activity may be viewed to be essentially a negative demand for crime or, conversely, a positive demand for defense against crime. In general, potential victims may wish to self-protect against victimization, both privately and collectively. Our present discussion is confined to collective self-protection via law-enforcement activity and ignores private self-protection and other collective methods of combating crime, since data exigencies rule out a comprehensive analysis of social defense against crime. (A theoretical analysis of self-protection by victims is implicit, however, in Ehrlich and Becker, 1972.) For a simple exposition, assume the following probability distribution of losses from crime to the ith person in a given period: he has either a potential real wealth I_i^c with probability $1 - k_i$, or a lower wealth, $I_i^c - L_i$, with probability k_i, where L_i is his potential loss from crime and k_i the probability of victimization. If the number of persons in the community were large enough, and their probabilities of victimization largely independent, their actual per capita wealth would be known with certainty and

---

31. The elasticity of P with respect to Q/N, β_2, is not likely to be lower than -1, however, since this would imply that, given E/N, an increase in Q/N reduces the absolute number of offenses cleared by conviction, and not only their proportion among all offenses.

32. Since $0 < P < 1$, the natural logarithm of P is bounded between $-\infty$ and 0, and its distribution cannot be assumed normal. Nevertheless, the normal distribution may approximate that of $\ln P$ over its observed range of variation. For example, the observed mean and standard deviation of our measures of $\ln P$ of all offenses in 1960 are -3.1670 and 0.5365, respectively. Moreover, since our regression estimates are derived by method of two-stage least-squares, they are asymptotically unbiased.

would equal the expected personal wealth, $Y = I - kL$, where

$$k = \frac{1}{N} \sum_{i=1}^{N} k_i = \frac{Q}{N}, \ I = \frac{1}{N} \sum_{i=1}^{N} I_i, \ \text{and} \ L = \frac{\sum_{i=1}^{N} k_i L_i}{\sum_{i=1}^{N} k_i}. \quad (3.4)$$

Effective law enforcement by police, courts, and legislative bodies is expected to reduce the crime rate (i.e., the objective probability of victimization to a person) by increasing the probability and severity of punishment for crime. In addition, such activity may also reduce the actual loss to victims by recovering stolen property, guarding property, and other related actions. Consequently, we may write $k = k(r, j)$ and $L = L(r, j)$, where $r = E/N$ is real per capita expenditure on direct law enforcement and j represents expenditure on the determination and actual implementation of imprisonment or other punitive measures, private expenditure on self-protection against crime, and other outlays affecting the level of criminal activity in a state. Both k and L are assumed to have continuous first- and second-order derivatives with respect to r, so that $k'(r)$ and $L'(r)$ are negative and $k''(r)$ and $L''(r)$ are positive in sign. To further simplify matters, we ignore any functional dependence between r and j and treat j as an exogenous variable. If the public were interested in maximizing the expected utility of the average person,[33] optimal per capita expenditure, r^*, would be derived under the foregoing assumptions by maximizing the expected personal wealth,

$$Y = I - k(r)L(r) - r - j, \quad (3.5)$$

with respect to r. The first-order optimality condition can be written

$$r^* = (e_1 + e_2)L(r^*)k(r^*), \quad (3.6)$$

where $e_1 = - k'(r^*)(r^*/k)$ and $e_2 = -L'(r^*)(r^*/L)$ are assumed constant. Optimal expenditure on apprehending and convicting offenders, $r^* =$

---

33. Collective self-protection may be viewed as a voluntary pooling of resources by potential victims of crime (all members of the community) to provide a common service—decreasing the probabilities of (private) states of the world involving victimization—the benefits of which are to be divided among all members. Maximization of the utility of an average member would then be the appropriate decision rule. Note that the loss to a victim of crime, even in the case of property crimes, is a net social loss, not just a transfer payment: if criminal activity were competitive, and offenders' risk neutral, then the potential marginal payoff to an average offender would equal the marginal value of the foregone resources he would devote to achieve it, including his marginal expected opportunity costs of imprisonment (see our analysis in Sec. I, A).

$(E/N)^*$, is thus seen to be proportional to the resulting crime rate and potential loss to a victim of crime. The latter may be forecast in practice as the actual crime rate and the average loss to a victim. The demand function for law-enforcement expenditure may thus be specified as

$$\left(\frac{E}{N}\right)^* = \Gamma \frac{Q}{N} L. \tag{3.7}$$

Equation (3.7) shows the desired level of per capita expenditure on law enforcement in the absence of adjustment costs. In practice, one may expect only partial adjustment of public expenditure on law enforcement to its desired level in a given period due to positive costs of adjustment in a relatively short run. If the ratio of current to lagged expenditure were a power function of the ratio of the desired to lagged expenditure, the relevant demand function could be written as

$$\frac{E}{N} = \Gamma L^\gamma \left(\frac{Q}{N}\right)^\gamma \left(\frac{E}{N}\right)_{t-1}^{1-\gamma} \exp(\epsilon), \tag{3.8}$$

where $0 < \gamma < 1$ is an adjustment coefficient and ϵ is assumed a normally distributed random variable. Equations (3.2), (3.3), and (3.8) [34] form the structure of our simultaneous-equation model of law enforcement and crime.[35]

---

34. Available information regarding expenditure on police relates to fiscal years, whereas the other variables used in the regression analysis relate to calendar years. The appropriate forecasts of $k(r^*)$ and $L(r^*)$ may therefore be defined as weighted geometrical means of current and lagged crime rates and average losses. At present no data on losses to victims of crime are available on a statewide basis, and no serious attempt has been made to estimate eq. (3.8). Lagged crime rates are included in the reduced-form regression equations.

35. Stability conditions associated with this system of equations require that the product of the elasticities b_1 and β_2 in eqq. (3.2) and (3.3) — both assumed negative in sign — does not exceed unity. This arises because when solving for the value of Q/N in terms of reduced-form variables, lagged expenditure $(E/N)_{t-1}$, for example, is raised to the power $[(1 - \gamma)b_1\beta_1]/(1 - b_1\beta_2 - \gamma b_1\beta_1)$. This coefficient would be negative for all possible values of γ — the simultaneous-equation system would have a stable solution — if the denominator were positive. A sufficient condition is $b_1\beta_2 < 1$. Note that unlike Becker's optimality conditions for the minimization of the social loss from crime (see Becker, 1968, included in this volume, pp. 14–18), our stability conditions do not require that $|b_2| < 1$ or that $|b_2| < |b_1|$: they do not require that in equilibrium offenders must be, on balance, risk preferrers. Indeed, some of our empirical estimates of $|b_{2i}|$, exceed those of $|b_{1i}|$ (see Sec. IV below).

IV. ANALYSIS OF CRIME VARIATIONS ACROSS STATES IN THE UNITED STATES

We have applied the economic and econometric framework developed in the preceding sections in a regression analysis of variations of index crimes across U.S. states in 1960, 1950, and 1940.[36] A short description of the variables used in the empirical investigation as counterparts of the theoretical constructs entering equations (3.2), (3.3), and (3.8) are given in Table 1, and the interested reader is referred to Appendix 1 to Section

TABLE 1
LIST OF VARIABLES USED IN REGRESSION ANALYSIS

$\left(\dfrac{Q}{N}\right)_i, \left(\dfrac{Q_i}{N}\right)_{t-1}$ = current and 1-year lagged crime rate: the number of offenses known per capita

$\left(\dfrac{C}{Q}\right)_i = P_i$ = estimator of probability of apprehension and imprisonment: the number of offenders imprisoned per offenses known

T_i = average time served by offenders in state prisons

W = median income of families

X = percentage of families below one-half of median income

NW = percentage of nonwhites in the population

A_{14-24} = percentage of all males in the age group 14–24

U_{14-24}, U_{35-39} = unemployment rate of civilian urban males ages 14–24 and 35–39

L_{14-24} = labor-force participation rate for civilian urban males ages 14–24

Ed = mean number of years of schooling of population 25 years old and over

$SMSA$ = percentage of population in standard metropolitan statistical areas

$\dfrac{E}{N}, \left(\dfrac{E}{N}\right)_{t-1}$ = per capita expenditure on police in fiscal 1960, 1959

M = number of males per 100 females

D = dummy variable distinguishing northern from southern states (south = 1)

NOTE. — Variables are time- and state-specific; i denotes a specific crime category.

---

36. Due to data exigencies, the empirical investigation deals with only seven felony offenses (index crimes) punishable by imprisonment. The data regarding (and definitions of) these crimes are available in the *Uniform Crime Reports* of the FBI. Samples from 1960 include 47 state observations and those from 1950 include 46. The 1940 sample sizes vary between 36 and 43.

III for a more elaborate analysis and discussion of this list. Since data on police expenditure across states are available for 1960, but not for 1950 and 1940, crime statistics relating to earlier decennial years are used only to derive ordinary-least-squares (OLS) estimates of supply-of-offenses functions. Data from 1960 are also used to derive two-stage least-squares (2SLS) and seemingly unrelated (SUR) estimates of supply-of-offenses functions and a production function of law-enforcement activity.

A. Supply-of-Offenses Functions: The Effect of Probability and Severity of Punishment, Income and Income Inequality, and Racial Composition

Despite the shortcomings of the data and the crude estimates of some of the desired variables (see Appendix 1 to Section III), the results of the regression analysis lend credibility to the basic hypotheses of the model. The major consistent findings are:

1. The rate of specific crime categories, with virtually no exception, varies inversely with estimates of the probability of apprehension and punishment by imprisonment, $P = C/Q$, and with the average length of time served in state prisons, T.

2. Crimes against property (robbery, burglary, larceny, and auto theft) are also found to vary positively with the percentage of families below one-half of the median income (income inequality), X, and with the median income, W; in contrast, these variables are found to have relatively lower effects on the incidence of crimes against the person, particularly murder and rape. Also, the regression coefficients associated with X and W have relatively high standard errors in the case of crimes against the person.

3. All specific crime rates appear to be positively related to the percentage of nonwhites in the population, NW. (For the reasons for including this, and other demographic variables, see Appendix 1 to Section III.) These findings hold consistently across samples from 1960, 1950, and 1940, independently of the regression technique employed or the specific set of (additional) variables introduced in the regression analysis. We therefore present them separately from other results.[37]

---

37. The FBI's estimates of crime rates across states in 1950 and 1940 relate to urban areas, whereas no such data are available in 1960. Also, our estimates of income inequality in 1940 are derived from a sample of wage and salary workers, whereas in 1960 they are derived from a census of family income. Because of these differences we have not integrated the three samples for a more comprehensive regression analysis. Also, the point estimates of the regression coefficients are not exactly comparable across the different samples.

OLS ESTIMATES

Tables 2 and 3 present a summary of weighted OLS estimates of elasticities associated with P, T, W, X, and NW. The regression equation used is a natural logarithmic transformation of equation (3.2):

$$\ln \left(\frac{Q}{N}\right)_i = a + b_{1i} \ln P_i + b_{2i} \ln T_i + c_{1i} \ln W$$
$$+ c_{2i} \ln X + e_{1i} \ln NW + \mu_i,^{38} \quad (4.1)$$

with the weighting factor being the square root of the population size.[39]

The OLS estimates of the elasticity of offenses with respect to P_i and T_i, $\hat{b}_{1i}$, and $\hat{b}_{2i}$, respectively, are generally lower than unity in absolute value. Also, the difference $|\hat{b}_{1i}| - |\hat{b}_{2i}|$ exceeds twice its standard error in regressions dealing with murder, rape, and robbery, while the converse holds in the case of burglary in 1960. However, estimates of b_{1i} are likely to be biased in a negative direction relative to those of b_{2i} (provided that the true absolute values of b_{1i} were lower than unity) because of a potential negative correlation between $(Q/N)_i$ and $P_i = (C/Q)_i$ arising from errors of measurement in Q_i[40] (see our discussion in Appendix 1 to Section III). In addition, the OLS estimates of b_{1i} and b_{2i} may be subject to a simultaneous-equation bias. More reliable estimates are therefore provided by our simultaneous-equation estimation methods.

The estimated elasticities of specific crimes against property with respect to both W and X, $\hat{c}_{1i}$ and $\hat{c}_{2i}$, respectively, are positive, statistically

---

38. When grouping specific crime categories in broader classes, the probability and severity of punishment, P_g and T_g, were measured as weighted averages of the P's and T's associated with the single categories:

$$P_g = \left(\sum_{i=1}^{g} C_i\right) \bigg/ \left(\sum_{i=1}^{g} Q_i\right) \text{ and } T_g = \sum_{i=1}^{g} C_i T_i \bigg/ \sum_{i=1}^{g} C_i.$$

It should be pointed out that the coefficient b_{2i} in eqq. (4.1) and (4.3) below is expected to be lower than b_{2i} in eq. (3.2) by a positive constant factor (see our discussion in Appendix 1 to Section III, item 3).

39. A residual analysis of unweighted regressions generally showed a negative correlation between the absolute value of estimated residuals and the population size. This apparent heteroscedasticity is consistent with the assumption that unspecified random variables which affect participation in crime are homoscedastic at the individual level. Thus, $\sqrt{N}$ may be an appropriate weighting factor.

40. Since the variances of errors of measurement in Q_i are likely to be greater in 1950 and 1940 than in 1960, the bias in the difference between b_{1i} and b_{2i} is likely to be relatively large in regressions using data from the former 2 years. Indeed, this may explain why the differences $|b_{2i}| - |b_{1i}|$ in regressions concerning burglary and larceny in 1960 are positive and significant, while in 1940 they are negative but insignificant.

TABLE 2

OLS (WEIGHTED) REGRESSION ESTIMATES OF COEFFICIENTS ASSOCIATED WITH
SELECTED VARIABLES IN 1960, 1950, AND 1940: CRIMES AGAINST THE
PERSON AND ALL OFFENSES (DEPENDENT VARIABLES ARE SPECIFIC
CRIME RATES)

Offense and Year	Estimated Coefficients Associated with Selected Variables						
	a Intercept	b_1 with ln P_i	b_2 with ln T_i	c_1 with ln W	c_2 with ln X	e_1 with ln NW	Adj. R^2
Murder:							
1960	−0.6644 [a]	−0.3407	−0.1396 [a]	0.4165 [a]	1.3637 [a]	0.5532	.8687
1950 [b]	−0.7682 [a]	−0.5903	−0.2878	0.6095 [a]	1.9386	0.4759	.8155
Rape:							
1960 [b]	−7.3802 [a]	−0.5783	−0.1880 [a]	1.2220	0.8942 [a]	0.1544	.6858
Assault:							
1960	−13.2994	−0.2750	−0.1797 [a]	2.0940	1.4697	0.6771	.8282
1950	−0.7139 [a]	−0.4791	−0.3839	0.5641 [a]	0.9136 [a]	0.5526	.8566
1940	−0.2891	−0.4239	−0.6036	0.7274 [a]	0.5484 [a]	0.7298	.8381
Murder and rape:							
1960 [b]	−1.8117	−0.5787	−0.2867	0.6773 [a]	0.9456	0.3277	.6948
Murder and assault:							
1950 [b]	1.0951 [a]	−0.7614	−0.3856	0.3982 [a]	1.1689 [a]	0.4281	.8783
Crimes against persons:							
1960 [b]	−4.1571 [a]	−0.5498	−0.3487	1.0458	0.9145	0.4897	.8758
All offenses:							
1960	−7.1657	−0.5255	−0.5854	2.0651	1.8013	0.2071	.6950
1950	−1.5081 [a]	−0.5664	−0.4740	1.3456	1.9399	0.1051	.6592
1940	−5.2711	−0.6530	−0.2892	0.5986	2.2658	0.1386	.6650

NOTE.—The absolute values of all regression coefficients in Tables 2 and 3, except those marked [a], are at least twice those of their standard errors; [b] indicates regressions in which the absolute difference $(\hat{b}_1 - \hat{b}_2)$ is at least twice the value of the relevant standard error $S(\hat{b}_1 - \hat{b}_2)$.

TABLE 3
OLS (Weighted) Regression Estimates of Coefficients Associated with Selected Variables in 1960, 1950, and 1940: Crimes against Property (Dependent Variables Are Specific Crime Rates)

Offense and Year	Estimated Coefficients Associated with Selected Variables						
	a Intercept	b_1 with $\ln P_i$	b_2 with $\ln T_i$	c_1 with $\ln W$	c_2 with $\ln X$	e_1 with $\ln NW$	Adj. R^2
Robbery:							
1960 [b]	−20.1910	−0.8534	−0.2233 [a]	2.9086	1.8409	0.3764	.8014
1950 [b]	−10.2794	−0.9389	−0.5610	1.7278	0.4798	0.3282	.7839
1940	−10.2943	−0.9473	−0.1912 [a]	1.6608	0.7222	0.3408	.8219
Burglary:							
1960 [b]	−5.5700 [a]	−0.5339	−0.9001	1.7973	2.0452	0.2269	.6713
1950	−1.0519 [a]	−0.4102	−0.4689	1.1891	1.8697	0.1358	.4933
1940	−0.6531 [a]	−0.4607	−0.2698	0.8327 [a]	1.6939	0.1147	.3963
Larceny:							
1960	−14.9431	−0.1331	−0.2630	2.6893	1.6207	0.1315	.5222
1950	−4.2857 [a]	−0.3477	−0.4301	1.9784	3.3134	−0.0342 [a]	.5819
1940	−10.6198	−0.4131	−0.1680 [a]	0.6186	3.7371	0.0499 [a]	.6953
Auto theft:							
1960	−17.3057	−0.2474	−0.1743 [a]	2.8931	1.8981	0.1152	.6948
Burglary and robbery:							
1960	−9.2683	−0.6243	−0.6883	2.1598	2.1156	0.2565	.7336
1950	−3.0355 [a]	−0.5493	−0.4879	1.3624	1.6066	0.1854	.5590
Larceny and auto theft:							
1960	−14.1543	−0.2572	−0.3339	2.6648	1.8263	0.1423	.6826
1950	−3.9481 [a]	−0.3134	−0.4509	1.9286	2.9961	−0.0290 [a]	.5894
Crimes against property:							
1960	−10.1288	−0.5075	−0.6206	2.3345	2.0547	0.2118	.7487
1950	−2.8056	−0.5407	−0.4792	1.5836	2.2548	0.0755	.6253

Note. — Same references as in Table 2.

significant, and generally greater than unity. Note, however, that $\hat{c}_{1i}$ may reflect, in part, the effect of "urbanization" (the percentage of the population in standard metropolitan statistical areas, SMSA), since W and $SMSA$ are highly correlated.[41] This may explain why the absolute values of $\hat{c}_{1i}$ in regressions using 1940 and 1950 data are lower than their estimates in the 1960 regressions: the dependent variables in the 1940 and 1950 regressions are urban crime rates, while in 1960 they are state crime rates. The fact that variations in X and W are found to have a lower effect on the incidence of crimes against the person relative to crimes against property supports our selection of them as indicators of the relative opportunities associated with these latter crimes. Moreover, the introduction of X and W in the regression analysis helps to obtain significant results concerning the effect of T, which is to be expected since variations in these variables presumably account in large part for the variation in the opportunity costs of imprisonment.

The positive correlation between the percentage of nonwhites, NW, and the rate of specific crimes is found to be independent of a regional effect tested via the introduction of a dummy variable distinguishing northern and southern states: the dummy variable loses its statistical significance when NW is also introduced in the regression analysis. Moreover, virtually the same elasticities of crime rates with respect to NW have been derived in an OLS regression analysis including northern states only. The significant effect of NW on the rate of specific crimes may essentially reflect the effect of the relatively inferior legitimate market opportunities (and lower opportunity cost of imprisonment) of nonwhites, since our measures of average relative legitimate opportunities in a state do not fully reflect opportunities available to nonwhites.

The simple multiple regressions appear to account for a large part of the variation in crime rates across states: the adjusted R^2 statistics range from .87 for murder to .52 for larceny in 1960. Apparently, the ranking of the R^2 statistics by crime categories is negatively related to the ranking of these crimes by the extent of their underreporting errors and by the extent to which they involve punishment other than imprisonment. The R^2 statistics may partly reflect, however, the extent of negative correlation between $(Q/N)_i$ and P_i, due to measurement errors in Q_i. This may

---

41. Urbanization may serve as a measure of accessibility to (lower direct costs of engaging in) various criminal activities due, for example, to the concentration of business activity, the massive communication networks, and the density of the population in metropolitan areas. The positive simple-regression coefficient associated with SMSA becomes insignificant, however, when P and W are also introduced in regressions concerning specific crimes against property.

explain why the R^2 statistics associated with the 1940 regressions are not lower than those associated with the 1960 ones.

THE 2SLS AND SUR ESTIMATES

The set of equations (4.1) has also been estimated via a 2SLS procedure, applying our simultaneous-equation model and using data from 1960. The set of exogenous and predetermined variables introduced in the reduced-form regression analysis has been

$$\ln P_i = a_0 + a_{1i} \ln T_i + a_{2i} \ln \left(\frac{E}{N}\right)_{t-1}$$

$$+ a_{3i} \ln \left(\frac{Q_i}{N}\right)_{t-1} + a_{4i} \ln W + a_{5i} \ln X$$

$$+ a_{6i} \ln U_{35-39} + a_{7i} \ln NW + a_{8i} \ln A_{14-24} \quad (4.2)$$

$$+ a_{9i} \ln \text{SMSA} + a_{10i} \ln M$$

$$+ a_{11i} \ln N + a_{12i}D + a_{13i} \ln Ed + \mu_i.[42]$$

Estimates of specific regression equations are presented in Tables 4, A, and 5, A.

The 2SLS estimates do not take account of disturbance correlations. However, random changes (disturbance terms) relating to the rate of, say, burglary may be positively associated with those relating to the rate of robbery if these crimes were complements. To derive efficient estimates of the supply-of-offenses functions we have also employed an asymptotically efficient simultaneous-equation estimation method proposed by Zellner (1962) for estimating seemingly unrelated regression equations (SUR).[43] Such estimates have been derived separately for crimes against property and crimes against the person and are presented in Tables 4, B, and 5, B.

---

42. It should be pointed out that the coefficients associated with $(E/N)_{t-1}$ in the reduced-form regressions are generally found to be statistically insignificant (a few having wrong signs), presumably because of a multicollinearity between $(E/N)_{t-1}$ and $(Q_i/N)_{t-1}$. Similar weak results were obtained in the reduced-form regression analysis when $\ln (Q/N)_i$ were regressed on the set of independent variables included in eq. (4.2). The presumed existence of multicollinearity in these regressions should not bias the computed (expected) values of both $(Q/N)_i$ and P_i, however, and should not affect the consistency of the estimates of our structural coefficients.

43. We have not attempted to derive 3SLS or FIML estimates of eq. (4.1) because of the absence of data requisite for estimating eqq. (3.3) and (3.8) in the case of specific crime categories; in particular, data are lacking for police expenditure on combating *specific* crimes and for average losses from crime to victims.

TABLE 4

2SLS AND SUR (WEIGHTED) REGRESSION ESTIMATES OF COEFFICIENTS ASSOCIATED WITH SELECTED VARIABLES IN 1960: CRIMES AGAINST PROPERTY

Offense	Coefficient (β) Associated with Selected Variables					
	a Intercept	b_1 with $\ln \hat{P}_i$	b_2 with $\ln T_i$	c_1 with $\ln W$	c_2 with $\ln X$	e_1 with $\ln NW$
A. 2SLS Estimates						
Robbery:						
$\hat{\beta}$	−11.030	−1.303	−0.372	1.689	1.279	0.334
$\hat{\beta}/S\hat{\beta}$	(−1.804)	(−7.011)	(−1.395)	(1.969)	(1.660)	(4.024)
Burglary:						
$\hat{\beta}$	−2.121	−0.724	−1.127	1.384	2.000	0.250
$\hat{\beta}/S\hat{\beta}$	(−0.582)	(−6.003)	(−4.799)	(2.839)	(4.689)	(4.579)
Larceny:						
$\hat{\beta}$	−10.660	−0.371	−0.602	2.229	1.792	0.142
$\hat{\beta}/S\hat{\beta}$	(−2.195)	(−2.482)	(−1.937)	(3.465)	(2.992)	(2.019)
Auto theft:						
$\hat{\beta}$	−14.960	−0.407	−0.246	2.608	2.057	0.102
$\hat{\beta}/S\hat{\beta}$	(−4.162)	(−4.173)	(−1.682)	(5.194)	(4.268)	(1.842)
Larceny and auto:						
$\hat{\beta}$	−10.090	−0.546	−0.626	2.226	2.166	0.155
$\hat{\beta}/S\hat{\beta}$	(−2.585)	(−4.248)	(−2.851)	(4.183)	(4.165)	(2.603)
Property crimes:						
$\hat{\beta}$	−6.279	−0.796	−0.915	1.883	2.132	0.243
$\hat{\beta}/S\hat{\beta}$	(−1.937)	(−6.140)	(4.297)	(4.246)	(5.356)	(4.805)
B. SUR Estimates						
Robbery:						
$\hat{\beta}$	−14.800	−1.112	−0.286	2.120	1.409	0.346
$\hat{\beta}/S\hat{\beta}$	(−2.500)	(−6.532)	(−0.750)	(2.548)	(1.853)	(4.191)
Burglary:						
$\hat{\beta}$	−3.961	−0.624	−0.996	1.581	2.032	0.230
$\hat{\beta}/S\hat{\beta}$	(−1.114)	(−5.576)	(−4.260)	(3.313)	(4.766)	(4.274)
Larceny:						
$\hat{\beta}$	−10.870	−0.358	−0.654	2.241	1.785	0.139
$\hat{\beta}/S\hat{\beta}$	(−2.52)	(−2.445)	(−1.912)	(3.502)	(2.983)	(1.980)
Auto theft:						
$\hat{\beta}$	−14.860	−0.409	−0.233	2.590	2.054	0.101
$\hat{\beta}/S\hat{\beta}$	(−4.212)	(−4.674)	(−1.747)	(5.253)	(4.283)	(1.832)

NOTE. —The underlying regression equation is

$$\ln\left(\frac{Q}{N}\right) = a + b_{1i} \ln \hat{P}_i + b_{2i} \ln T_i + c_{1i} \ln W + c_{2i} \ln X + e_{1i} \ln NW + \mu_i. \quad (4.3)$$

TABLE 5

2SLS AND SUR (WEIGHTED) REGRESSION ESTIMATES OF COEFFICIENTS
ASSOCIATED WITH SELECTED VARIABLES IN 1960: CRIMES AGAINST
THE PERSON AND TOTAL OFFENSES

Offense	Coefficient (β) Associated with Selected Variables					
	a Inter-cept	b_1 with $\ln \hat{P}_i$	b_2 with $\ln T_i$	c_1 with $\ln W$	c_2 with $\ln X$	e_1 with $\ln NW$
A. 2SLS Estimates						
Murder:						
$\hat{\beta}$	0.316	−0.852	−0.087	0.175	1.109	0.534
$\hat{\beta}/S\hat{\beta}$	(0.085)	(−2.492)	(−0.645)	(0.334)	(1.984)	(8.356)
Rape:						
$\hat{\beta}$	−0.599	−0.896	−0.399	0.409	0.459	0.072
$\hat{\beta}/S\hat{\beta}$	(−0.120)	(−6.080)	(−2.005)	(0.605)	(0.743)	(0.922)
Murder and rape:						
$\hat{\beta}$	2.703	−0.828	−0.350	0.086	0.556	0.280
$\hat{\beta}/S\hat{\beta}$	(0.732)	(−6.689)	(−3.164)	(0.172)	(1.188)	(5.504)
Assault:						
$\hat{\beta}$	−7.567	−0.724	−0.979	1.650	1.707	0.465
$\hat{\beta}/S\hat{\beta}$	(−1.280)	(−3.701)	(−2.301)	(2.018)	(2.111)	(3.655)
Crimes against the person:						
$\hat{\beta}$	1.635	−0.803	−0.495	0.328	0.587	0.376
$\hat{\beta}/S\hat{\beta}$	(0.380)	(−6.603)	(−3.407)	(0.570)	(1.098)	(4.833)
All offenses:						
$\hat{\beta}$	−1.388	−0.991	−1.123	1.292	1.775	0.265
$\hat{\beta}/S\hat{\beta}$	(−0.368)	(−5.898)	(−4.483)	(2.609)	(4.183)	(5.069)
B. SUR Estimates						
Murder:						
$\hat{\beta}$	−1.198	−0.913	−0.018	0.186	1.152	0.542
$\hat{\beta}/S\hat{\beta}$	(−0.033)	(−3.062)	(−1.710)	(0.361)	(2.102)	(8.650)
Rape:						
$\hat{\beta}$	0.093	−0.930	−0.436	0.333	0.425	0.065
$\hat{\beta}/S\hat{\beta}$	(0.019)	(−6.640)	(−2.318)	(0.502)	(0.692)	(0.841)
Assault:						
$\hat{\beta}$	−6.431	−0.718	−0.780	1.404	1.494	0.460
$\hat{\beta}/S\hat{\beta}$	(−1.103)	(−4.046)	(−2.036)	(1.751)	(1.871)	(3.801)

NOTE. — Same reference as in Table 4.

The results of the 2SLS and SUR regression analyses strongly support the qualitative results of the simple regressions analyzed in the preceding discussion. They show that the rates of all specific crimes are inversely and significantly related to the appropriate P_i and T_i and directly related to NW, the estimated regression coefficients generally exceeding twice their standard errors. Crimes against property are found to be positively and significantly related to W and X, whereas the estimated elasticities of crimes against the person with respect to these variables are relatively lower—and their standard errors relatively higher—especially those associated with W in the regressions concerning murder and rape.[44] Moreover, estimates derived via the 2SLS and SUR methods are similar in magnitude, the latter generally having lower standard errors. However, these estimates only have the desirable large-sample property of consistency, and their small-sample properties are for the most part unknown.[45]

Unlike the OLS estimates of the elasticities of specific crimes with respect to P_i, the elasticities derived via 2SLS and SUR methods are expected to be free of a potential negative bias (due to measurement errors in Q_i) between current values of $(Q/N)_i$ and $P_i = (C/Q)_i$, since $\hat{P}_i$ is a linear combination of a set of variables that does not include (current) $(Q/N)_i$.[46] Nevertheless, estimates of both b_{1i} and b_{2i} appear even higher than those reported in Tables 3 and 4. It is interesting to note that the absolute values of the estimated elasticities of crimes against the person with respect to probability and severity of punishment are not lower on the average than those associated with crimes against property. This suggests that law enforcement may not be less effective in combating crimes of hate and passion relative to crimes against property.[47]

---

44. To some extent crimes against the person may be complementary to crimes against property since they may also occur as a by-product of the latter. This is particularly true in the case of assault, for it is generally agreed that some incidents of robbery are classified in practice as assault. This may be one reason why assault exhibits a greater similarity to crimes against property in its estimated functional form, and why the incidence of murder is positively correlated with W and X.

45. See Zellner (1970). A more elaborate analysis of this problem in the context of this study is given in Ehrlich (1970).

46. The 2SLS estimates might still be affected by spurious correlation if errors of measurement in $(Q/N)_i$ were serially correlated in each state. We have therefore derived alternative 2SLS estimates of the supply-of-offenses functions by excluding $(Q_i/N)_{t-1}$ from the reduced-form regressions. The results, reported in Ehrlich (1970, Table 15 of Appendix R), are nevertheless highly consistent with those reported in Tables 4 and 5.

47. Note, however, that this may be partly due to the preventive effect of imprisonment which is expected to be generally higher for crimes against the person (see Sec. II, C).

The absolute values of b_{1i} in Tables 4 and 5 are found to exceed those of b_{2i} in the case of murder, rape, and robbery, while they fall short of b_{2i} in the case of burglary and larceny (the differences exceeding twice the value of their standard errors). It should be emphasized, however, that the various T_i are less than proportionally related to the discounted cost of imprisonment and, therefore, our estimates of b_{2i} necessarily understate the true elasticities of the various crimes with respect to severity of punishment, F_i—especially in the case of crimes punishable by long imprisonment terms (see our discussion in item 3 of Appendix 1 to Section III). In view of these results we may venture the conclusion that burglars and thieves are risk avoiders (see the analysis in Sec. I, B). Whether other offenders are risk preferrers cannot be determined unambiguously, however, without knowledge of offenders' discount rates: the higher the latter, the larger would be the absolute values of our revised estimates of b_{2i}.[48] Following our analysis in Section I, A, we can therefore expect that in a real income sense, crime does pay at the margin to burglars and thieves, while it may not pay to robbers.[49]

It is difficult to determine accurately on the basis of available data to what extent the estimated values of b_{1i} and b_{2i} are attributable to a preventive effect of imprisonment (see eq. [2.7]) because the absolute values of our estimates of P_i may not be accurate.[50] Since our 2SLS and SUR cross-states estimates of b_{1i} and b_{2i} appear to differ significantly in the case of murder, rape, robbery, burglary, and larceny (some of these estimates approach or even exceed unity in absolute value), the independent deterrent effect of law enforcement appears to be confirmed because the preventive effect of probability and severity of imprisonment,

---

48. We have computed estimates of correction factors $1/\lambda$ (where λ is defined in Appendix 1 to Section III) based on arithmetic mean values of T_i and alternative arbitrary discount rates. We find that only when using a yearly rate of 36 per cent do the revised estimates of b_{2i} for murder and rape (but not for robbery) approach our estimates of b_{1i} associated with the same crimes.

49. We have attempted to test these implications directly by calculating the net monetary gains associated with an average robbery, burglary, larceny, and auto theft. Surprisingly, our crude estimates of the expected net gains are compatible with their predicted values according to the regression results discussed above, for the net gain is estimated to be negative in the case of robbery and positive in the case of burglary and larceny (see Appendix 2 to this section).

50. Estimates of σ based on our estimates of P and T are found to account for less than 10 per cent of the magnitude of the 2SLS estimates of b_1 and b_2 associated with all offenses. The latter may be regarded as estimates of steady state elasticities of the crime rate with respect to P and T, because the variation in these variables across states is likely to exhibit persistent differences.

P_i and T_i, is expected to be virtually identical, and, in view of the available information regarding average values of T_i and reasonable estimates of P_i in the United States, considerably lower than unity.

B. SUPPLY-OF-OFFENSES FUNCTIONS: THE EFFECT OF UNEMPLOYMENT, LABOR-FORCE PARTICIPATION, AND AGE COMPOSITION

We have also investigated in our regression analysis the partial effects of unemployment and labor-force participation rates of urban males in the age groups 14–24, U_{14-24} and L_{14-24}, respectively, as well as the effect of the variation in the proportion of all males belonging to that age group, A_{14-24}, by adding these variables to the regression equations (4.1) and (4.3). The expanded regression equation is

$$\ln \left(\frac{Q}{N}\right)_i = a_i + b_{1i} \ln P_i + b_{2i} \ln T_i + c_{1i} \ln W + c_{2i} \ln X + d_{1i} \ln U_{14-24}$$

$$+ d_{2i} \ln L_{14-24} + e_{1i} \ln NW + e_{2i} \ln A_{14-24} + \mu_i, \qquad (4.4)$$

and the results concerning these variables are shown in Table 6.[51]

The partial effect of age is found to be inconclusive in the regressions dealing with crimes against property. The signs of e_{2i} vary across different crimes with their values falling short of their standard errors, especially when estimates are derived via a 2SLS procedure. Possibly, then, not age per se, but the general opportunities available to offenders determine their participation in crimes against property. The percentage of young age groups does appear to be positively correlated with the rate of crimes against the person in 1960, independently of the regression method employed.

The results concerning the partial effect of the unemployment rate U_{14-24} are generally disappointing: the signs of d_{1i} are not stable across different regressions and do not appear significantly different from zero. One reason may be that variations in U_{14-24} across states reflect considerable variation in voluntary unemployment due to the search for desirable employment, since this source of unemployment is particularly important among young workers. Indeed, we have achieved somewhat

---

51. We have generally excluded A_{14-24} from eq. (4.4) whenever the ratio of e_2 to its standard deviation fell short of 1. In the 2SLS regressions, P_i were replaced by estimates of specific probabilities of imprisonment, $\hat{P}_i$, derived through a modified version of the reduced-form regression eq. (4.2), including U_{14-24} and L_{14-24}, in addition to the explanatory variables entering eq. (4.2), and excluding U_{35-39}.

ALTERNATIVE ESTIMATES OF ELASTICITIES OF OFFENSES WITH RESPECT TO UNEMPLOYMENT AND LABOR-FORCE PARTICIPATION OF YOUNG AGE GROUPS IN 1960 (DEPENDENT VARIABLES ARE SPECIFIC CRIME RATES)

| Crime Category | Ordinary Least-Squares (OLS) | | | | | | Two-Stage Least-Squares (2SLS) | | | | | |
| | Unweighted | | | Weighted | | | Unweighted | | | Weighted | | |
	d_1	d_2	e_2	d_1	d_2	e_2	d_1	d_2	e_2	d_1	d_2	e_2
Robbery:												
$\hat{\beta}$	0.148	−0.346	—	−0.297	−0.431	—	−0.634	−0.793	—	−0.749	−0.920	—
$\hat{\beta}/S\hat{\beta}$	(−0.383)	(−1.145)	—	(−0.838)	(−1.208)	—	(−1.281)	(−2.006)	—	(−1.968)	(−1.754)	—
Burglary:												
$\hat{\beta}$	−0.078	0.059	0.9092	−0.084	0.216	—	−0.306	−0.136	—	−0.033	0.334	—
$\hat{\beta}/S\hat{\beta}$	(−0.333)	(0.301)	(1.4150)	(−0.380)	(0.944)	—	(−1.115)	(−0.559)	—	(−0.154)	(1.107)	—
Larceny:												
$\hat{\beta}$	0.186	0.573	—	0.091	0.430	—	0.214	0.487	—	−0.103	−0.033	—
$\hat{\beta}/S\hat{\beta}$	(0.955)	(2.056)	—	(0.326)	(1.395)	—	(0.711)	(1.188)	—	(−0.306)	(−0.067)	—
Auto theft:												
$\hat{\beta}$	0.147	0.435	1.062	−0.137	0.373	—	0.516	0.401	—	−0.315	0.174	—
$\hat{\beta}/S\hat{\beta}$	(0.534)	(1.984)	(1.328)	(−0.553)	(1.360)	—	(0.188)	(1.396)	—	(−0.365)	(0.519)	—
Murder:												
$\hat{\beta}$	−0.132	−0.656	1.803	−0.178	−0.602	1.622	−0.151	−1.510	2.072	−0.324	−0.822	1.293
$\hat{\beta}/S\hat{\beta}$	(−0.388)	(−2.264)	(1.875)	(−0.636)	(−2.018)	(2.043)	(−0.268)	(−2.456)	(1.298)	(−0.227)	(−1.966)	(1.698)
Rape:												
$\hat{\beta}$	0.238	−0.728	1.339	0.222	−0.654	1.605	0.286	−0.851	1.430	0.209	−0.576	2.043
$\hat{\beta}/S\hat{\beta}$	(0.853)	(−3.232)	(1.660)	(0.828)	(−2.363)	(2.080)	(0.428)	(−3.366)	(1.603)	(0.774)	(−1.902)	(2.583)
Assault:												
$\hat{\beta}$	−0.073	−0.325	2.792	−0.083	−0.314	2.164	−0.132	−0.162	3.403	−0.389	−0.168	1.345
$\hat{\beta}/S\hat{\beta}$	(−0.219)	(−1.044)	(2.885)	(−0.268)	(−0.903)	(2.431)	(−0.283)	(−1.370)	(2.492)	(−0.938)	(−1.272)	(1.938)
All offenses:												
$\hat{\beta}$	0.037	0.159	1.044	0.049	0.275	1.157	−0.129	−0.481	1.386	−0.169	0.004	—
$\hat{\beta}/S\hat{\beta}$	(0.172)	(0.768)	(1.709)	(0.262)	(1.264)	(2.051)	(−0.421)	(−1.288)	(1.606)	(−0.806)	(0.012)	—

better results when using the unemployment rates of urban males in the age group 35–39 in lieu of U_{14-24}. Another reason may be that the effect of variations in the true probability of involuntary unemployment is impacted in the effect of income inequality, X, since a decline in legitimate market opportunities leading to an increase in involuntary unemployment is likely to affect disproportionately those with lower schooling and training and may therefore increase income inequality. Finally, it may be noted that our theoretical analysis indicates some ambiguity regarding the effect of an increase in the probability of unemployment on offenders engaging in both legitimate and illegitimate activities, if unemployment is regarded as an uncertain event (see footnote 14).

Interesting results have been obtained with respect to the partial effect of labor-force participation on the rate of specific crimes. The effect of L_{14-24} is somewhat inconclusive in the case of crimes against property but is found consistently negative and significantly different from zero in the case of specific (as well as all) crimes against the person. Are these results compatible with the theory developed in Section I of this paper?

One important question is what do variations in labor-force participation rates indicate in the context of this investigation? On the one hand, if all offenders specialized in crime and also chose to register as not in the labor force, then L_{14-24} could be viewed as a rough index of time spent in *legitimate* market activities by young persons in a state: movements in L_{14-24} would then be likely to reflect opposite movements in the rate of participation in crimes against property. On the other hand, if most offenders were partly engaged in legitimate market activities, L_{14-24} would be an index of time spent by the average young person in *all* market activities, legitimate as well as illegitimate.

Traditional economic theory predicts that labor-force participation is a function of real income, the market wage rate if employed, and the probability of unemployment. If variations in these variables were effectively accounted for by the variation in W, X, and U_{14-24}, the variation in L_{14-24} would mainly capture the effect of exogenous factors determining labor-force participation of young age groups (e.g., the rate of school enrollment or the degree of enforcement of child labor laws). Assuming that L_{14-24} is an index of total time spent in market activities by the average young person, variations in L_{14-24} would then produce a pure scale effect on participation in crime. We have expected such a scale effect to be positive in the case of crimes against property and negative in the case of crimes against the person (see our discussion in Secs. I, B, and I, C). However, since variations in legitimate wage rates available to potential young offenders are only indirectly accounted for by the variation in family income inequality, X, they, too, are likely to be reflected by the variation in L_{14-24}. Specifically, with the distribution of family income held constant, an increase in legitimate wages available to young workers is expected to reduce their incentive to participate in all crimes. This negative substitution effect is likely to offset the positive scale effect of an increase in L_{14-24} on the rate of crimes against property, but may reinforce the negative scale effect of an increase in L_{14-24} on the rate of crimes against the person, as our analysis in the last paragraphs of Sections I, B, and I, C, predicts. The results reported in Table 6 are compatible with these expectations.

It should be pointed out that the introduction of A_{14-24}, U_{14-24}, and L_{14-24} in the regression analysis has had virtually no effect on the estimated elasticities and only a marginal impact on the extent of the R^2 statistics reported in Tables 2 and 3.[52]

C. THE EFFECTIVENESS OF LAW ENFORCEMENT: SOME TENTATIVE ESTIMATES

Is law enforcement effective in combating crime? Is there at present too much or too little enforcement of existing laws against felonies? The answer to these questions can be obtained, in principle, by considering two related issues. First, what would be the effect of an increase in the probability and severity of punishment on the level of felony offenses and the resulting social loss? Second, to what extent would an additional expenditure on law-enforcement agencies increase their effectiveness in apprehending and punishing felons?

Our empirical estimates of supply-of-offenses functions provide consistent results pertaining to the first issue. In addition, an attempt has

---

52. The regression models employed thus far have implicitly assumed that specific illegal activities, i, were independent of each other. Specific crimes may be substitutes (or complements) in the sense that an increase in opportunities available in one crime would have opposite (or similar) effects on the rate of related crimes. (For example, offenders charged for robbery are often convicted of burglary; an increase in the penalty for burglary might then deter participation in both crimes.) To test interdependencies among specific crimes, we have introduced in the regression eq. (4.3) the (estimated) probability and severity of imprisonment relating to subsets of these crimes, $\hat{P}_g$ and T_g, respectively, in addition to own variables. The 2SLS estimates of the regression coefficients associated with $\hat{P}_g$ and T_g indicate that robbery and burglary are complements, and that burglary and theft are substitutes, but the absolute values of the coefficients associated with these variables are found to be quite low relative to their standard errors. Moreover, the estimated coefficients of the explanatory variables introduced in eq. (4.3) are virtually unaffected by the introduction of these other variables (see Ehrlich, 1970, pp. 86–89).

been made to estimate the effectiveness of public outlays on police in determining the probability of apprehending and punishing felons, P, by estimating an aggregate production function of law-enforcement activity (equation (3.3) defined for all felony offenses) via a 2SLS weighted-regression procedure using state data from 1960. In the first stage of the analysis, the rate of all felony offenses, Q/N, and per capita expenditure on police, E/N, were regressed on the set of exogenous and predetermined variables specified in the reduced-form regression equation (4.2). In the second stage, P was regressed on values of $\hat{Q}/N$ and $\hat{E}/N$ computed from the estimated reduced-form regression equations, and on other environmental variables, some of which were discussed in connection with equation (3.3). The results are given in equation (4.5) below (the numbers in parentheses denote the ratios of the regression coefficients to their standard errors).[53]

$$\ln P = 1.489 + 0.219 \ln \left(\frac{\hat{E}}{N}\right) - 0.854 \ln \left(\frac{\hat{Q}}{N}\right) - 0.226 \ln N$$
$$\quad (0.601) \quad (0.611) \qquad (-3.784) \qquad (-2.980)$$

$$\quad - 0.059 \ln SMSA + 1.094 \ln X + 0.267 \ln NW + 2.37 \ln Ed'$$
$$\quad (-1.505) \qquad (1.755) \qquad (2.893) \qquad (2.637)$$

$$\quad - 1.074 \ln A_{14-24} + 0.428D. \quad (4.5)$$
$$\quad (-1.313) \qquad (2.268)$$

As expected, the probability of apprehending and convicting felons is found to be positively related to the level of the current expenditure on police and negatively related to the crime rate, the estimated elasticities being $\hat{\beta}_1 = 0.219$ and $\hat{\beta}_2 = 0.854$, respectively. The productivity of law-enforcement activity is found to be negatively affected by the size and density of the population, as indicated by the negative signs of the coefficients associated with N and SMSA, and positively affected by the extent of relative poverty, the schooling level of the adult population, and the proportion of nonwhites, as indicated by the positive signs of the co-

---

53. The reader may note that the results reported in equation (4.5) of this essay, as well as other calculations in this section which are based on these results, differ to some extent from the corresponding results in my original article in the *Journal of Political Economy*. Subsequent to the publication of my article it was discovered that the computer program used to derive the latter results did not weight the dummy variable, D, by the weighting factor applied to all other variables. There is, of course, little technical justification for such an incomplete weighting procedure. The qualitative conclusions reached here on the basis of the new results are consistent, however, with those reached in my original article.

efficients associated with X, Ed, and NW.[54] Also, P appears to be greater in southern states and lower in states with a greater proportion of juveniles.[55] Note, however, that the standard error of the coefficient associated with E/N is 0.358 which implies, for example, that the lower and upper 95 per cent confidence limits of $\hat{\beta}_1$ (calculated from the normal distribution) are -0.483 and 0.920, respectively. Put differently, the probability that $\hat{\beta}_1$ takes on a *positive* value, given that β_1 is normally distributed with mean 0.219 and standard deviation 0.358, is only .7291. This somewhat weak result may be attributed both to measurement errors in E/N and aggregation biases involved in estimating an aggregate production function of law-enforcement activity. First, E/N measures all expenditures on police activity, including, for example, traffic control, but not on criminal courts. The latter is presumably an important determinant of felony conviction rates. (Also see our discussion of item 6 in Appendix 1 to Section III.) Second, monetary expenditure on police is an imperfect measure of the real outlays on police activity across states because of possible regional differences in the rates of pay to policemen across states that are not due to differences in productivity. Finally, to the extent that the coefficients of the production function of law-enforcement activity against *specific* crimes differ for different crime categories (in particular, crimes against the person as against crimes against property), the estimated coefficients in equation (4.5) may be subject to aggregation biases, since the distribution of specific crimes among total felonies (especially crimes against property) varies significantly across states.[56] This implies, of course, that all the estimated coefficients in equation (4.5), not only $\hat{\beta}_1$, must be viewed with caution.

Assuming for a methodological purpose the validity of our estimates of the aggregate production function (4.5), we may now combine these

---

54. The positive association between P and both X and NW suggests that those with lower income spend less resources on legal counsel and legal defense. The positive (partial) effect of Ed on P, given E/N, is interesting, for it may reflect the degree and effectiveness of private self-protective efforts and other assistance provided by victims and law-enforcement agents in bringing about the apprehension and conviction of offenders (also see Appendix 1 to Section III, item 6).

55. One reason why P—the probability of punishment by imprisonment—may be negatively related to A_{14-24} is that many young convicts are sent to reformatories and other correctional institutions rather than to state and federal prisons.

56. Indeed, the value of the coefficient associated with E/N is found to exceed twice the value of its standard error in a regression analysis estimating a production function of law-enforcement activity that relates to crimes against the person only (see Ehrlich, 1970, p. 92). In general, estimates of both β_1 and β_2 have been found to be quite sensitive to the specification of the reduced-form regression equation.

with estimates of the aggregate supply-of-offenses function to derive a preliminary estimate of the effectiveness of public expenditure on law enforcement in a given year in reducing the rate of crime in that year. Substituting equation (3.3) in equation (3.2), it is easily seen that the elasticity of the crime rate, Q/N, with respect to current expenditure, E/N, is $e = (b_1\beta_1)/(1 - b_1\beta_2)$. In terms of our 2SLS estimates of b_1, β_1, and β_2, e is, then, estimated at -1.42: a 1 per cent increase in expenditure on direct law enforcement would result in about a 1.4 per cent decrease in all felony offenses. However, the standard error of this estimate calculated through a Taylor's series approximation of e as a function of b_1, β_1 and β_2 is found to be 3.8. This implies that the probability that $\hat{e}$ takes on a negative value, given that e is asymptotically normally distributed with mean -1.42 and standard deviation 3.8, is only .6443.

The total social loss from crimes against property and crimes against the person in 1965 has been estimated in monetary terms at \$5,968 million (see PCL, 1967(b), p. 44), which is probably an underestimate of the true social loss due to these crimes. On the other hand, total expenditure on police, courts, prosecution, and defense in 1965 was \$3,178 million (see PCL, 1967(b), p. 54), which obviously is an overestimate of the public expenditure devoted to combating these crimes alone. Nevertheless, if one accepted the tentative estimate of $e = -1.42$, one would conclude that in 1965 the marginal cost of law enforcement against felonies fell short of its marginal revenue, or that expenditure on direct law enforcement was less than optimal.[57] In view of the imperfections inherent in our estimate of e, however, this result cannot be considered very reliable. More accurate and specific data on expenditure on various kinds of law-enforcement activity, on payoffs on specific crimes against property, on private self-protection against crime, and on the private losses from crime would be required in order to derive more reliable simultaneous-equation estimates of production functions of law-enforcement activities

---

57. Assuming that the social loss from crime is proportionally related to the number of offenses committed, an increase in the expenditure on police and courts in 1965 by \$32 million (1 per cent of \$3,178 million) could have reduced the loss from felonies by about \$83 million (1.4 per cent of \$5,968 million). Furthermore, our tentative estimates of β_1 and e indicate that a 1 per cent increase in the expenditure on police and courts might have reduced the flow of offenders committed to prisons, $C/N = P(Q/N)$ and thus the total costs of their imprisonment by $\beta_1 + e = 1.2$ per cent. Since expenditures on state adult institutions in 1965 amounted to \$385 million (see PCL, 1967(b), p. 54; this represents approximately the total costs of imprisonment of a yearly flow of offenders committed to state prisons throughout their effective prison terms), the additional cost of law enforcement associated with a 1 per cent increase in the expenditure on police and courts in 1965 might have amounted to about \$27 million only (\$32 million less \$4.6 million savings in imprisonment costs).

and the effectiveness of these activities in reducing specific crimes and the resulting social losses.

CONCLUSION

The basic thesis underlying our theory of participation in illegitimate activities is that offenders, as a group, respond to incentives in much the same way that those who engage in strictly legitimate activities do as a group. This does not necessarily imply that offenders are similar to other people in all other respects, or that the extent of their response to incentives is the same. Indeed, our theory suggests that the extent of individual offenders' response to incentives may vary (negatively) with the extent of their specialization in illegitimate activity and so may not be uniformly high or low. We do emphasize, however, the role of opportunities available in competing legitimate and illegitimate activities in determining the extent of an offender's participation in the latter and thus, indirectly, also in determining the extent of his response to incentives.

The results of our regression analysis of variations in the rate of index crimes across states in the United States are not inconsistent with this basic thesis. In spite of the shortcomings of the crime statistics used, the indirect estimates of some of the theoretical constructs, and the somewhat stringent econometric specification of functional relationships, the signs and alternative point estimates of the coefficients of specific regression equations exhibit a remarkable consistency with the theoretical predictions, as well as with one another, across independent samples. The rate of specific felonies is found to be positively related to estimates of relative gains and negatively related to estimates of costs associated with criminal activity. In particular, and contrary to some popular arguments, the absolute magnitudes of the estimated elasticities of specific crimes with respect to estimates of probability and severity of punishment are not inconsistent with the hypothesis that law-enforcement activity has a deterrent effect on offenders that is independent of any preventive effect of imprisonment. Moreover, the elasticities associated with crimes against the person are not found to be lower, on the average, than those associated with crimes against property.

Viewing the decision to participate in crimes involving material gains as an occupational choice is not inconsistent with the evidence concerning the positive association between income inequality and the rate of crimes against property. Moreover, the relative magnitude of estimates of the elasticities of burglary and larceny with respect to probability and severity of punishment indicate that burglars and thieves are risk avoiders. These findings indicate, in turn, that many crimes against property, not unlike legitimate market activities, pay in the particular sense that their expected gains exceed their expected costs at the margin. This approach may be useful in explaining not only variations in the rate of felonies and many other types of crime across states or over time, but also a variety of specific characteristics associated with individual offenders: for example, why many appear to be relatively young males with little schooling and other legitimate training; why some are occasional offenders who combine legitimate and illegitimate market activities, while others specialize in crime; and why many continue their participation in illegitimate activities even after being apprehended and punished. Such characteristics, the analysis suggests, may be largely the consequence of the relative opportunities available to offenders in legitimate and illegitimate activities rather than the result of their unique motivation.

More important, the analytical and econometric framework developed in this paper appears useful in evaluating the effectiveness of public expenditure on law-enforcement activity. Some tentative estimates of the effectiveness of police and court activity against felonies in 1965 indicate that such activity paid (indeed, "overpaid") in the sense that its (partial) marginal revenue in terms of a reduced social loss from crime exceeded its (partial) marginal cost. Our empirical investigation also indicates that the rates of all felonies, particularly crimes against property, are positively related to the degree of a community's income inequality. This suggests a social incentive for equalizing training and earning opportunities across persons, which is independent of ethical considerations or any social welfare function. Whether it would pay society to spend more resources in order to enforce existing laws would then depend not only on the effectiveness of such expenditure in deterring crime, but also on the extent to which alternative methods of combating crime pay. Our ability to analyze these important issues would undoubtedly improve as more and better data concerning the frequency of illegitimate activities, self-protection by both offenders and victims, and alternative private and collective methods of combating crime became available.

APPENDIX 1 TO SECTION I: THE ALLOCATION OF TIME TO ILLEGITIMATE ACTIVITIES

A.

The expected utility associated with a one-period consumption prospect can be written generally as

$$EU = U^* = \sum_{s=a}^{n} \pi_s U(X_s, t_c), \qquad (A.1)$$

where s denotes the state of the world and π_s its probability. If returns from i were contingent upon the occurrence of only two events: "no punishment," with probability $(1 - p)$, and "apprehension and punishment," with probability p, and if the returns from l were fully insured, then (A.1) would reduce to

$$U^* = (1 - p)U(X_b, t_c) + pU(X_a, t_c), \qquad (A.2)$$

where

$$X_b = W' + W_i(t_i) + W_l(t - t_i),$$

$$X_a = W' + W_i(t_i) - F_i(t_i) + W_l(t - t_i),$$

and

$$t = t_i + t_l \equiv t_o - t_c$$

is the amount of "working time." Given the value of t_c, hence t, the value of t_i that maximizes this function in case of an interior solution must satisfy the first-order condition

$$(1 - p)U'(X_b)(w_i - w_l) + pU'(X_a)(w_i - w_l - f_i) = 0, \qquad (A.3)$$

where $w_k = (dW_k/dt_i^*)k = i, l; f_i = (dF_i/dt_i^*)$; and t_i^* denotes the optimal value of t_i. Clearly, equation (A.3) may be satisfied only if

$$w_i - f_i > w_l. \qquad (A.4)$$

The second-order condition is

$$\Delta = (1 - p)U''(X_b)(w_i - w_l)^2 + pU''(X_a)(w_i - w_l - f_i)^2$$

$$+ (1 - p)U_b' \left(\frac{dw_i}{dt_i} + \frac{dw_l}{dt_l}\right) + pU_a' \left(\frac{dw_i}{dt_i} - \frac{df_i}{dt_i} + \frac{dw_l}{dt_l}\right) < 0. \quad (A.5)$$

If the rates of change in w_i, f_i and w_l were constant, equation (A.5) would always be satisfied if everywhere $U'' < 0$. However, if w_i and w_l were a decreasing function of "working time" and f_i were not a decreasing function of t_i (if the production transformation curve were concave to the origin as in Figure 1), (A.5) would also be satisfied if everywhere $U'' = 0$ and might be satisfied even if $U'' > 0$. In the following analysis it is therefore assumed that equation (A.5) is satisfied regardless of attitudes toward risk, and that equilibrium is consistent with regular interior maxima with the values of both t_i and t_l being positive.

The partial effects of equal percentage changes in p and $f = F/t_i$ on the value of t_i^* in case the latter is positive have been analyzed in Section I, B, and in footnote 13 in the text. However, the theorem presented in equation (1.10) in footnote 13 concerning the relative elasticity of t_i^* with respect to p and f_i is more general, since it also holds in case of a boundary solution in which a person specializes in legitimate activity. To prove this proposition note, first, that for any given value of t_c, a person would be indifferent between entering i or devoting his full working time to l if the expected utility from a single offense were the same as that from the marginal unit of time allocated to l; that is, if

$$U_i^* \equiv (1 - p)U(W + w_i) + pU(W + w_i - f_i) = U_i^*(W + w_l), \tag{A.6}$$

where $W = W' + w_l(t - dt)$, and $t = t_o - t_c$. Clearly,

$$\frac{\partial U_i^*}{\partial p} = -[U(X_b) - U(X_b - f_i)] < 0,$$

and $\hspace{12cm}$ (A.7)

$$\frac{\partial U_i^*}{\partial f_i} = -pU'(X_b - f_i) < 0,$$

where $X_b = W + w_i$. An increase in either p or f_i decreases the incentive to *enter* i. Furthermore, by the set of equations (A.7) the relative effects of equal percentage changes in p and f_i on the incentive to enter or exit from i can be summarized as follows:

$$-\frac{\partial U_i^*}{\partial p} p \gtrless -\frac{\partial U_i^*}{\partial f_i} f_i,$$

as

$$U(X_b) - U(X_b - f_i) \gtrless U'(X_b - f_i)f_i. \tag{A.8}$$

Applying Taylor's theorem around the point $X_b - f_i$ one can write

$$U(X_b) = U(X_b - f_i) + f_i U'(X_b - f_i) + \frac{f_i^2}{2!} U''(X_b - f_i + \theta f_i),$$

where $0 < \theta < 1$. Hence, $U(X_b) - U(X_b - f_i) \gtrless U'(X_b - f_i)f_i$, as $U'' \gtrless 0$. Equation (A.8) thus implies that a 1 per cent change in p has a greater effect on the incentive to enter i than a 1 per cent change in f_i if a person is risk preferring, and a relatively lower effect if a person is risk avoiding. A geometrical proof for this result is given in Becker (1968), included in this volume.

The effect of an equal proportional increase in the wage rates obtained in i, hence in the average wage $\bar{w}_i$ with p, f_i, w_l and W' held constant, would be given by

$$\frac{dt_i^*}{d\bar{w}_i} \bar{w}_i = \frac{(A + B)\bar{w}_i}{\Delta}, \tag{A.9}$$

where

$$A = -(1 - p)U_b' - pU_a'$$

and

$$B = -(1 - p)U_b''(w_i - w_l)t_i^* - pU_a''(w_l - w_l - f_i)t_i^*.$$

Because the value of A is always negative, equation (A.9) would have a positive value if $U'' = 0$ or if B did not have an algebraic sign opposite to that of A. Substituting equation (A.3) in B it can be shown that B would equal zero if

$$-\frac{U_a''}{U_a'} = -\frac{U_b''}{U_b'},\qquad\text{(A.10)}$$

i.e., there is constant absolute risk aversion (or preference).[58] This assumption also guarantees that a reduction in $\bar{w}_l$ would always increase participation in i since then

$$-\frac{dt_i^*}{d\bar{w}_l}\,\bar{w}_l = \frac{(A - C)w_l}{\Delta} = \frac{(-)}{(-)}\quad),\qquad\text{(A.11)}$$

where

$$C = -(1 - p)U_b''(w_i - w_l)t_i^* - pU_c''(w_i\quad w_l - f_i)t_l.$$

If we now relax the assumption that legitimate earnings are known for certain and assume that earnings in l, too, were contingent upon the occurrence of two events: "employment" with probability $(1 - u)$, and "unemployment" with probability u, and if the probability of unemployment were independent of the probability of apprehension and conviction, then equation (A.1) would become

$$U^* = (1 - p)(1 - u)U(X_a, t_c) + (1 - p)uU(X_b, t_c)$$
$$+ p(1 - u)U(X_c, t_c) + puU(X_d, t_c),\quad\text{(A.12)}$$

where

$$X_a = W' + W_i(t_i) + W_l(t - t_i),$$
$$X_b = W' + W_i(t_i) + W_l(t - t_i) - D_l(t - t_i),$$
$$X_c = W' + W_i(t_i) - F_i(t_i) + W_l(t - t_i),$$
$$X_d = W' + W_i(t_i) - F_i(t_i) + W_l(t - t_i) - D_l(t - t_i),$$

and D_l denotes the reduction in real earnings due to unemployment. Given the value of t_c, the first-order optimality condition is

$$\frac{dU^*}{dt_i^*} = (1 - p)(1 - u)U_a'(w_i - w_l) + (1 - p)uU_b'(w_i - w_{l2})$$
$$+ p(1 - u)U_c'(w_{i2} - w_l) + puU_d'(w_{i2} - w_{l2}) = 0,\quad\text{(A.13)}$$

---

58. See the discussion in Ehrlich and Becker (1972). Since both absolute and relative risk aversion are constant along the certainty line (Ehrlich and Becker, op. cit.), equations (A.9) and (A.11) would always have a positive sign when most working time is spent in l. Of course, both might have a positive sign even when there is increasing or decreasing absolute risk aversion.

where $w_{i2} = w_i - f_i$ and $w_{l2} = w_l - d_l$, and the second-order condition is

$$\frac{d^2 U^*}{dt_i^{*2}} = \Sigma < 0. \tag{A.14}$$

If $w_i > w_l$ equations (A.13) and (A.14) would be satisfied by the same conditions satisfying equations (A.3) and (A.5).[59]

The effects of changes in p, f_i, w_i and w_l on the value of t_i^* discussed above can be shown to apply in this more general case as well. In particular,

$$\frac{dt_i^*}{dp} = \frac{1}{\Sigma} \left[(1 - u)U_a'(w_i - w_l) + uU_b'(w_i - w_{l2}) + S \right] = \frac{(+)}{(-)} < 0, \tag{A.15}$$

since $S = -(1 - u)U_c'(w_{i2} - w_l) - uU_d'(w_{i2} - w_{l2})$ must have a positive sign for equation (A.13) to be satisfied. On the other hand, the effect of an increase in u on t_i^* would be given by

$$\frac{dt_i^*}{du} = \frac{1}{\Sigma} [(1 - p)U_a'(w_i - w_l) - (1 - p)U_b'(w_i - w_{l2})$$
$$+ pU_c'(w_{i2} - w_l) - pU_d'(w_{i2} - w_{l2})]. \tag{A.16}$$

The sign of equation (A.16) would always be positive if $U'' = 0$, since then equation (A.16) reduces to $-(U'd_l/\Sigma) = (-)/(-) > 0$. If $U'' < 0$ and $w_{i2} - w_{l2} \geq 0$ it also can be seen that (A.16) would be positive. In contrast, if $w_{i2} - w_{l2} < 0$, which would be the case if $f > w_i$ and $d \leq w_l$, equation (A.16) would have a positive sign only if p were small and U were not too concave. It is then possible, in principle, that an increase in the probability of unemployment will not induce offenders to allocate more time to i, essentially because an increase in u increases the demand for wealth in the less desirable states of the world. Note, however, that regardless of attitudes toward risk, an increase in u would always increase the incentive to enter i, since as a result of this change the expected utility from the marginal unit time spent in l would decrease relative to the expected utility from entering i. This can be easily shown by differentiating the term U_i^* in equation (A.6) above with respect to u.[60]

---

59. A necessary condition for entry into i is that the expected utility from entering i would exceed the expected utility from "full-time" participation in l. If earnings in l are known for certain, it has been shown in the text that this condition would be satisfied for a risk avoider if the expected wage in i, $E(w_i)$, exceeded w_l. Since earnings in l are here assumed subject to uncertainty, then given that the variance of earnings in i is greater than that in l, a risk avoider would enter i only if $E(w_i)$ were initially sufficiently greater than $E(w_l)$.

60. Equation (A.16) shows the partial effect of u on t_i^* when the extent of punishment is held constant. If punishment were by imprisonment, an increase in u that was expected to persist over a sufficiently long period might also imply a reduction in the expected opportunity costs of imprisonment, provided these were largely determined by the expected legitimate earnings. In this case, an increase in u might unambiguously induce a greater participation in crime.

So far we have assumed in our analysis that the probability of being apprehended and punished in a given "period," p, was independent of the amount of time spent in i. This assumption may be justified in part in view of the opposite effects an increase in t_i may have on p. On the one hand, an increase in the number of offenses committed within a given period may increase the likelihood that the offender will be apprehended on any one offense committed.[61] However, an increase in t_i is also likely to enhance an offender's ability to elude apprehension and punishment through "learning by doing." [62] The net effect of t_i on p is therefore not clear a priori. However, even if p were positively related to t_i at the margin, the results derived in the preceding discussion would essentially be unaffected.

Given that $\partial p / \partial t_i^* = p'(t_i^*) > 0$, equation (A.3) becomes

$$[1 - p(t_i^*)]U_b'(w_i - w_l) + p(t_i^*)U_a'(w_i - w_l - f_i) - p'(t_i^*)[U_b - U_a] = 0, \quad \text{(A.17)}$$

and equation (A.15) becomes

$$\Delta' = \Delta - p''(t_i^*)(U_b - U_a) - p'(t_i^*)[U_b'(w_i - w_l) - U_a'(w_i - w_l - f_i)], \quad \text{(A.18)}$$

where Δ is defined as in equation (A.5). As Δ has been assumed negative in value, Δ' would be negative in value – the second-order equilibrium condition would be satisfied – if $p''(t) \geq 0$, and $f > w_i - w_l$.

Since p is a function of the amount of time spent in i,[63] a 1 per cent increase in p may generally be interpreted as a 1 per cent increase in both $p(t_i^*)$ and $p'(t_i^*)$. In this case, holding the value of all the other parameters constant, the effect on t_i^* would be

$$\frac{dt_i^*}{dp} p = \frac{[-U_a'(w_i - w_l - f_i)p + U_b'(w_i - w_l)p] + p'(t_i^*)(U_b - U_a)}{\Delta'}$$

$$= \frac{(+)}{(-)} < 0. \quad \text{(A.19)}$$

Similarly, the effect of a 1 per cent increase in all the penalty rates, hence in the aggregate rate f, would be

$$\frac{dt_i^*}{df} f = \frac{[U_a'pf_i + U_a''(w_i - w_l - f_i)] + p'(t_i^*)U_a'ft_i^*}{\Delta'} = \frac{(+)}{(-)} < 0 \quad \text{(A.20)}$$

if $U'' \leq 0$. The implications of equation (1.10) in footnote 13 are thus shown to hold in this case as well. Moreover, the implications of equation (A.18) also hold

---

61. If the probability of being apprehended on a single offense π were independent of the number of offenses committed, t, then the probability of being apprehended on any one offense committed would be $\tau = 1 - (1 - \pi)^t$. Clearly, then, $\partial \tau / \partial t > 0$.

62. Moreover, it is shown in Appendix 2 to Section I that an increase in t_i is likely to enhance the offender's expenditure on self-protection and thus decrease at least the probability of apprehension and punishment for a single offense.

63. Formally, $p(t_i^*) = \int_0^{t_i^*} p'(t_i)dt_i$.

in this case. Note, first, that in equilibrium $X_a = X_b - F^*$, where $F^* = ft_i^*$. Using a theorem summarized by equation (A.8) above, given the value of t_c,

$$U(X_b) - U(X_b - F^*) \gtreqless U'(X_b - F)F,$$

as $U'' \gtreqless 0$. Therefore, the second term in the numerator of equation (A.19) exceeds, is equal to, or falls short of, the second term in the numerator of (A.20) as U'' is greater than, equal to, or lower than, zero. Exactly the same condition determines the relative magnitudes of the first terms in the numerators of equations (A.19) and (A.20), as was shown in footnote 13 in the text. The results summarized in equation (1.10) in footnote 13 therefore hold unambiguously in this case as well.[64]

B.

The analysis so far has focused on effects of changes in exogenous factors on the allocation of working time, $(t_o - t_c)$, between i and l. In this section, the assumption of t_c being constant is relaxed in order that behavioral implications can be developed regarding the absolute, as well as the relative, allocation of time to i and l. In general, the effect of changes in legitimate and illegitimate costs and returns on the absolute magnitude of t_c^*, hence of t_i^* and t_l^*, are ambiguous because of competing wealth and substitution effects. Also, changes in the overall amount of time allocated to market activities, $t_o - t_c$, may have systematic effects on the incentive to participate in either i or l. Abstracting from such possible effects, it can be shown, however, that the same implications discussed in Part A of this appendix hold also in reference to the absolute allocation of time to i and l. In the following analysis, this assertion is demonstrated with regard to effects of exogenous changes in p and f.

For methodological convenience, let us define $t_i \equiv s(t_o - t_c)$, and $t_l = (1 - s) \times (t_o - t_c)$, where s and $(1 - s)$ denote the fractions of working time devoted to i and l, respectively. Optimal values of t_i, t_l, and t_c may thus be determined through an unconstrained maximization of equation (A.2) with respect to the independent variables s and t_c. It is assumed throughout the analysis that the utility function, U, is strongly separable in t_c and $X_j, j = a, b$, so that $\partial U/\partial X; \partial t_c = 0$. It is also assumed that $\partial U^*/\partial s \partial t_c = 0$, so that the relative allocation of working time between i and l is independent of the scale of working time itself. Values of s and t_c that maximize equation (A.2) locally in case of an interior solution under these assumptions must satisfy the following necessary conditions:

$$U_s^* = (1 - p)U'(X_b)(w_i - w_l)(t_o - t_c^*)$$
$$+ pU'(X_a)(w_i - f_i - w_l)(t_o - t_c^*) = 0, \quad (A.21)$$

---

64. The results discussed in reference to equations (A.10) and (A.11) can also be shown to hold with some modifications in this more general case.

and

$$U_t^* = U'(t_c) - (1 - p)U'(X_b)[w_i s^* + w_l(1 - s^*)]$$

$$- pU'(X_a)[(w_i - f_i)s^* + w_l(1 - s^*)] = 0, \quad (A.22)$$

where U_s^* and U_t^* denote $\partial U^*/\partial s$ and $\partial U^*/\partial t_c$, respectively, $U'(X_j) = \partial U/\partial X_s$, and $U'(t_c) = \partial U/\partial t_c$. The variables w_i, w_l and f_i were defined in Part A above. The set of sufficient conditions in this case requires that

$$U_{ss}^* = (1 - p)U''(X_b)(w_i - w_l)^2(t_o - t_c^*)^2$$

$$+ pU''(X_a)(w_i - f_i - w_l)^2(t_o - t_c^*)^2 + (1 - p)U'(X_b) \left(\frac{dw_i}{dt_i} + \frac{dw_l}{dt_l}\right)(t_o - t_c^*)$$

$$+ pU'(X_a) \left(\frac{dw_i}{dt_i} - \frac{df_i}{dt_i} + \frac{dw_l}{dt_l}\right)(t_o - t_c^*) < 0, \quad (A.23)$$

$$U_{tt}^* = U''(t_c) - (1 - p)U''(X_b)[w_i s^* + w_l(1 - s^*)]^2$$

$$- pU''(X_a)[(w_i - f_i)s^* + w_l(1 - s^*)]^2$$

$$+ (1 - p)U'(X_b) \left[\frac{dw_i}{dt_i}(s^*)^2 + \frac{dw_l}{dt_l}(1 - s^*)^2\right]$$

$$+ pU'(X_a) \left[\left(\frac{dw_i}{dt_i} - \frac{df_i}{dt_i}\right)(s^*)^2 + \frac{dw_l}{dt_l}(1 - s^*)^2\right] < 0, \quad (A.24)$$

and

$$U_{ss}^* U_{tt}^* - (U_{st}^*)^2 > 0. \quad (A.25)$$

Clearly, values of s^* and t_c^* that satisfy equations (A.23) and (A.24) also satisfy equation (A.25) since, by assumption, $U_{st}^* = \partial U^*/\partial s \partial t_c = 0$.

Consider, now, the effects of an exogenous increase in p on s^* and t_c^* with w_i, f_i, w_l and W' held constant. These effects are summarized in equations (A.26) and (A.27) as follows:

$$\frac{\partial s^*}{\partial p} = \frac{1}{U_{ss}^*} \left\{(t_o - t_c^*)[U'(X_b)(w_i - w_l) - U'(X_a)(w_i - f_i - w_l)]\right\} = \frac{(+) + (+)}{(-)} < 0,$$

$$(A.26)$$

and

$$\frac{\partial t_c^*}{\partial p} = \frac{1}{U_{tt}^*} \left\{-U'(X_b)[w_i s^* + w_l(1 - s^*)] + U'(X_a)[(w_i - f_i)s^* + w_l(1 - s^*)]\right\}$$

$$= \frac{(-) + (-)}{(-)} > 0, \quad (A.27)$$

provided that $(w_i - f_i)s + w_l(1 - s) < 0$. The latter condition requires that the punishment imposed on the offender exceed his current income from both legitimate and illegitimate activity, which is likely to be satisfied in the case of most felonies. This analysis shows that an increase in p increases t_c^* and decreases s^*. Thus, it decreases unambiguously the absolute amount of time spent in illegitimate activities.

Similarly, the effects of an exogenous increase in all the penalty rates dF_i/dt_i, hence in the average penalty f, on s^* and t_c^*, with p, w_i, w_l, and W' held constant, are given by

$$\frac{\partial s^*}{\partial f} = \frac{1}{U_{ss}^*} [pU'(X_a)(t_o - t_c^*) + pU''(X_a)(w_i - f_i - w_l)s^*(t_o - t_c^*)^2]$$

$$= \frac{(+) + (+)}{(-)} < 0, \text{ if } U'' \leq 0, \quad (A.28)$$

and

$$\frac{\partial t_c^*}{\partial f} = \frac{1}{U_{tt}^*} \left\{ -pU'(X_a)s^* - pU''(X_a)[(w_i - f_i)s^* \right.$$

$$\left. + w_l(1 - s^*)]s^*(t_o - t_c^*) \right\} = \frac{(-) + (-)}{(-)} > 0 \text{ if } U'' \leq 0. \quad (A.29)$$

Furthermore, the effect of a 1 per cent increase in p on t_c^* can be easily shown to exceed that of a 1 per cent increase in f if a person were a risk avoider, with the converse holding for a person who was a risk preferrer. Formally, by equations (A.27) and (A.29),

$$\frac{\partial t_c^*}{\partial p} p = \frac{1}{U_{tt}^*} \left\{ -pU'(X_a)f_i s^* + p[U'(X_a) - U'(X_b)][w_i s^* \right.$$

$$\left. + w_l(1 - s^*)] \right\} \gtrless \frac{\partial t_c^*}{\partial f} f = \frac{1}{U_{tt}^*} \left\{ -pU'(X_a)f_i s^* \right.$$

$$\left. - pU''(X_a)[(w_i - f_i)s^* + w_l(1 - s^*)]s^*(t_o - t_c^*)f_i \right\} \text{ as } U'' \gtrless 0. \quad (A.30)$$

The theorem summarized in equation (A.29) has already been shown in equation (1.10) in footnote 13 to hold unambiguously in reference to the relative effects of equal percentage changes in p_i and f_i on the relative allocation of working time between i and l, indicated by s^*. Thus, under the assumptions imposed in this analysis, equation (1.10) in footnote 13 holds in reference to the effects of p and f (or f_i) on the absolute as well as the relative allocation of time to i and l.

APPENDIX 2 TO SECTION I:
CRIME AND SELF-PROTECTION

The maximization of equation (A.2) in Appendix 1 has been carried out on the assumption that both the probability and severity of punishment are independent of an offender's actions. This assumption is not always true; for example, an offender can reduce the probability of being apprehended and punished by spending resources on "covering" his illegal activity, by fixing policemen and witnesses, by disposing of stolen goods through selected fences, or, in general, by providing self-protection. An explicit analysis of self-protection may be useful primarily because decisions concerning participation in illegal activity are generally influenced by the extent to which the former is provided; some behavioral implications should therefore be developed within the context of a more comprehensive decision problem.

Assuming for simplicity that expenditure on self-protection only affects the probability of apprehension and conviction, and that self-protection does not involve the use of an offender's time, we may write

$$p = p(r, s), \tag{B.1}$$

where r is public expenditure on law enforcement and s is an offender's total expenditure on self-protection, with $\partial p/\partial r > 0$ and $\partial p/\partial s = p'(s) \leq 0$.

Given the value of time spent in nonmarket activities, t_c, and the value of r, equation (A.2) can be written as a function of t_i and s:

$$U^* = [1 - p(s)]U[X_b(t_i) - s] + p(s)U[X_a(t_i) - s]. \tag{B.2}$$

The values of t_i and s that maximize this function in the case of an interior solution must satisfy the first-order conditions

$$U_{t_i}^* = (1 - p)U_b'(w_i - w_l) + pU_a'(w_i - w_l - f_i) = 0, \tag{B.3}$$

and

$$U_s^* = -p'(s)[U_b - U_a] - (1 - p)U_b' - pU_a' = 0. \tag{B.4}$$

The second-order conditions are

$$U_{t_it_i}^* = (1 - p)U_b''(w_i - w_l)^2 + pU_a''(w_i - w_l - f_i)^2$$

$$+ (1 - p)U_b'\left(\frac{dw_i}{dt_i} - \frac{dw_l}{dt_l}\right) + pU_a'\left(\frac{dw_i}{dt_i} - \frac{df_i}{dt_i} + \frac{dw_l}{dt_l}\right) < 0, \tag{B.5}$$

$$U_{ss}^* = -p''(s)(U_b - U_a) + 2p'(s)(U_b' - U_a') + (1 - p)U_b'' + pU_a'' < 0, \tag{B.6}$$

and

$$\Sigma = U_{t_it_i}^* U_{ss}^* - (U_{t_is}^*)^2 > 0, \tag{B.7}$$

which are assumed to be satisfied regardless of the sign of U''.[65]

Equation (B.4) implies that the incentive to provide self-protection is related to the level of participation in i, for the marginal gain from self-protection, given

---

65. A more detailed discussion of these optimality conditions and other related issues can be found in Ehrlich and Becker (1972) in reference to the joint determination of self-insurance and self-protection.

by $-p'(s)(U_b - U_a)$, is a positive function of the difference between income in different states, which is positive if $t_i > 0$. Moreover, an exogenous increase in t_i is expected to increase the amount spent on self-protection because its main effect is to widen the differences between income in different states:

$$\frac{ds}{dt_i} = \frac{-U_{st_i}^*}{U_{ss}^*} = \frac{(-)}{(-)} > 0, \tag{B.8}$$

where

$$U_{st_i}^* = -p'(s)[U_b'(w_i - w_l) - U_a'(w_i - w_l - f_i)] - (1 - p)U_b''(w_i - w_l)$$

$$- pU_a''(w_i - w_l - f_i) > 0,$$

provided that U'' and U' do not have opposite signs if $U'' \leq 0$, and that they do not have the same signs if $U'' > 0$.[66] This analysis provides an explanation for the fact that professional criminals—those who engage in crime on a relatively full-time basis—also tend to exercise more self-protection relative to other offenders [67] (see PCL, 1967(b), p. 97). Furthermore, it predicts that the proportion of professional offenders (and, generally, those who are relatively efficient in providing self-protection due to age, experience, or appropriate training) among those arrested and convicted of crime would understate their share in the total number of crimes committed.

Since self-protection and illegitimate activity are generally seen to be complements, the direction of the effect of changes in exogenous factors on the extent of participation in crime when self-protection is available would be the same as that predicted in the absence of such protection only if the direct effects of these changes on t_i and s are not in opposite directions, but might be different otherwise. For example, an increase in expenditure on law enforcement—f_i, w_i, w_l, W', and $p'(s)$ [68] held constant—would reduce the optimal values of both t_i and

---

66. Note that by equation (B.3): $(1 - p)(w_i - w_l) \gtrless -p(w_i - w_l - f_i)$; i.e., $E(w_i) \gtrless w_l$ as $U'' \lessgtr 0$, respectively.

67. Given the value of s, if p were positively related to t_i equation (B.3) would become (A.17) and equation (B.6) would become (A.18). U_{st_i} would then have a positive sign if in addition to the assumptions made above $\partial p'(s)/\partial t_i \geq 0$, i.e., the marginal productivity of a given expenditure on self-protection does not increase with more offenses committed within a given period. The results discussed in reference to equations (B.9) to (B.12) can then be shown to hold in this more general case as well.

68. If part of the increased expenditure on law enforcement is directed to combating collaboration of law-enforcement agents with offenders and other means of self-protection employed by offenders, then

$$-A_2 = -\frac{\partial p'(s)}{\partial r}[U_b - U_a] + [U_b' - U_a']\frac{\partial p}{\partial r},$$

where $-\partial p'(s)/\partial r < 0$ and $-A_2$ is defined following equation (B.10) below. In this case $-A_2$ has a negative sign even if $U'' = 0$; the incentive to exercise self-protection would be smaller and, consequently, the decrease in t_i would be greater.

s, provided that $U'' \leqslant 0$, since then

$$\frac{dt_i}{dr} = \frac{A_1 U_{ss}^* - A_2 U_{st_i}^*}{\Sigma} = \frac{(-)}{(+)} < 0, \tag{B.9}$$

and

$$\frac{ds}{dr} = \frac{A_2 U_{t_i t_i}^* - A_1 U_{st_i}^*}{\Sigma} \leqslant 0, \tag{B.10}$$

where

$$-A_1 = -[U_b'(w_i - w_l) - U_a'(w_i - w_l - f_i)] \frac{\partial p}{\partial r} < 0,$$

and

$$-A_2 = [U_b' - U_a'] \frac{\partial p}{\partial r} \leqslant 0 \text{ if } U'' \leqslant 0.$$

In contrast, an exogenous increase in the severity of punishment on the optimal values of t_i and s, with $p'(s)$, r, w_i, w_l, and W' held constant, and with $U'' \leqslant 0$, is generally ambiguous:

$$\frac{dt_i}{df} = \frac{B_1 U_{ss}^* - B_2 U_{st_i}^*}{\Sigma}, \tag{B.11}$$

and

$$\frac{ds}{df} = \frac{B_2 U_{t_i t_i}^* - B_1 U_{st_i}^*}{\Sigma}, \tag{B.12}$$

where

$$-B_1 = -pU_a' - pU_a''t_i(w_i - w_l - f_i) < 0 \text{ if } U'' \leqslant 0,$$

while

$$-B_2 = -p'(s)U_a't_i + pU_a''t_i > 0 \text{ if } U'' \geqslant 0.$$

The direct effect of an increase in punishment on the incentive to self-protect would be positive if $U'' = 0$ and may be positive even if $U'' < 0$, provided U was not too concave. This effect would at least partly offset the deterrent effect on t_i. Therefore, the observation that efforts to apprehend and convict offenders have a greater deterrent effect on some offenders relative to an increase in the severity of punishment may be explained simply by the interaction between self-protection and crime, and may be consistent with neutral (or even negative) attitudes toward risk.[69]

In analogy to the incentive offenders have to self-protect against the hazard

---

69. Note that the results derived in Appendix 1 to Section I (as well as in the text) regarding the relative deterrent effect of the probability and the severity of punishment refer to the partial effect of p and f when either alone changes. The analysis above is concerned with the effect of a change in f when r, not p, is held constant. It does not affect, therefore, the results summarized in equation (A.8) in Appendix 1 to Section II, and in equation (1.10) in footnote 13 in the text, or the corresponding hypotheses tested in the empirical investigation.

of apprehension and punishment, potential victims of crime have an incentive to self-protect against the hazard of becoming victims to crime. For example, the probability of becoming a victim to burglary or robbery can be reduced by installing security locks and burglar alarm systems, or by keeping watchdogs; that of becoming a victim to assault or rape can be lowered by using appropriate means of transportation and escorts when traveling at certain locations and hours. Another option available to individuals is to reduce the potential size of their losses if victimized (self-insurance), for example, the loss from a house burglary can be reduced by keeping money in saving accounts and valuables in safe deposit boxes. Since the formal analysis of these methods of shifting risks is virtually identical to that presented in Ehrlich and Becker (1972) the interested reader is referred to this source for a detailed discussion of the behavioral implications. An example of aggregate self-protection by potential victims through law enforcement activity is discussed in Section IV, C, of this paper.

APPENDIX 1 TO SECTION III:
THE EMPIRICAL COUNTERPARTS OF OUR
THEORETICAL CONSTRUCTS

The empirical counterparts of our constructs can be itemized as follows:

1. $(Q/N)_i$, the crime rate of a specific crime category, is measured as the number of offenses known to the police to have occurred in a given year per 100,000 (state) population. Statistics of offenses known are based on a count of complaints of crimes filed with the police by victims and other sources and subsequently substantiated. Since reporting a crime is time consuming and may involve psychic and other disadvantages, an underreporting of crime is expected, especially in the case of milder offenses where the various costs of reporting may exceed its benefits (the potential recovery of stolen property, the collection of insurance benefits, or vengeance).[70] If relative underreporting of specific crimes did not differ systematically across states and percentage reporting errors were random, the relative variation in the rate of offenses known would serve as an unbiased approximation to that of the true crime rate (see Appendix 1 to Section IV).

2. P_i, an average offender's subjective probability that he will be apprehended and punished for his engagement in a specific crime category in a given year, may be approximated by the objective probability that a single offense will be cleared by the conviction of an offender.[71] At present, no judicial statistics on

---

70. Evidence consistent with this argument is presented in PCL, 1967(b), pp. 18, 19.

71. If the probability that an offender will be apprehended and convicted of his criminal activity in a given year were independent of the amount of time he devoted to illegal activity, as our model has assumed for simplicity, an objective measure of P would be the ratio of the number of offenders convicted, C', to the number of active offenders in the same year, or $P_i = (C'/\theta)_i$. This ratio would be the same as the ratio of offenses cleared by conviction to the total number of offenses committed, or K/Q, if those convicted committed the same number of offenses per period, ζ, as other offenders in the same state, or $(K/Q) = (\zeta C'/\zeta \theta)$.

the number of convictions are available on a statewide basis. Instead, we have computed the ratio of the number of commitments to state (and in the case of auto theft also federal) prisons in a given state to the number of offenses known to have occurred in the same year, $(C/Q)_i$.[72] Of course, not all those convicted are committed to prisons; some (especially young offenders) are sent to correctional institutions or released on probation. To the extent that the proportion of such convicted offenders did not differ systematically across states, the relative variation in $(C/Q)_i$ could serve as an efficient approximation to that in P_i.

It is possible that a purely statistical exaggeration of the expected negative sign of the regression coefficient associated with $(C/Q)_i$ in equation (4.1), b_{1i}, would result from spurious correlation. Recall that the dependent variable is $(Q/N)_i$. If Q_i were not measured appropriately, the errors in the numerator of the dependent variable and in the denominator of the probability measure would move in the same direction. This spurious correlation would bias b_{1i} to a higher (absolute) value if and only if the absolute value of the true regression coefficient were lower than unity (a proof is given in Appendix 1 to Section IV).[73] A spurious correlation may also exist in an opposite direction, however, for if the recovery of stolen merchandise or vengeance played an important role in determining the reporting of an offense, or if the fraction of reported offenses were positively related to law enforcement activity, a low probability of apprehending and convicting offenders would be associated with a low rate of *reported* crimes, thus biasing the correlation between $(Q/N)_i$ and $(C/Q)_i$ toward a positive value. A similar argument can be made regarding the correlation between the severity of punishment and reported crime.

3. F_i, the average cost of punishment for a specific crime category, is measured by the average time actually served by offenders in state prisons for that crime before their first release, T_i. As with our measure of P_i, if the relative variation in T_i also reflected the relative variation in the severity of other punitive measures imposed for the same crime, and if, in addition, current values of T_i in different states indicate effectively the long-run levels of these variables, as forecast by potential offenders in those states, then T_i would serve as an efficient indicator of F_i. Note, however, that T_i is not proportionately related to F_i. For example, the opportunity costs of imprisonment, F', which may be assumed to be proportionally related to the total cost of punishment, would be measured under a continuous discounting process as $F' = \int_0^T \omega e^{-rt}\, dt$, where ω denotes an average prisoner's (constant) foregone value of time per period of imprisonment and r is the relevant discount rate. The elasticity of crime rates with respect to T, σ_{kT}, can therefore be expected to be consistently lower than that with

---

72. Data for both this and the following variable, T_i, are collected from the National Prisoner Statistics. These variables were first used by Smigel-Leibowitz (1965).

73. If the number of offenses committed by the average offender, ζ, were positively related to the crime rate, then our probability measure C/Q would underestimate the relative level of the true probability in states with higher crime rates. This might inject a further negative bias on the regression estimates of b_1.

respect to F, σ_{kF}, the difference being particularly significant in the case of crimes punishable by long imprisonment terms.[74]

4. As indicators of differential returns in property crimes we use W and X (see the discussion in Sec. III, B).

5. U, the average probability of unemployment in legitimate activities in a given year, is measured by census estimates of yearly unemployment rates in the civilian labor force. The variation in unemployment rates may not fully capture the variation in the average unemployment duration across states, for which data were not available in our sample years, and thus it may not reflect the true variation in the relevant probability of unemployment with sufficient accuracy. One way to minimize potential biases is by narrowing the base of the unemployment index to apply to relatively homogeneous groups of labor-force participants. Alternative estimates used have been the unemployment rate of urban males in the age group 14–24, U_{14-24}, and 35–39, U_{35-39}. Another way is by introducing census estimates of labor-force participation rates jointly with unemployment rates. We have actually used the labor-force participation rate of civilian urban males in the age group 14–24, L_{14-24}.

6. E/N, the per capita amount of resources allocated to law-enforcement activity in a given year, is measured as the per capita yearly expenditure on police activity by state and local governments (collected from *Governmental Finances in 1960*). Data on expenditures on courts by local governments, which bear the bulk of these expenditures, are not available on a statewide basis. To the extent that the proportion of total expenditure on direct law enforcement devoted to courts did not differ systematically across states (the production functions (3.3) were homogeneous with respect to police and court activity [75] and the ratio of factor costs were constant), and if, in addition, the absolute prices of the relevant factors were constant, the relative variation in our measure of E/N would approximate its true variation. However, the absence of data on private expenditure on self-protection might bias our estimates of equation (3.3) if the former had a direct effect on apprehending and convicting offenders and were not related proportionally to the per capita expenditure on police. To some extent,

---

74. Assuming that losses due to the criminal record effect and other disadvantages of punishment for crime are proportionally related to F', it is easily shown that $(d \ln F)/(d \ln T) = (rT\,e^{-rT})/(1 - e^{-rT}) = \lambda < 1$. This implies that the coefficient b_{1i} in eqq. (4.1) and (4.3) is lower than b_{1i} in eq. (3.2) by a constant proportion, λ. Clearly, λ tends to zero as T tends to infinity. Another difficulty with the use of T is that it measures the average penalty per offender, not per offense. To the extent that the number of offenses committed by the average offender was positively related to the crime rate across states, estimates of b_2 might be biased toward positive values.

75. By definition, the probability of apprehension and conviction is $P \equiv P_a \cdot P_{c|a}$, where P_a is the probability of apprehension and $P_{c|a}$ is the conditional probability of conviction, given apprehension. If $P_a = g(E_p')$ and $P_{c|a} = h(E_c')$ were homogeneous with respect to real per capita expenditure on police (E_p') and courts (E_c'), so would P be with respect to both.

we may have accounted for the variation in private self-protection by the variation in the schooling level of the adult population across states, Ed. The latter can be shown to be positively related to optimal expenditures on the former (see Ehrlich and Becker, 1972).

7. The percentage of young males aged 14–24, A_{14-24}, and the percentage of nonwhites in the population, NW, are introduced in the regression analysis to account for variations in the demographic composition of the population. One reason for standardizing the observations for age and racial composition is to increase the efficiency of our estimators of probability and severity of punishment. For example, there is likely to be a positive correlation between the age of offenders and the use of punitive methods other than imprisonment across states. In addition, since the variation in differential returns from criminal activities is only indirectly accounted for in the regression analysis via X and W, the effect of both A_{14-24} and NW may partly reflect the effect of such differential returns, or a lower opportunity cost of imprisonment, for the legitimate employment opportunities of young age groups and nonwhites are well below the average, whereas their returns from illegitimate activity may not be significantly different. (For a more detailed discussion of schooling, age, race, and crime, see Ehrlich, NBER and Carnegie Commission on Higher Education (1974).) Given P and T, both NW and A_{14-24} may thus be positively related to all crime rates. Other demographic variables used in some of the cross-state regressions are listed in Table 1.

APPENDIX 1 TO SECTION IV:
ANALYSIS OF MEASUREMENT ERRORS

This discussion analyzes the impact of errors of measurement in the crime rates and the probabilities of apprehension and conviction on the least-squares estimates of the coefficients of the supply of offenses function. We start with the simple stochastic equation:

$$\left(\frac{Q^o}{N}\right)_i = A_{oi} \left(\frac{C^o}{Q^o}\right)_i^{\beta_i} e^{\epsilon_i}, \tag{C.1}$$

where Q_i^o denotes the true number of offenders engaged in crime category i (the latter subscript will henceforth be omitted), C^o is the number of offenders convicted of such crimes, N is the state population, A_o is a constant term, e is the base of natural logarithms, and ϵ is a stochastic variable, independently and identically distributed, with a zero mean and a constant variance. Equation (C.1), thus, relates the crime rate to the probability of apprehension and conviction.

If the number of reported offenses, Q, and the number of convicts entering state prisons, C, were related to Q^o and C^o by

$$Q = Q^o(1 - g)e^w, \tag{C.2}$$

and

$$C = C^o(1 - d)e^\mu, \tag{C.3}$$

where g and d are constants and w and μ are measurement errors, each a random variable independently and identically distributed, with a zero mean and a constant variance, then (C.1) could be written in terms of Q and C as

$$\left(\frac{Q}{(1 - g)e^w N}\right) = A_o \left(\frac{C(1 - g)e^w}{Q(1 - d)e^\mu}\right)^\beta e^\epsilon. \tag{C.4}$$

The regression model would thus be

$$(q - n) = \alpha_o + \ln (1 - g)(1 + \beta) - \ln (1 - d)\beta$$
$$+ \beta(c - q) + [\epsilon + (1 + \beta)w - \beta\mu], \tag{C.5}$$

where q, n, c, and α_o are the natural logarithms of Q, N, C, and A_o, respectively, and $\alpha_1 = \ln (1 - g)(1 + \beta) - \ln (1 - d)\beta$ is an additional constant term.[76]

The least-squares estimates of (C.5) are both biased and inconsistent. Note, first, that

$$\operatorname*{plim}_{N \to \infty} (\hat{b} - \beta) = \operatorname{var} (c - q)^{-1} \operatorname{cov} [(c - q), (\epsilon + (1 + \beta)w - \beta\mu)] \tag{C.6}$$

is not zero. Specifically, if ϵ, w, μ, q^o, and c^o were mutually uncorrelated, (C.6) would equal

$$\operatorname*{plim}_{N \to \infty} (\hat{b} - \beta) = -\operatorname{var} (c - q)^{-1}[(1 + \beta) \operatorname{var} (w) + \beta \operatorname{var} (\mu)]. \tag{C.7}$$

The direction of bias in $\hat{b}$ cannot be determined unambiguously, however, without making specific assumptions regarding the value of β and the relative magnitudes of var (w) and var (μ). If var (μ) were zero, (C.7) would imply that

$$\operatorname{plim} \hat{b} < \beta \text{ if } \beta \geqslant 0,$$
$$\operatorname{plim} \hat{b} \leqslant \beta \text{ if } 0 > \beta \geqslant -1, \tag{C.8}$$
$$\operatorname{plim} \hat{b} > \beta \text{ if } 0 > \beta < -1.$$

Put differently, the absolute magnitude of the regression coefficient $\hat{b}$ is likely to be biased upward if the absolute value of β were lower than unity, and downward if the latter were greater than unity (provided that $\beta < 0$). In general, var (μ), hence the second term on the right-hand side of (C.7), are positive. Consequently, plim $\hat{b}$ may be smaller than β in absolute value, even if $\beta \geqslant -1$. Moreover, since (C.7) is a weighted average of var (w) and var (μ), the weights being $(1 + \beta)$ and β, respectively, the importance of var (μ) in determining the direction of bias in $\hat{b}$ would increase as the value of β was closer to -1.

Finally, the direction of bias in $\hat{b}$ also determines the direction of bias in the

---

76. Note that if $\beta > -1$, a_1 would be negative in sign, since g and d are, in general, lower than 1.

least-squares estimate of the intercept $\alpha = \alpha_0 + \alpha_1$, since $\plim_{N \to \infty} \hat{\alpha} = \alpha + (\beta - \plim \hat{b})E(c - q)$.

Errors of measurement in Q/N and C/Q affect not only α and β in (C.5), but, in general, all the regression coefficients in the multiple regression regarding the supply-of-offenses function. To evaluate these effects, the foregoing discussion may be generalized following a model developed by Lindley and applied for a similar problem by Chow (1957). Let y^o be a vector $(N \times 1)$ of the natural logarithms of the true crime rates $(q^o - n)$ and let $X^o = [x_1^o, x_2^o, \ldots, x_k^o]$ be a matrix $(N \times p)$ of p predetermined variables of which x_k^o designates the true probability of apprehension and punishment $(c^o - q^o)$. It is assumed that the regression of y^o on all the x^o's is linear, that is,

$$y^o = X^o\beta + \epsilon. \tag{C.9}$$

Hence

$$\text{cov}\ (X^o)\beta = \text{cov}\ (X^o, y^o), \tag{C.10}$$

where cov (X^o) designates the variance-covariance matrix of X^o in the population. If y^o and X^o were related to their measured values by

$$y = y^o + w, \tag{C.11}$$

and

$$X = X^o + U \tag{C.12}$$

where w and U are an $(n \times 1)$ vector and an $(n \times p)$ matrix of measurement errors, respectively, and if all errors of measurement were random variables, independently and identically distributed, independent of y^o and all the X^o's and normally distributed, Lindley shows that the regression of y on the X's would be linear provided that the latter have a multivariate normal distribution. In this case, therefore,

$$\text{cov}\ (X)b = \text{cov}\ (X, y), \tag{C.13}$$

where

$$b = \plim_{N \to \infty} \hat{b}.$$

Substituting for the x^o's and the y^o their values from (C.11) and (C.12) equation (C.10) becomes

$$\text{cov}\ (X - U)\beta = \text{cov}\ [(X - U), (y - w)]. \tag{C.14}$$

Since cov $(XU) = \text{cov}\ (U)$, and using equation (C.13), (C.14) reduces to

$$\text{cov}\ (X)(b - \beta) = -[\text{cov}\ (U)\beta - \text{cov}\ (U, w)], \tag{C.15}$$

or

$$b - \beta = -\text{cov}\ (X)^{-1}[\text{cov}\ (U)\beta - \text{cov}\ (U, w)]. \tag{C.16}$$

Henceforth, the analysis is a straightforward application of Chow's development (op. cit.). Assuming that only $x_k = (c - q)$ was subject to a measurement error: $e = (\mu - w)$, and denoting cov $(e) = e^2 = $ cov $(\mu) + $ cov $(w) = \mu^2 + w^2$ it can be shown that

$$b_k - \beta_k = -\frac{w^2}{s^2 + e^2}(1 + \beta_k) - \frac{\mu^2}{s^2 + e^2}\beta_k, \qquad (C.17)$$

and

$$b_{p(\neq k)} - \beta_p = d_{kp}\left[\frac{w^2}{s^2 + e^2}(1 + \beta_k) + \frac{\mu^2}{s^2 + e^2}\beta_k\right], \qquad (C.18)$$

where d_{kp} is the partial regression coefficient of x_k on $x_{p(\neq k)}$ in the multiple regression of the former on all the other x_p's $(p \neq k)$; $(s^2 + e^2)$ is the variance of the residual term in the same regression; and s^2 is the variance of the residual term in the regression of x_k^0 on all the x_p's. Clearly, (C.17) has the same implications as (C.7). In addition (C.18) implies the following generalization: the least-squares estimates of the regression coefficients of variables other than x_k would be biased in the same direction as $\hat{b}_k$ if d_{kp} were *negative*, and in an opposite direction if d_{kp} were *positive*.[77]

APPENDIX 2 TO SECTION IV:
DOES CRIME PAY?

Crime always pays, according to the assumption underlying our model, if the variety of all monetary and psychic costs and returns offenders derive from engaging in crime as well as their utility from assuming risk are taken into ac-

---

77. Simple least-squares estimates of d_{kp} associated with the basic explanatory variables in the supply of offenses functions in 1960 are shown below in Table A.1.

TABLE A.1
THE PROBABILITY OF IMPRISONMENT FOR VARIOUS FELONIES
REGRESSED AGAINST SELECTED VARIABLES

Estimate of d_{kp} Associated with p

k = Probability of Punishment for:	T_i	W	X	NW
Murder	−0.2468	−0.7297	−0.6373	−0.1532
Rape	−0.1818	−2.1461	−1.3940	−0.2800
Assault	−1.2165	−0.7502	0.5878	−0.4885
Robbery	−0.3715	−1.9805	−0.9631	−0.0997
Burglary	−1.0511	−1.5533	0.1415	0.0790
Larceny	−1.1913	−0.4920	2.2799	0.0324
Auto theft	−0.5098	0	2.1744	−0.0531

count, and if offenders act rationally. Since psychic costs and gains cannot be measured directly, one may attempt to measure the monetary costs and returns from a single offense in those crimes in which the payoff is measurable in monetary terms. Whether crime pays in the monetary sense alone, however, would, in general, depend on the importance of the monetary relative to the nonmonetary aspects of crime. In particular, if psychic costs and returns average out to a constant magnitude, equal for the property crimes considered in this discussion (auto theft is excluded in this analysis), the algebraic value of the net expected gain on a single offense at the margin would indicate the relative premium required by offenders in order to compensate themselves for assuming the risk involved in these crimes. An independent test for the offenders' attitudes toward risk may thus be obtained for the three property crimes considered (robbery, burglary, and larceny).

The expected net monetary return on a single crime against property is

$$E(w_i) = (1 - p)w_i + p[(1 - d)w_i - f],$$

or

$$E(w_i) = (1 - dp)w_i - pf,$$

where w_i, w_l and f_i are here defined to include monetary elements only, and d denotes the conditional probability that the stolen property would be recovered by the police if the offender were apprehended.

In the following calculations of the expected net monetary returns, w_i is measured by the average reported value of property stolen in a single offense type i.[78] The cost of conviction on a single offense is measured by the average disposable income foregone while serving an actual prison term T_i in state prisons in 1960. Disposable income is computed on the basis of the median income of males with eight years of schooling, net of the average income tax actually paid in 1960, with the data being corrected for the age and race of those sent to state prisons and for the likelihood of being unemployed in legitimate markets.[79] Finally, the expected cost of conviction is calculated as the product of the latter statistic and the probability of being punished by imprisonment

---

78. The relevant statistic should be the market value of stolen property in each crime category, which may be considerably lower than its reported value. No information is given in the UCR on the market value of stolen merchandise by type of crime. It is possible, however, that the discount rates charged by fences when purchasing stolen goods are approximately the same except for auto-theft, which is why auto-theft is excluded from property crimes whose expected net pecuniary returns are compared below.

79. The available information concerns income rather than earnings, although the latter statistic may be a more appropriate measure of market opportunity costs of incarceration. No attempt is made to measure the nonmarket opportunity costs of incarceration, the criminal record effect, or the value of direct benefits received during imprisonment, nor to discount the value of earnings foregone in relatively distant incarceration periods.

(approximated by $(C/Q)_i$), with the expected cost of other forms of punishment omitted.[80]

The results are presented in Table A.2.

TABLE A.2

PECUNIARY COSTS AND RETURNS ON CRIMES OF THEFT

Crime	Average Gross Return [a]	Average Expected Cost
Robbery	$256	$620
Burglary	183	102
Larceny	178 [b]	83

[a] Estimates of the conditional probability that stolen property would be recovered by the police, d_i, are not broken down by these specific crimes. UCR estimates of the percentage of stolen property recovered by the police range below 10 per cent for all goods except autos.

[b] Average gross return on larceny over and under $50 is only $74 in 1960. However, since the measures of the probability of imprisonment and the average time served in prisons for larceny (C/Q) may essentially relate to larceny over $50 (data on the number of larcenies relate to larcenies over $50 only, and offenders committed to prisons for larceny are presumably mainly those convicted of more serious larcenies), the average gross return on larceny over $50 has been estimated on the basis of data provided by the UCR for 1965.

80. The true expected cost of conviction is pf, where p is the probability of being convicted of an offense and f is the "average punishment" imposed in the case of conviction. Assuming that the various forms of punishment are mutually exclusive,

$$p = p_1 + p_2,$$

where p_1 is the probability of being punished by imprisonment and p_2 is the probability of being put under probation, released into parents' custody, and so on. Similarly,

$$f = \frac{p_1}{p} f_1 + \frac{p_2}{p} f_2,$$

where f_1, f_2 are the monetary losses associated with the two forms of punishment discussed. It follows that

$$pf = p_1 f_1 + p_2 f_2,$$

which is approximated by $p_1 f_1$ on the assumption that f_2 is small.

Even though expected cost of punishment $p_1 f_1$ in each class of offenses is computed for a single offender rather than for a single offense $p_1' f_1'$, these two measures may be approximately equal. Assume that each offender committed ζ offenses. Then the relevant probability and severity of punishment estimates may be, according to n. 71,

$$p_1' = \frac{\zeta C'}{Q}, \text{ and } f_1' = \frac{f_1}{\zeta},$$

assuming the actual punishment to the offender is proportional to the number of offenses committed. Thus,

$$p_1' f_1' = p_1 f_1.$$

The estimated probabilities of punishment employed in Table A.2 above are based on the ratio of commitments over the *reported* number of offenses. If these probabilities were calculated adjusting for the percentage of unreported crimes in each crime category according to estimates from the President's Commission on Law Enforcement and Administration of Justice (1967(a), p. 22), average expected costs would become:

TABLE A.3
REVISED ESTIMATES OF PECUNIARY COSTS AND
RETURNS IN CRIMES OF THEFT

Crime	Average Gross Return	Average Expected Cost
Robbery	$256	$459
Burglary	183	71
Larceny	178	59

Given the estimates of costs and returns reported in Table A.3, the expected net gain in robbery appears negative, while the expected net gains in burglary and larceny appear positive. Clearly in view of serious omissions of various nonpecuniary costs and returns in our calculations the absolute values of these estimates are unreliable. However, if the same percentage errors applied to all specific estimates of costs and gains respectively, the *ranking* of the three property crimes investigated above might not be affected. By this ranking robbers appear to be risk preferrers *relative* to burglars and thieves.

REFERENCES

Becker, G. S. "A Theory of the Allocation of Time." *Economic Journal* 75 (September 1965).
———. "Crime and Punishment: An Economic Approach." *Journal of Political Economy* 78 (March/April 1968).
Bentham, J. *Theory of Legislation.* New York: Harcourt Brace, 1931.
Chow, G. C. *The Demand for Automobiles in the United States—a Study in Consumer Durables.* Amsterdam: North-Holland, 1957.
Ehrlich, I. "The Supply of Illegitimate Activities." Unpublished manuscript, Columbia Univ., 1967.
———. "Participation in Illegitimate Activities: An Economic Analysis." Ph.D. dissertation, Columbia Univ., 1970.
———. "On the Relation between Education and Crime." In *Education, Income, and Human Behavior,* edited by F. T. Juster. Berkeley: NBER and Carnegie Commission on Higher Education, 1974.
Ehrlich, I., and Becker, G. S. "Market Insurance, Self-Insurance and Self-Protection." *Journal of Political Economy* 80 (July/August 1972).

Fama, E. F. "Multiperiod Consumption-Investment Decisions." *American Economic Review* 60 (March 1970).

Fleisher, B. M. *The Economics of Delinquency*. Chicago: Quadrangle, 1966.

Fuchs, V. R. "Redefining Poverty and Redistributing Income." *Public Interest* 8 (Summer 1967).

President's Commission on Law Enforcement and Administration of Justice (PCL). *The Challenge of Crime in a Free Society*. Washington: U.S. Government Printing Office, 1967(*a*).

———. *Crime and Its Impact — an Assessment*. ("Task Force Reports.") Washington: U.S. Government Printing Office, 1967(*b*).

Smigel-Leibowitz, Arleen. "Does Crime Pay? An Economic Analysis." M.A. thesis, Columbia Univ., 1965.

Stigler, George J. "The Optimum Enforcement of Laws." *Journal of Political Economy* 78 (May/June 1970).

Taft, D. R., and England, R. W., Jr. *Criminology*. 4th ed. New York: Macmillan, 1964.

Tobin, J. "A Statistical Demand Function for Food in the U.S.A." *Journal of the Royal Statistical Society*, Ser. A, 113 (1950).

U.S., Department of Commerce, Bureau of the Census. *Prisoners in State and Federal Prisons and Reformatories*. Washington: U.S. Government Printing Office, 1943.

———. *Governmental Finances in 1959*. Washington: U.S. Government Printing Office, 1960.

———. *Governmental Finances in 1960*. Washington: U.S. Government Printing Office, 1961.

U.S., Department of Justice, Bureau of Prisons. *Prisoners in State and Federal Institutions, 1950*. National Prisoner Statistics. Washington: U.S. Government Printing Office, 1956.

———. *Prisoners Released from State and Federal Institutions, 1951*. National Prisoner Statistics. Washington: U.S. Government Printing Office.

———. *Characteristics of State Prisoners, 1960*. National Prisoner Statistics. Washington: U.S. Government Printing Office.

———. *Federal Prisons, 1960*. Washington: U.S. Government Printing Office.

———. *Prisoners Released from State and Federal Institutions, 1960*. National Prisoner Statistics. Washington: U.S. Government Printing Office.

———. *Prisoners Released from State and Federal Institutions, 1964*. National Prisoner Statistics. Washington: U.S. Government Printing Office.

U.S., Department of Justice, Federal Bureau of Investigation. *Uniform Crime Reports for the U.S.* (UCR). Printed annually 1933 to date. Washington: U.S. Government Printing Office.

Zellner, A. "An Efficient Method of Estimating Seemingly Unrelated Regressions and Tests for a Regression Bias." *Journal of the American Statistical Association* 57 (June 1962).

———. "Estimation of Regression Relationships Containing Unobservable Independent Variables." *International Economic Review* 11 (October 1970).

The Bail System: An Economic Approach

William M. Landes

University of Chicago and National Bureau of Economic Research

Widespread dissatisfaction with the current state of criminal justice in the United States has revived interest in the long-standing problem of determining what to do with a person charged with a crime between the time of his arrest and trial.[1] Should the accused be released or detained during this time interval? What factors are relevant to this decision? What requirements, if any, should be imposed on the accused as a condition of his release? The fundamental issue these questions raise is the difficulty of reconciling the defendant's rights to freedom before his guilt has been formally adjudicated with the community's interest in protecting itself from possible future harm.[2] In practice, most societies try to

This study has been supported by a grant for the study of law and economics from the National Science Foundation to the National Bureau of Economic Research. I would like to thank Gary Becker, Barry Chiswick, John Hause, Benjamin Klein, and Elisabeth Landes for their criticisms and helpful comments, Elisabeth Parshley for her assistance, and H. Irving Forman for charting the graphs. I also benefited from comments at economic seminars at Columbia University, the University of Chicago, and the University of Massachusetts.

1. See, *e.g.*, John N. Mitchell, Bail Reform and the Constitutionality of Pretrial Detention, 55 Va. L. Rev. 1223 (1969); Laurence H. Tribe, An Ounce of Detention: Preventive Justice in the World of John Mitchell, 56 Va. L. Rev. 371 (1970).

2. The definition of harm is itself an important source of controversy. See, *e.g.*, John N. Mitchell, *supra* note 1; Laurence H. Tribe, *supra* note 1. One definition includes only

resolve this conflict by means of a bail system that establishes rules and procedures to guide decisions on whether or not to release a defendant. These rules may specify which classes of defendants are eligible for release, and require an eligible defendant to make a monetary payment to the court, pledge an asset that will be forfeited if he does not appear for trial, or have a third party assume responsibility for his presence at trial.

In the U.S., the typical procedure is for the court to set a bond as security for the defendant's appearance at trial. If he can post the amount of the bond by pledging acceptable assets or by having a professional bondsman do it for him, he is released; otherwise he is imprisoned. Data presented in Table 1 reveal that a substantial fraction of defendants are in fact imprisoned. A survey of more than 4,000 felony defendants across 70 counties in 1962 showed that 53 per cent of these defendants were confined. A sample of defendants arraigned in New York City in 1971 indicates that 68 per cent of those charged with felonies and 51 per cent of those charged with misdemeanors were imprisoned for average periods of 38 days and 14 days respectively. Moreover, among felony defendants both the likelihood of detention and the average days detained rose the more serious the offense. Table 2 views pretrial detention from a different perspective. It shows that of the more than 127,000 adult inmates in local jails in March 1970 (excluding 25,356 adults not yet arraigned or being held for other authorities), 41 per cent were pretrial detainees. The President's Commission reports that nearly 40 per cent of adults in prison are in local jails.[3] Thus, about one in 6 adults in prison are persons whose guilt has not been formally determined.

The fact that large numbers of defendants are denied pretrial liberty —whether this is desirable or not—has important implications for the overall operation of the criminal justice system. In the first place, the greater the proportion of defendants not released, the lower the number of trials relative to guilty pleas. The disposition of cases is affected in this way because the costs of going to trial (specifically, the costs of waiting due to court delay) are greater for detained defendants than those re-

---

the expected losses (e.g., a weakening in the deterrent effect of criminal sanctions) that result when some defendants flee, tamper with evidence, or intimidate witnesses during the period of pretrial release. This leads to the view that the only justification for denying or placing restraints on pretrial liberty is that the defendant's release would seriously impair the proceedings against him. A broader definition of harm also includes predictions about the losses from crimes committed by released defendants. According to this view the potential dangerousness of the defendant is a legitimate reason for denying pretrial liberty.

3. See U.S. President's Comm'n on Law Enforcement & Admin. of Justice, The Challenge of Crime in a Free Society 172 (1967).

TABLE 1
PRETRIAL DETENTION

Area (Year)	Type of Charge	No.	Bond	%	Days De-tained	Prior Felony Arrests								
						None			1–3			4 or More		
						No.	Bond	%	No.	Bond	%	No.	Bond	%
N.Y.C. (1971)	Felony	526	$1,339	68	38	304	$ 973	55	189	$1,842	85	33	$1,848	91
	Felony B	61	3,087	90	84	31	2,637	87	25	3,704	92	5	2,800	100
	Felony C	120	1,563	69	53	66	1,207	56	45	2,056	84	9	1,722	89
	Felony D	258	1,070	65	22	150	705	49	93	1,538	88	15	1,833	87
	Felony E	87	604	57	18	57	502	49	26	769	69	4	1,000	100
	Misdemeanor	329	477	51	14	190	286	36	119	722	73	20	850	65
U.S.— 70 Counties (1962)	Felony	4,569	$3,437	53										

NOTE.— No. = number of defendants.

Bond = average size of bail bond.

% = per cent of defendants detained prior to the disposition of their case.

Days Detained = average days detained for defendants whose cases were not dismissed.

SOURCES.—(1) N.Y.C. data provided to me by the Legal Aid Society based on a random sample of Legal Aid defendants in Manhattan during several months of 1971.

(2) U.S. data from Lee Silverstein, Bail in the State Courts—A Field Study and Report, 50 Minn. L. Rev. 621 (1966), and Lee Silverstein, Defense of the Poor in Criminal Cases in American State Courts, A Field Study and Report (1965). Silverstein presents data for more than 200 counties. I have used only those counties where information was available on pretrial status and size of bond.

TABLE 2

DEFENDANTS NOT RELEASED ON BAIL IN LOCAL JAILS, MARCH 1970 [a]

Total Inmates [b]	Inmates Not Released on Bail and Awaiting Trial	% Not Released	Annual Operating and Capital Costs Attributed to Inmates Not Released	
			Total [c] ($000)	Per Inmate ($)
127,707	52,565	41.2	161,950	3,081
			106,081 [d]	2,017 [d]

SOURCE. — U.S. Dep't of Justice, Law Enforcement Assistance Admin., 1970 National Jail Census 9-11 (Nat'l Crim. Justice Inf. & Stat. Serv. 1971).

[a] Local jails are those operated locally in municipalities which in 1960 had a population of 1,000 or more. Facilities which normally detain persons for 2 days or less were excluded.

[b] Excludes 25,356 adults who were not yet arraigned or who were being held for other authorities, and 7,800 juveniles.

[c] Total was 203,967,000 but this was multiplied by .794 to take account of inmates who were excluded. Operating costs were for 1969 while capital costs were those planned for 1970.

[d] Operating costs alone.

leased. Secondly, defendants not released are likely to have higher conviction probabilities in a trial and receive longer sentences if they plead guilty than defendants released on bail. This occurs because detention adversely affects the productivity of the defendant's resources (both market and time inputs). For example, in the case of market inputs detention would hamper consultation with lawyers, and in the case of time inputs detention would make it more difficult to seek out witnesses and engage in other investigatory activities. Finally, if making bail is a positive function of wealth, then the effects of pretrial imprisonment would fall most heavily on low-income defendants.[4] Recent empirical research on the criminal court system provides some support for these hypotheses.[5]

4. See William M. Landes, An Economic Analysis of the Courts, this volume, for a further development of these arguments.

5. See William M. Landes, *supra* note 4, for an empirical analysis across state county courts using multiple regression techniques. A study by the New York City Legal Aid Society (Brief for Appellee, Bellamy v. Abruczo (N.Y. Sup. Ct., March 1972)) of defendants in New York City also finds a positive relationship between pretrial detention and the likelihood of a prison sentence, holding constant the defendant's prior record,

The purpose of this essay is to reexamine the important questions of pretrial liberty and bail determination from a different viewpoint than the usual one. Instead of focusing on the desirability of actual bail practices or proposed reforms and their constitutionality, we begin by developing an economic model of an optimal bail system. Our approach is to derive the social benefit from pretrial liberty that incorporates both the gains to defendants from being released on bail and the costs and gains to the rest of the community from their release. We then determine the number of defendants to release and the level of resource expenditures on the bail system that are consistent with the maximization of the social benefit.[6] After developing the basic model we consider the consistency of the rules derived from an optimal system with some existing practices in the United States: for example, the practice of setting higher bail for more serious offenses and for defendants with prior arrests (see Table 1 for evidence on this), and the rationale of legislation that guarantees a right to bail except for certain classes of defendants (e.g., those accused of capital offenses). Two common views on the proper function of a bail system—deterring flight and preventing future crime—are incorporated into the model as special cases and compared to the more general criterion of maximizing the social benefit.

The main contribution of this essay, however, is the development of alternative methods to select defendants for release. Two basic methods and variations on them are analyzed. Both are consistent with the criterion of maximizing the social benefit function. The first, which corresponds to most existing bail systems, requires defendants to pay for their release. The second compensates defendants for their detention via a monetary or other form of payment. The latter proposal is not only novel but, as we show, is superior in a number of ways to existing bail systems.[7] The final part of the paper brings into the analysis the advantage of crediting a defendant's pretrial detention against his eventual sentence,

---

family ties, employment status, and seriousness of the charge. For an early study that supports some of these hypotheses see Anne Rankin, The Effect of Pretrial Detention, 39 N.Y.U.L. Rev. 641 (1964).

6. This model is based on one presented by Gary S. Becker in Crime and Punishment: An Economic Approach, included in this volume. Becker determines the optimal supply of criminal offenses by selecting values for the probability of conviction and the penalty that minimize the community's loss from crime. He does not explicitly consider the bail system, although his approach is applicable to devising rules for an optimal bail system.

7. Gordon Tullock discusses the possibility of compensating defendants not released on bail in The Logic of Law 194–95 (1971), and I have briefly analyzed it. See William M. Landes, pp. 178–79 this volume.

the possibility of tort suits by detained defendants who are acquitted, and the role of bail bonds and bondsmen.

THE MODEL

GAINS FROM RELEASE

Let us assume that n defendants have been arrested and accused of committing similar types of crimes. From this group some will be detained in jail while others will be released during the period between arrest and trial. Let us also assume that each of the n defendants is expected to do the same amount of harm prior to trial if released on bail.[8] There are two sources of gains to the community from releasing defendants: the gains to the defendants (whom we assume are members of the community) and the gains to the rest of the community. The gain to the defendant from being released on bail (which is rigorously specified in a later section) depends in part on his earnings outside prison, his wealth, the value he places on the nonpecuniary aspects of pretrial liberty net of the consumption provided him in prison, and any changes in the expected future value of these variables resulting from pretrial liberty (*e.g.*, higher expected future earnings if pretrial release lowers the probability of conviction).[9] The aggregate gain to all defendants released is the sum of the individual gains and can be written as

$$G = G(b, t, p, u) \tag{1}$$

where b is the number released on bail ($b \leq n$),[10] t is the time from arrest to disposition of a case (or, equivalently, the length of pretrial detention),

---

8. The assumption of equal harm is not unreasonable in view of the earlier assumption that defendants are accused of similar crimes, which is one indicator of potential harm. We make the assumption of equal harm in order to simplify the presentation of the model. Differences in harm can be handled by dividing n into subgroups of defendants (*i.e.*, $n_1, n_2, \ldots, n_n$) where each subgroup consists of persons who are each expected to do the same amount of harm if released on bail. We would then derive the number of defendants to release in each subgroup instead of simply the total number released. The implications of differences in harm are discussed later.

9. All gains and costs in the paper are measured in terms of monetary equivalents.

10. Aggregating the individual gains into the G function depends on which of the n defendants are released. That is, if b, t, p and u were given and defendants differed in their gains from release, G would still be unknown unless one specified which defendants were released. Therefore, we make the following assumption: if only one person is released, it is the defendant with the highest gain; if two are released, it is the first defendant plus the defendant with the second highest gain, etc. The justification for this ordering will become

p is the probability of reapprehension for a defendant not appearing at trial, and u is the influence of other factors affecting the gains from release. (Hereafter, residual terms such as u are deleted.) One would expect G to increase as more defendants are released, as the period of release lengthens, and as the probability of recapture falls. That is, $G_b > 0$, $G_t > 0$, and $G_p < 0$ where $\partial G/\partial b = G_b$ (etc.). (The latter notation is used for all derivatives in the paper.)

The second gain from releasing defendants on bail, accruing primarily to members of the community who are not defendants, is the reduction in direct costs of providing detention services, which includes savings on expenditures for jails, guards, food, etc. These savings would increase with b and t as in

$$J = J(b, t) \tag{2}$$

where $J_b > 0$ and $J_t > 0$. The savings from releasing defendants are not insignificant. The President's Commission estimates that the costs per defendant of pretrial detention are between \$3 and \$9 per day.[11] The data presented in Table 2 indicate that the annual operating and capital costs of pretrial detention facilities are more than \$161 million, which comes to a cost per defendant of about \$3,000 annually and \$8.50 per day.

COSTS OF RELEASE

It is not costless to release defendants on bail. As previously indicated, harm or damage may result to the community that would not have occurred had these defendants been in custody. The harm will include losses from crimes committed by defendants during the period of pretrial liberty and from a possible reduction in the effectiveness of the legal system as some defendants disappear, tamper with evidence, or intimidate witnesses.[12] Thus the expected harm from all defendants released on bail can be written:

---

clearer when methods for releasing defendants are considered. The ordering of b in the functions that are specified later is identical to the ordering in the G function; however, since defendants can be assumed identical with respect to the other functions, the values of these functions are independent of the ordering of b.

11. See U.S. President's Comm'n on Law Enforcement & Admin. of Justice, The Courts 38 (Task Force Report, 1967).

12. As noted earlier (see *supra* note 2), considerable controversy exists over the desirability of including predictions about future crime in decisions on pretrial liberty. Although we include it, the model would essentially be unchanged by its exclusion. This point is developed later on.

$$H = H(b, t, p). \qquad (3)$$

H will tend to be greater, the greater the number of defendants released on bail, the longer the period of release and the less likely that defendants are reapprehended. That is, $H_b > 0$, $H_t > 0$, and $H_p < 0$.[13]

A second source of costs (which for convenience are grouped together) consists of expenditures by the state to reapprehend defendants and to affect the length of pretrial release. These costs may be written as

$$C = C(b, p, t). \qquad (4)$$

Since an increase in the probability of reapprehension (p) and a decrease in the period of pretrial release (t) require greater resources, $C_p > 0$ and $C_t < 0$. C_b is assumed positive for two reasons. First, an increase in b is likely to increase the number of released defendants who flee. With p constant, this implies a proportionate increase in reapprehensions and hence greater costs. Second, defendants released on bail are more likely to go to trial (and less likely to plead guilty) than defendants not released, so that an increase in b will increase trial demand.[14] This in turn will increase court delay and raise t for a given supply of trials. Thus an increase in b with t constant requires greater expenditures on the court system and hence an increase in C.[15] Note that C is set at 0 when $b = 0$

---

13. Since we assume the expected harm from each released defendant is the same, H can be written as $b \cdot h(t, p)$ where $h(t, p)$ is the expected harm per defendant.

14. See William M. Landes, pp. 176–82 this volume.

15. This point is not as obvious as it may first appear. If one believes that the "quality" of justice resulting from plea bargaining and guilty pleas is about as good as the "quality" from trials, then any additional demand and subsequent expenditures for trial services that result from increasing the number of defendants released is a cost to the community. It is a cost in the following sense: the "quality" of justice is not being enhanced by releasing more defendants but a more expensive method of disposing of cases (*i.e.*, more trials) is being used. Alternatively, if one believed that "quality" is raised by more trials and fewer pleas, then part or all of these additional expenditures on trials should be excluded from the above cost function. These two views come close to those described in "The Crime Control Model" and "The Due Process Model" in Herbert L. Packer, The Limits of the Criminal Sanction 210–21 (1968). For example, "The Crime Control Model" rests on the belief that most persons charged with a crime are "factually guilty" and hence a major cost of making pretrial liberty the norm is that "the increase in time required to litigate cases that don't really need to be litigated would put an intolerable strain on what is already an overburdened process." In contrast, "The Due Process Model" starts from the assumption that the accused "is not a criminal." Pretrial detention and guilty pleas are often undesirable because they lead one "to waive the various safeguards against unjust conviction that the system provides." When large numbers of defendants are detained and plead guilty, "the adversary system as a whole suffers, because its vitality depends on effective challenge."

because there are no expenditures on p, and only the increment in expenditures on the criminal court system that result from a positive b are included in C.

NET BENEFIT FUNCTION

The net benefit from releasing defendants on bail depends on the gain and cost components specified above, which in turn are functions of b, p, and t. In principle, a number of additional considerations could enter the net benefit function.[16] But in the analysis that follows we restrict ourselves to a simple formulation of the net benefit function, which is the sum of the cost and gain components. This measures the monetary equivalent of the net gain from releasing defendants and is denoted by

$$\pi = G(b, t, p) + J(b, t) - H(b, t, p) - C(b, t, p). \tag{5}$$

Optimality requires that we simultaneously select values for b, t, and p that maximize the value of π. By assumption, defendants are selected for release in a way that yields the highest G and therefore the highest π. Two methods for selecting defendants that satisfy the above assumption are considered. In the first, the defendant pays for his release; in the second, the defendant is paid for remaining in jail prior to trial.

THE DEFENDANT PAYS

The n defendants will have a demand function for release on bail that can be written as

$$b = b(m, t, p), \tag{6}$$

where m is the price defendants must pay for pretrial release, and b, t, and p are defined as before. Since defendants generally differ in the maximum amount they would pay for release, depending on differences in the opportunity cost of their time, wealth, and tastes for nonprison compared to prison life, a decline in m (holding t and p constant) would lead more

---

16. For example, if one believed that the harm defendants were expected to do was too vague and difficult to predict, H might be given a small weight in the calculation of net benefits. If part of G included the gains to persons from further crimes and this was deemed an inappropriate source of utility, G could be discounted in estimating the net benefit function. Alternatively, if it was strongly felt that defendants later found innocent should not be detained, a greater weight could be given to G. (In the extreme, G would be so large that all defendants were released.)

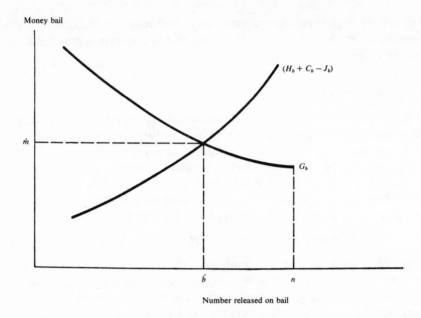

Money bail

$\hat{m}$

$(H_b + C_b - J_b)$

G_b

b n

Number released on bail

FIGURE 1

defendants to choose release on bail in preference to jail.[17] Similarly, an increase in t and a decrease in p would raise the relative attractiveness of pretrial release and increase its demand. Therefore, we would expect that $b_m < 0$, $b_p < 0$, and $b_t > 0$.

Now consider the optimality conditions for maximizing the net benefit π. The variables subject to direct control by the state are C, the costs of recapturing defendants and reducing the period of pretrial release, and m, the level of money bail or the price of release. These variables determine b, p, and t which then determine π. Maximizing π first with respect to m yields

$$G_b = H_b + C_b - J_b. \tag{7}$$

In words, money bail should be set at a level where the marginal gain from pretrial release of an additional defendant (G_b) equals the marginal harm

---

17. Evidence from samples of defendants in the U.S. supports the view that money bail is both negatively related to and an important determinant of the number of defendants released. See, *e.g.*, Note, A Study of the Administration of Bail in New York City, 106 U. Pa. L. Rev. 693 (1958); Charles E. Ares, Anne Rankin & Herbert Sturz, The Manhattan Bail Project: An Interim Report on the Use of Pre-Trial Parole, 38 N.Y.U.L. Rev. 67 (1967); Note, Compelling Appearance in Court: Administration of Bail in Philadelphia, 102 U. Pa. L. Rev. 1031 (1954); U.S. Atty. Gen'l's Comm. on Poverty & Admin. of Crim. Justice, Report, app. 1 (1963).

(H_b) plus marginal costs of reapprehension and expanding court services (C_b) minus the marginal savings in detention costs (J_b).[18] Since a defendant would choose release if his gain exceeded m, and prefer jail if m exceeded his gain, the optimal number of defendants would be released if m were set at $\hat{m}$ where

$$\hat{m} = G_b = H_b + C_b - J_b. \tag{8}$$

Thus, defendants are charged a price for release that compensates for the marginal harm and costs minus the savings in detention costs.[19] The optimum is illustrated in Figure 1 at $\hat{b}$ and $\hat{m}$.[20]

Several implications of the optimality conditions are worth noting.

(1) Wealthier defendants would be willing to pay a higher price for their release on bail because forgone earnings tend to rise with wealth,

---

18. Although C is the remaining variable subject to control, it is more convenient to maximize π with respect to t and p. This would determine the optimal level of C given the value of b that satisfies equation (7). In addition to equation (7), the first-order optimality conditions would then include

$$G_t + J_t - H_t - C_t = 0 \tag{i}$$

$$G_p - H_p - C_p = 0 \tag{ii}$$

where (i) and (ii) have been simplified by the substitution of equation (7). We largely ignore (i) and (ii) in the subsequent analysis since our main interest is the determination of b and m.

19. At this stage I am ignoring difficulties of financing m. These difficulties could lead a person to remain in jail although his gain exceeded m so that the number of defendants released at a price of $\hat{m}$ would be less than optimal.

20. Second-order conditions require that $G_{bb} < H_{bb} + C_{bb} - J_{bb}$ at $\hat{b}$ (where $G_{bb} = \partial^2 G/\partial b^2$, etc.). Figure 1 assumes that $G_{bb} < 0$ and $(H_{bb} + C_{bb} - J_{bb}) > 0$. It seems plausible that $G_{bb} < 0$ because the ordering of b in the G function is such that additional defendants released value their release by smaller and smaller amounts. $(H_{bb} + C_{bb} - J_{bb})$ would probably be positive beyond some level of b for two reasons. If the marginal costs of detention rise with the number detained, J_{bb} will be negative (and hence $-J_{bb} > 0$) since the cost saving will fall as more defendants are released. If there are diseconomies of scale in recapturing defendants and reducing court delay, C_b would be a rising function of b and hence $C_{bb} > 0$. Note that $H_{bb} = 0$ because all defendants are assumed to do the same amount of harm if released. Corner solutions are possible. For example, if $G_b > H_b + C_b - J_b$ for all values of b, then $b = n$, and if $G_b < H_b + C_b - J_b$ for all b, then $b = 0$.

All defendants are charged the same price for release. In view of our assumptions of similar offenses and equal harm, the use of a single price appears to be consistent with the way bail actually operates. For example, the President's commission reports that "... bail rates are often preordained by stationhouse or judicial schedules: so and so many dollars for such and such a crime. The effect of standard rates and their disparity from place to place is to leave out of consideration not only the important question of a defendant's financial means but also the equally important ones of his background, character, and ties to the community." U.S. President's Comm'n on Law Enforcement & Admin. of Justice, *supra* note 3, at 131.

and "days free" are likely to be, in part, a consumption good with a wealth elasticity greater than zero. Other things being equal, this would lead to a greater frequency of pretrial release for defendants with higher incomes, independent of capital market difficulties in financing bail. Although released defendants would be buying their freedom, they would nevertheless be compensating society for the marginal harm and costs of their release via the payment of money bail.[21]

(2) We have assumed that differences among defendants in expected harm do not exist. Suppose these differences exist and are detectable. We could then separate defendants into subgroups where persons in each subgroup were expected to inflict the same harm if released on bail. Subgroups expected to do more marginal harm (*i.e.*, a higher H_b with H_{bb} still equal to zero for each subgroup) would generally have money bail set at a higher level and a smaller proportion of defendants released.[22] In terms of Figure 1, the supply curve would be further to the left for subgroups expected to do more harm, resulting in a higher m and lower b for a given G function.

(3) Suppose there was an exogenous increase in congestion in the court system which increased the delay between arrest and trial. This

---

21. It has been suggested that bail would be more equitable if it were set with regard to the defendant's ability to pay (*i.e.*, his wealth). In our model this would have the effect of increasing the state's revenue without altering the number or composition of released defendants. Higher prices to wealthier defendants would enable the state to extract some of the defendants' surplus (*i.e.*, consumers' surplus) in Figure 1.

22. The net benefit function can be redefined as follows:

$$\pi = G(b_1, b_2, \ldots, b_n, t, p) + J(b, t) - H(b_1, b_2, \ldots, b_n, t, p) - C(b, t, p),$$

where $b = b_1 + b_2 \ldots + b_n$, and where defendants continue to be identical with respect to the J and C functions. Maximizing π with respect to the b_i's ($i = 1, \ldots, n$) and setting optimal prices for release yields

$$\hat{m}_i = G_{b_i} = H_{b_i} - C_b + J_b.$$

If we assume that the demand curve for release is the same for the n groups and $\partial(H_{b_i})/\partial_{b_i} = 0$, then the greater the group's marginal harm, the lower the proportion released and the higher the price of release. One might argue that a group's demand curve for release would be positively correlated with its marginal harm (*i.e.*, the more harm a defendant is likely to do, the greater is his gain from release on average). Our prediction of a decline in the proportion released as the marginal harm rises would still hold if the G_b function shifted up by a smaller amount than the $(H_b + C_b - J_b)$ function. However, it is by no means obvious that the marginal harm and gain are positively correlated. Innocent defendants are likely to do the least harm if released, and their gain from release may be even greater than for guilty defendants. The former, if detained, incur losses not only in current but also future income resulting from any stigma attached to being in jail. They also may incur sizable search costs to obtain employment after being found innocent and released.

would raise the defendant's gain from release and shift G_b to the right in Figure 1. If increases in H_b and J_b offset each other as t rises (and C_b does not change), there will be no shift in the supply curve and both the optimal m and the number of defendants released on bail will rise. If the change in H_b more than offset the change in J_b, one could no longer predict the direction of change in the number released.

OPTIMAL BAIL AND CURRENT PRACTICES

Having set forth the basic model, we now compare some actual bail practices with the prescriptions of an optimal system.[23] Table 1 shows that the size of the bail bond tends to increase with both the severity of the charge and the number of prior arrests (though this does not hold for every charge and prior arrest class). Not surprisingly, the proportion of defendants released declines with both the severity of the charge and the number of prior arrests. These results are consistent with an optimal system under the assumption that the severity of the charge and prior arrests are indicators of greater marginal harm (H_b) and marginal costs (C_b). The severity of the charge may provide information on marginal harm for two reasons: (1) present charges are one predictor of the damages from possible offenses during the period of pretrial release (holding constant the rate of recidivism); and (2) the more serious the charge, the greater the possible punishment and hence the greater the defendant's gain (the avoidance of punishment being one component) from not appearing for trial. It follows from (2) that the marginal cost of reapprehending defendants (C_b) and the seriousness of the charge are positively correlated since defendants faced with more serious charges have a lower probability of voluntarily appearing for trial. Similar reasoning can be used to relate the number of prior arrests to greater marginal harm and marginal costs. Admittedly, the above arguments are tenuous in the absence of empirical data connecting present charges and prior arrests with marginal harm and marginal costs. Nevertheless, they provide some rationale for present practices in the framework of an optimal system.

---

23. One difference should be noted at the outset. Money bail, m, in the optimal system is a cash payment not returned to the defendant. In actual practice, most defendants are required to post a bond for which they pay a cash fee to a bondsman. However, this difference is not important for the analysis because we can redefine m in the optimal system as the cash fee paid the bondsman. Optimality would then require the state to maximize the net benefit by setting a value for the bond that resulted in the defendant paying the bondsman an amount equal to the payment derived in equation (8). Hence, the use of bonds has little effect on the analysis at this stage and is left for a later section and the appendix.

For certain offenses, the marginal harm and marginal cost may be so great that it is not feasible for the defendant to compensate the community for his pretrial release. (In terms of Figure 1, the supply curve would be everywhere above the demand curve.) Optimality would be consistent with legislation that prohibited pretrial liberty or permitted the denial of bail for these offenses. In the United States, state and local laws provide defendants with a right to bail in noncapital offenses but permit the denial of bail in capital offenses. Since capital offenses are the most serious, existing laws would appear to conform to the rules of an optimal system. The classic capital offense, murder, does not entirely fit the argument for denying bail to defendants accused of more serious offenses. Since "most persons who are charged with this offense murder family members or paramours and therefore are the least likely of all offenders to be recidivists," [24] the denial of bail could not be based on predictions about committing more murders during the time of pretrial release. Instead, it would have to rest on the contention that persons faced with the prospect of such severe penalties would be most likely to flee.[25]

One can interpret the joint effect of the Eighth Amendment, which states that "excessive bail shall not be required," and legislation that grants a right to bail (except for capital offenses), as requiring that money bail be set according to the amount the defendant can afford without regard to marginal harm and marginal costs. A less extreme position would require setting an upper limit to money bail at a "reasonable" level. If this level were less than the amount that maximized the net benefit function, some defendants would be released even though marginal damages and costs exceeded the gains from their release. In response, one might expect the development of measures that circumvented constitutional and legislative restrictions on setting bail: for example, "preventive detention" in noncapital offenses (in effect, the setting of an infinite bail charge) or the imposition of travel restrictions, requirements of weekly appearances, etc., on released defendants to reduce marginal harm and cost.

ALTERNATIVE VIEWS OF OPTIMAL BAIL

There are two views of bail that dominate much of the current discussion on the topic. The first asserts that the primary function of a bail system is to ensure the defendant's appearance at trial. Money bail should be set, if at all, to prevent flight or more generally to prevent the defendant from

---

24. See John N. Mitchell, *supra* note 1, at 1236.
25. This point is made forcefully by Laurence H. Tribe, *supra* note 1.

interfering with the proceedings against him. Wherever possible, alternatives to money bail and detention should be encouraged. The second view asserts that the prevention of crimes by defendants during the period of pretrial liberty is a proper concern of the bail process. Accordingly, the potential "dangerousness" of the defendant is a legitimate reason for setting high bail or denying bail altogether. For convenience, the former position is termed the "deterring flight" model and the latter is called the "preventive detention" model.[26] Both models are special cases of the basic model developed earlier in the paper and, therefore, both can be incorporated into net benefit functions as follows.

Deterring Flight: $\qquad \pi_1 = G_1(b, t, p) - H_1(b, t, p) - C_1(b, p) \qquad$ (5a)

Preventive Detention: $\quad \pi_2 = G_2(b, t, p) - H_2(b, t, p) - C_2(b, t, p).$ (5b)

There are several important differences between (5a) and (5b) at equal values of b, t, and p. The marginal harm from increasing the number of defendants released (H_b), from lengthening the period of pretrial release (H_t), and from lowering the probability of reapprehension (H_p) are greater in the "preventive detention" than the "deterring flight" model since the former adds another dimension to harm—namely predictions about future crime. Hence, $H_{1b} < H_{2b}$, $H_{1t} < H_{2t}$, and $H_{1p} > H_{2p}$. The marginal cost of increasing the number released (C_b) is less in the "deterring flight" model because it does not regard the additional demand for trials that results from releasing more persons as a cost of the bail system. In contrast, a willingness to include the costs of added congestion and greater demand for trials is more characteristic of the "preventive detention" model. Thus, $C_{1b} < C_{2b}$. It also follows that the direct costs of reducing the period of pretrial detention or court delay (C_t) would be excluded from the "deterring flight" model.[27]

We can now compare the optimal values of m, b, t, and p that are

---

26. These descriptions are simplifications of the two positions and their many variations. Two recent papers that provide more detailed descriptions are John N. Mitchell, *supra* note 1, and Laurence H. Tribe, *supra* note 1. Mitchell argues in favor of the "preventive detention" model, while Tribe argues against it and in favor of the "deterring flight" model. An excellent discussion is also contained in Herbert L. Packer, *supra* note 15, where "preventive detention" is part of his "Crime Control Model" and "deterring flight" is part of his "Due Process Model."

27. One should note that the savings in detention costs (the J function) have been excluded from (5a) and (5b) since both models give little or no weight to these savings. We also assume that G_1 and G_2 are equal, although it may be argued that the "preventive detention" model tends to overlook these gains. However, the differences already noted in the text between (5a) and (5b) are sufficient for comparing the main implications of the two models.

obtained from maximizing the net benefit functions in (5a) and (5b). The "deterring flight" model results in a lower money bail and a greater proportion of defendants released than the "preventive detention" model since both the marginal harm and marginal costs (and hence the supply curve in Figure 1) are lower in the former than in the latter. The optimal period of pretrial detention is less in the "deterring flight" model as the marginal cost of reducing this time interval is excluded from the model's specification. This means that court delay or pretrial detention is kept at a minimum (i.e., where $G_{1t} = H_{1t}$) in the "deterring flight" model. Anything greater lowers the net benefit. Supporters of this model would therefore favor a greater allocation of resources to the judiciary to reduce delay. On the other hand, advocates of the "preventive detention" model would put less emphasis on expanding the court's resources because the resulting marginal benefits (a lower H) would eventually be offset by the costs of reducing delay. In the latter model, the greater harm that results from longer periods of pretrial liberty is countered by releasing fewer persons. Finally, the optimal probability of reapprehending defendants would be set higher in the "preventive detention" than the "deterring flight" model because one element of harm from a lower probability (i.e., future crime) is explicitly excluded from the latter model.

THE DEFENDANT IS PAID

Let us return to the original model, summarized by the net benefit function in equation (5), with one important change: the defendant is paid to remain in prison instead of paying for his pretrial liberty. He is offered a choice between jail, where he receives m^* as compensation, or release on bail, where he receives nothing. To distinguish this system from the one in which the defendant pays, we first consider the effect on the defendant's choice between pretrial liberty and detention.

Figure 2 presents a set of indifference curves between the defendant's wealth and "days free" on bail. We assume that both wealth and "days free" are sources of utility, "days free" are fixed at t_0, and, provisionally, a defendant forgoes no current or future income if he is jailed. A defendant with an initial wealth of W_0 would be willing to pay up to $W_0 - W_1$ for his pretrial release. This puts him at E_1, which is on the same indifference curve as his original position W_0, and leaves his utility unchanged. Therefore, $W_0 - W_1$ is the monetary equivalent of the defendant's gain from pretrial release when "days free" are the property right of the state. Suppose the state is required to pay the defendant for detaining him. The defendant would now be at E_0 and not W_0 since "days free" have become

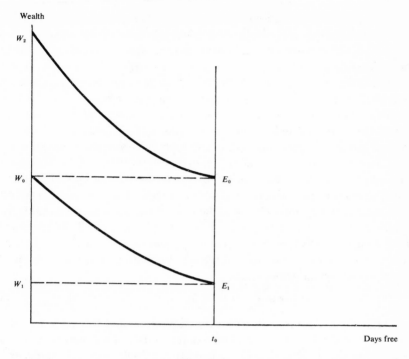

FIGURE 2

the property right of the individual. This shift in property rights puts the defendant on a higher indifference curve and increases his utility level. The minimum amount he will accept to forgo t_0 days is $W_2 - W_0$ which leaves him on the same indifference curve as the point E_0. Thus, $W_2 - W_0$ measures the gain from release when "days free" belong to the defendant. If the slopes of the two indifference curves in Figure 2 are equal at each value of t, the indifference curve passing through E_0 will be everywhere equidistant from the curve passing through E_1 and $W_0 - W_1$ will equal $W_2 - W_0$. In this instance, "days free" has a zero wealth elasticity so that the amount one will accept to give up his pretrial liberty is identical to the amount one will pay to retain it. The former sum will exceed the latter if "days free" has a positive wealth elasticity (which requires that the absolute value of the slope of the higher indifference curve be greater than the slope of the lower one at each t).[28] The analysis remains essentially the

---

28. With a positive wealth elasticity a further complication arises due to the uncertainty of conviction. To illustrate, suppose the defendant is paid for pretrial detention and there are two states of the world, a conviction state with a probability P and a nonconviction

same when present or future earnings are lost as a result of pretrial detention. The above monetary gains from release are merely increased by the discounted value of the forgone earnings (*i.e.*, the latter sum is added to both $W_2 - W_0$ and $W_0 - W_1$).

The main point of the preceding discussion is that the monetary equivalent of the defendant's gain from release, which is summarized by the G function, and hence the net benefit function depend on the type of bail system specified unless the wealth elasticity of "days free" is zero. To facilitate a comparison among different bail systems, therefore, we will make the simplifying assumption of a zero wealth elasticity and then point out the implications of a positive elasticity. If the defendant were paid to remain in custody, the net benefit function in equation (5) would remain unchanged, and m^* would be substituted for m in equation (6). Maximizing π with respect to m^* would yield equation (7). Since a defendant chooses freedom or jail depending on whether m^* is less than or greater than his gain from pretrial release, the optimal number of defendants released would occur when

$$\hat{m}^* = G_b = H_b + C_b - J_b = \hat{m}. \tag{9}$$

Thus, defendants would be paid $\hat{m}^*$ to stay in jail and this equals $\hat{m}$, the optimal payment in the system where defendants pay for their release. In terms of Figure 1, all schedules would remain unchanged and, therefore, the number and composition of defendants released would be identical in both systems. If the wealth elasticity of days free were positive, the G_b curve would be further to the right in Figure 1 and both $\hat{m}^*$ and the number released would be greater than their respective optimal values when defendants must pay for their release.

Although the optimality conditions are the same whether one pays defendants who are detained or defendants pay for their release, there are a number of distinctions to be drawn between the two bail systems.

1. The "presumption of innocence" is part of American legal tradition. Yet, when defendants must pay for their release, persons are jailed without compensation who by definition are not guilty. In effect, "innocent" persons are punished. The conflict between practice and the

---

state with a probability $(1 - P)$. The minimum amount the defendant will accept to forgo his pretrial freedom will be greater in the nonconviction state since he has a higher wealth. We can define the expected amount the defendant is willing to accept as the sum of the amounts in the two states weighted by their respective probabilities. However, the expected amount will differ from the amount he is willing to accept to forgo pretrial release if his tastes for risk are nonneutral. We do not explicitly introduce the latter result into our model since it does not affect the qualitative comparisons between the different bail systems.

"presumption of innocence" principle has so outraged some persons that they have advocated the virtual elimination of pretrial detention. Others, opposed to this view, cite the potential harm to the community from the release of dangerous persons. However, paying persons for the right to detain them simultaneously satisfies both views. It eliminates the punishment aspect of a bail system since those detained are detained voluntarily and are fully compensated for their losses, and it detains persons where the potential damages to the community exceed the gains from release.

2. A major criticism of requiring defendants to pay for their release is that it discriminates against low-income defendants.[29] This argument has some support even in the context of the simplified model presented above. Capital market difficulties may make it impossible for certain low-income defendants to finance their release, although their gain exceeds the money payment required for release. A system of loans from the court to finance release could be instituted, but this brings with it the problem of enforcing repayment.[30] In contrast, when defendants not released are paid, the charge of discrimination against the poor is eliminated.

3. In a voluntary bail system the community would often pay higher sums to detain defendants the greater the marginal harm and marginal costs of reapprehension that result from their release. In some instances, the payment would be extraordinarily large and possibly infinite. For example, a psychotic defendant accused of multiple premeditated murders and certain to be convicted is likely to value his release highly since it provides him with the opportunity both to escape conviction and to commit additional murders. Although this is an extreme example, it illustrates an obvious problem: a volunteer system provides greater rewards to persons the more dangerous they are or appear to be. The source of the problem is the strict adherence to the principle that "persons are presumed innocent until proven guilty" and, therefore, should not be punished until found guilty. The strict maintenance of a principle can be too costly. If we are willing to compromise, the problem of larger payments to more dangerous defendants becomes tractable. Suppose a particular group of defendants are deemed sufficiently dangerous so that the net benefit function is maximized when all are detained (i.e., the supply curve is everywhere above the G_b curve in Figure 1), but the payment to

---

29. See, for example, U.S. President's Comm'n on Law Enforcement & Admin. of Justice, *supra* note 11, at 37–39.

30. The institution of bondsmen for financing bail is relevant here. This is discussed later.

achieve a zero release rate is unacceptably large. We might simply fix a maximum payment and jail (voluntarily or involuntarily) the entire set of defendants. It must be emphasized that this modification substantially alters the nature of the bail system where defendants are paid. We no longer allow certain defendants the choice between pretrial release or jail. Instead, this decision is made by the court or prosecutor with the stipulation that a jailed defendant receives some compensation.

4. A problem related to the above is that arrested offenders have an incentive to exaggerate their potential harm and desire to escape if released on bail as a means of extracting a higher payment for remaining in jail. Note, however, that this problem exists in reverse when defendants must pay for their release. There, the prosecutor has an incentive to exaggerate the potential danger from releasing the defendant in order to persuade the magistrate to set a higher bail.[31]

5. The physical facilities and living conditions that are provided detained defendants are often deplorable.[32] This is not surprising because when defendants pay for their release there is little incentive for the state or court to improve these conditions. In contrast, a volunteer or partial volunteer system (*i.e.*, for some offenses the defendant is given the choice between release or jail) would provide such an incentive. Improved detention facilities would reduce the nonmoney costs of detention to defendants, which in turn would reduce the amount the state would have to pay to detain them. The less unpleasant these facilities, the lower the payments. An optimum degree of unpleasantness would be achieved when the marginal costs of improved facilities equaled the marginal savings in payments to jailed defendants.

6. Reducing the time between arrest and disposition has been urged as the best practical solution to problems of the existing bail system.[33]

---

31. The advantage of high bail to the prosecutor is that it raises the likelihood of convicting the defendant. See William M. Landes, pp. 176–77 this volume.

32. A major complaint of inmates who rioted in the N.Y.C. Tombs (a prison for persons not released on bail) was the overcrowding, inadequate food and presence of roaches, lice, etc. Their complaints were verified by public officials and prison guards. (See Newsweek, August 24, 1970.) Also see U.S. President's Comm'n on Law Enforcement & Admin. of Justice, *supra* note 11, at 38, on the poor quality of pretrial detention facilities.

33. Chief Judge Harold Greene of the Court of General Sessions in Washington, D.C., has argued as follows:
". . . A strict policy favoring the detention of criminal suspects is bound to lead to the incarceration of some who will ultimately be acquitted. On the other hand, a liberal release policy has caused and will continue to cause the pretrial freedom of many who will take advantage of their freedom to continue their criminal careers to the detriment of society. Opinions differ as to which is more harmful to our values. . . . Whatever one's view on this

Less pretrial delay would diminish the losses to detained defendants, the harm that released defendants might do, and the direct costs of detention. One could argue that delay would be reduced more when defendants are paid compared to when they pay because the former provides an additional incentive for the state to reduce delay — namely a reduction in the size of payments to attract a given number of volunteers.[34]

7. The two bail systems will have different effects on the deterrence of crime. When defendants are paid, the expected costs of committing crimes are lower than when defendants must pay for their release. In the former, the economic returns to the criminal are higher and, other things remaining the same, the amount of crime will tend to be greater. However, which bail system is preferable on deterrence grounds alone is not obvious. For example, if penalties and probabilities of conviction are optimally set without explicitly considering the bail system, then requiring defendants to pay for their release will impose added penalties that result in overdeterrence. On the other hand, if penalties or probabilities are inadequate, we may move closer to an optimal level of deterrence when defendants pay for their release. Thus, without knowledge of the existing penalties and probabilities, we cannot determine which bail system produces a more desired level of deterrence. Moreover, if penalties and probabilities are adjustable, one can adjust them to achieve the optimal deterrence level for each type of bail system.

SOME MODIFICATIONS

Two further problems in the development of an optimal bail system are now considered: the "moral hazard" problem, which occurs primarily when defendants are compensated for pretrial detention, and the provision of incentives for defendants released on bail to return for trial. The

---

issue, no one could reasonably quarrel with the proposition that the most desirable solution to this dilemma is to escape it altogether.

Escape is possible, but only through the construction of a judicial system which tries its suspects so quickly that the incarceration of innocent defendants or the pretrial freedom of potential repeat offenders is so brief as to be acceptable as a practical matter. . . ." (Washington Star, March 30, 1969, at F2, quoted in American Enterprise Institute for Public Policy Research, The Bail Reform Act 47–48 (April 1969).)

34. Note that the optimal amount of delay, t, is the same in both bail systems (assuming a zero wealth elasticity of days free) because payments made either by defendants or the state are viewed as transfer payments that do not enter the net benefit function. The inference in the text regarding "additional incentive" is clearly not derived from the optimality conditions but from a view of how the state would actually behave when confronted with a limited budget and having to pay defendants.

recognition of each problem leads us to devise alternative payment schemes to those previously set forth.

THE "MORAL HAZARD" AND CREDIT AGAINST SENTENCE

The "moral hazard" arising when defendants are paid is that a person may commit and confess to a crime, or confess to a crime he did not commit, for the sole purpose of collecting a payment for his detention prior to conviction. This would be most likely to occur for crimes in which the levels of pretrial payments were high relative to the eventual sentence, and for persons with low opportunity costs. One can avoid this difficulty by paying the defendant for pretrial detention only if he is found innocent, and giving him credit toward his sentence for pretrial detention if he is convicted.[35] With this modification the incentive to confess as a means of receiving pretrial payments would be eliminated since a confession would largely preclude receiving payments.[36]

The payment and credit scheme can be formally incorporated into our model as follows. Both the gains to defendants (the G function) and the savings in jail costs (the J function) from pretrial release will be less than when payments alone are used. The gains from release are less because one must deduct from each defendant's gain the amount he values the credit for pretrial detention.[37] The savings in jail costs are less when credit is given since we eliminate savings (ignoring discounting) to the community from the pretrial release of defendants who are subsequently

---

35. In most states pretrial detention is not by law deducted from the sentence received by the convicted defendant. However, some judges make allowance for this when fixing sentence by lowering the latter by the amount of time spent in jail prior to conviction. See Daniel J. Freed & Patricia M. Wald, Bail in the United States: 1964, at 89–90 (1964).

36. The "moral hazard" problem would not be entirely eliminated because a defendant might initially confess or "plant" evidence making him appear guilty and at the time of trial reveal evidence that resulted in his acquittal. Incentives for such frauds could be reduced by making them subject to penalties. However, it appears unlikely that one could design a bail system that was entirely free of "moral hazards." For example, we previously noted that either the defendant or the prosecutor has an incentive to exaggerate the potential harm from release depending upon which bail system is operative. Moreover, when the defendant pays for his release, the prosecution may purposely impose large costs (including detention) on a person known to be innocent by having a high bail set. Of course, even a system where defendants are paid allows the state to detain innocent persons; however, it raises the cost by shifting the burden of the payment from the accused to the state.

37. Let g_i and g_i^* equal the wealth equivalents of the ith defendant's gain from release when no credit is given and when credit is given, respectively. We want to show that $g_i > g_i^*$. As previously noted (see *supra* note 28), g_i is more correctly an expected gain that equals the gain if convicted times P_i, the probability of conviction, plus the gain if not convicted times $(1 - P_i)$. The concept of an expected gain is also applicable to g_i^*. Since

convicted; their release merely transfers jail costs from the present toward the future. In terms of Figure 1, these factors lead to a downward shift in the demand curve for release (as the gains to defendants fall) and an upward shift in the cost curve (as the deduction for savings in jail costs decline). This in turn results in the release of fewer defendants than when no credit is given. Other things remaining the same, the shifts in these curves will be greater, and hence the decline in defendants released will be greater, the higher the probabilities of conviction, the greater the value defendants attach to credits, and the lower the community's discount rate on savings in future jail costs. In sum, optimal policy will be to detain a greater proportion of defendants when credit is combined with payments than when payments alone are used.

As in the earlier analysis, suppose that varying the size of the payment to defendants is the means by which the state affects the number of defendants released and detained. Here the payment is received only if the defendant is not convicted, since credit is given if he is convicted. At what level should the payment be set to maximize the net benefit function? It can be shown that a uniform payment would not lead in general to the release on bail of the optimal number of persons from our sample of n defendants.[38] Instead, the state would first determine whether or not the defendant should be detained, and then offer to pay each detained defendant an amount that would induce him to remain in

---

the gain from pretrial release if convicted is less when credit is given than when it is not by the amount one values the credit (which is equivalent to a reduction in sentence), $g_i > g_i^*$ when $P_i > 0$. The value of the credit to the defendant will depend on the rate of discount of future "days free," the length of his sentence, and the value of "days free" in the future.

38. Consider two defendants, A and B, where their expected gains from pretrial release are respectively

$$\bar{g}_a = (1 - P_a)g_{n_a} + P_a g_{c_a}$$

$$\bar{g}_b = (1 - P_b)g_{n_b} + P_b g_{c_b},$$

where P_a and P_b are the probabilities of conviction, g_{n_a} and g_{n_b} are the gains from release if not convicted, and g_{c_a} and g_{c_b} are the gains if convicted. To simplify, assume that the credit fully compensates for pretrial detention if one is convicted so that g_{c_a} and g_{c_b} are both zero. Suppose $\bar{g}_a < \bar{g}_b$ but $g_{n_a} > g_{n_b}$, and optimality requires that A be detained and B be released (because A's expected gain is less than the net costs of his release while B's expected gain is greater). The minimum contingent payment that A will accept to remain in jail will equal g_{n_a}, and the minimum that B will accept will equal g_{n_b}. If a single payment were offered that was sufficient to induce A to remain in jail, then B would also be willing to remain in prison (as $g_{n_a} > g_{n_b}$), contrary to the optimality condition. A uniform payment would be consistent with optimality in the special case where the rank correlation between expected gains and gains if not convicted were equal to 1 (e.g., in the case where the probabilities of conviction were equal for all defendants or where defendants with higher g_n's had lower P's).

prison. The decision to detain or release would depend on the state's estimate of whether the expected gain to the particular defendant from his release was less or greater than the potential harm from his release plus the costs of reapprehending him and expanding trial services, minus the expected savings in jail costs. Such a policy would be consistent with the maximization of the net benefit function and would lead to the optimal number of defendants released. A more attractive payment scheme might be to defer the setting of payments until the completion of the defendant's case. At that time, if he were found innocent, he could bring a tort action against the state to collect payment both for damages suffered during the period of pretrial detention and for the costs of bringing the action. The sole question before the court would be the amount of compensation since the question of liability would have already been decided by the defendant's acquittal. One who favored a "voluntary" bail system (even if only for certain types of offenses) might initially object to a credit and tort remedy on the ground that it enables the state to detain persons prior to trial without their consent. However, if the tort action permitted the defendant to receive full compensation, the latter would equal what he would have accepted to remain voluntarily in prison prior to the disposition of his case.[39]

INCENTIVES FOR APPEARING AT TRIAL

In our model, the likelihood of appearing for trial is one of several factors relevant in maximizing the net benefit function. The likelihood of appearing determines in part the harm from releasing defendants and the costs of reapprehending them (since the frequency of attempts to flee will affect the cost of achieving a given probability of reapprehension); however, the net benefit function is also affected by considerations of possible new crimes, the costs of expanding trial services, and the savings in jail costs. Nevertheless, appearing for trial is an important factor and it is worthwhile to consider more explicitly what mechanisms can be devised to provide incentives for the defendant's appearance.

---

39. When defendants are paid to remain in prison prior to adjudication of their cases but no credit is given, detained defendants will have funds to replace their forgone earnings, enabling them to finance a defense. However, one could argue that with a tort remedy these funds would not be available, which would result in higher probabilities of conviction for those detained compared to those not detained, other things remaining the same. However, this inference is not correct because defendants would be able to make contingent contracts with lawyers who would agree to defend them in exchange for receiving a payment only if their client was acquitted. Similar contracts are common in many tort actions (*e.g.*, negligence cases).

The most direct method would be to make nonappearance a crime in itself and set appropriate penalties to achieve the optimum deterrence of this crime.[40] One objection is that the deterrent effect of these penalties is likely to be small because they represent only a marginal increment in the penalty for a defendant likely to be convicted. However, this implies that the appropriate degree of deterrence would require a relatively high penalty for nonappearance and one that is probably in proportion to the penalty for the crime the defendant is initially accused of committing. Moreover, it follows from the optimality conditions of the bail model that defendants accused of the most severe crimes (where penalties for non-appearance may have the smallest deterrent effect) are the least likely to be released on bail.

When defendants must pay for their release, another way to provide an incentive for the defendant's appearance would be to set a money payment or bond that is returned only if the accused appears at trial. In such a system firms are likely to arise that would be willing to accept the risk of nonappearance, and hence forfeiture of the bail bond, in exchange for a fee to compensate them for their expected losses. Thus, an institutional arrangement would come about for shifting the risks of nonappearance from defendants to bondsmen.[41] In the United States, this is precisely the system that has developed. Of those defendants free on bail, a large proportion were released because a bondsman posted a bail bond.[42] A formal analysis of the bail bond system is presented in the appendix.

It has been alleged that the shifting of potential financial loss to the bondsman removes the incentive for the defendant to appear at trial. This need not be true, for the following reasons: (1) Bondsmen usually require collateral from the defendant. This is a form of sharing or pooling the risks with the accused and thus both suffer losses from nonappearance. (2) The defendant is liable for the amount of the bond should it be forfeited. (3) The bondsmen have an incentive to protect their investment via the expenditure of resources to reduce the likelihood of the defendant's fleeing. This would include periodic checkups of the defendant's whereabouts and threats to revoke the bond (which would make the de-

---

40. See Gary S. Becker, this volume, for the derivation of optimal penalties for crimes.

41. The analogy to insurance is not perfect, since another important reason for firms specializing in bail bonds is to provide funds for defendants who cannot borrow from banks due, for example, to usury laws or poor collateral.

42. One survey of 19 counties in the U.S. in 1962 indicated that among defendants released, 45% used professional bondsmen, 35% had friends or relatives post a bond, 12% posted cash and 8% were released on their own recognizance. See Lee Silverstein, Bail in the State Courts—A Field Study and Report, 50 Minn. L. Rev. 621, 647 (1966). I computed these figures by taking averages for the counties where data were given.

fendant a fugitive). In addition, the bondsman is given the power to arrest a defendant who flees, and there are scattered reports of bondsmen relentlessly pursuing, apprehending, and returning the defendant.[43] (4) Professional criminals who regularly appear in court have little incentive to flee because bondsmen would be unwilling to post bail for them in the future.

CONCLUDING REMARKS

The main contribution of this essay has been to propose and analyze an alternative to the existing bail system. This alternative is a system in which the defendant is compensated for his pretrial detention in contrast to the present method of having the defendant pay for his release. Compensation to detained defendants can take a variety of forms that include money payments, credit against sentence for persons subsequently found guilty, and tort remedies for those acquitted.[44] Our approach was first to derive a net benefit function from releasing defendants prior to trial that incorporated both the gains to defendants and the costs and gains to the community from their release. The optimal number of defendants released was one that maximized the net benefit. Although the optimality conditions were largely unaffected by whether the defendant had to pay or was paid, there are some important advantages to a system in which defendants are compensated. The major one is reducing the punitive aspect of the bail system, since those detained are compensated for losses resulting from their detention. Other advantages include reducing discrimination against low-income defendants and providing incentives for the states to improve pretrial detention facilities.

Criticisms of the existing bail system and proposals for reform play an important role in current policy debates over effective law enforcement. Most proposals call for weakening or even eliminating the requirement that the defendant pay for his release. In its place, these proposals typically advocate extensive investigation of the defendant's background to determine suitability for pretrial release. If he is found suitable, the

---

43. See Daniel J. Freed & Patricia M. Wald, *supra* note 35, at 30–31. The incentive to return the defendant to custody, after he does not appear, is that the bondsman is usually given a grace period of about 30 days before he forfeits the bond.

44. The question of whether compensation is a realistic alternative to the existing bail system is beyond the scope of this paper. However, we should note that one difficulty in implementing this proposal is that the majority of voters do not expect to be defendants; therefore, it is unlikely that they would favor a proposal that reduced their wealth and increased the wealth of future defendants.

defendant may be released without having to post a bond or having only to pay a nominal sum. "Suitability" would be determined on the basis of the defendant's ties to the community, his employment record, past convictions, etc. In New York City some experiments have already been conducted along these lines by the Vera Foundation. The major defect of these proposals is the fate of the defendant not recommended for release. He would be jailed without compensation and thus punished although by law he is still "innocent." In contrast, the proposal advanced in this essay not only lessens the punitive aspect of the bail system by compensating jailed defendants but also provides an incentive to set up investigatory procedures that are advocated in the above proposals. The reason is that paying defendants shifts part of the burden of the bail system from the defendant to the state, and hence there is an incentive for the state to reduce this burden by allocating resources to discovering which defendants are likely to do little harm if released.

APPENDIX

THE BONDSMAN

In our model both bail bonds and firms specializing in the sale of these bonds (*i.e.,* bondsmen) were omitted. Let us now introduce them into the analysis, and assume the following: (1) a money payment, denoted by M, is set by the court for the defendant's release, but instead of M being paid directly by the defendant, a bondsman posts M with the court in behalf of the defendant; [45] (2) M will be forfeited only in the event the defendant does not show up for trial (*i.e.,* if the defendant shows up, the bondsman makes no payment to the court); (3) the bondsman charges the defendant a fee for this service equal to $f \cdot M$ where $0 < f < 1$ and he may also require some collateral; and (4) competition initially prevails among bondsmen.

Total costs (T) for the group of firms writing bonds will tend to increase with increases in the number of defendants not showing up for trial, the size of M, and the time from arrest to disposition.[46] That is

$$T = T(p, b, M, t), \tag{10}$$

---

45. This system would not prevent the defendant from depositing cash or another asset valued at M to secure release. However, we rule this out in the analysis in order to focus on the bondsman.

46. A longer t implies a greater average volume of bail bonds outstanding at any moment in time. Since we would expect bondsmen to hold reserves (which have an opportunity cost) against the contingency that a defendant will not appear for trial, a longer t will be associated with a greater volume of reserves and hence greater costs.

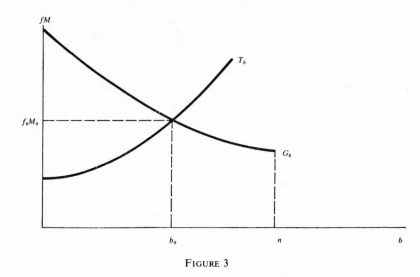

where $T_p < 0$, $T_b > 0$, $T_M > 0$ and $T_t > 0$. The demand function of defendants for release on bail is similar to the previous demand function (see equation (6)) and may be written as

$$b = b(fM, t, p, u),\tag{11}$$

where fM is the fee to the bondsman, and t, p and u are defined as before except that the residual u would also include the amount of collateral required by the bondsman. Both $b_f(= \partial b/\partial fM \cdot (M))$ and b_M are assumed to be negative. If M were set at M_o (and t and p are given), equilibrium in the market for bail bonds would take place at f_oM_o and b_0 in Figure 3. At higher levels of M, for example, T_b shifts to the left, fM rises and b falls. Thus, to maximize the net benefit function π (see equation (5)), M would be set by the court at a value where the number of defendants released on bail in Figure 3 was equal to the number that maximized π.[47] That is

$$fM = T_b = G_b = H_b + C_b - J_b.\tag{12}$$

Although the optimal M in (12) would be greater than the optimal money payment $(\hat{m})$ in the model that excluded the bondsman, the number of defendants released on bail and the actual payment for release would be the same.

   Let us drop the assumption of a competitive market in the sale of bail bonds, and instead assume a cartel agreement among bondsmen where entry is restricted and the fee for bonds is set above the competitive price. Both fee-fixing and entry

---

47. We do not explicitly consider the resource costs of bondsmen in the net benefit function.

restrictions are enforced by the state.[48] The cartel would take a curve marginal to the demand curve in Figure 3 (assuming no price discrimination) and for a given M this would result in a higher fM (*i.e.,* a higher f) and fewer defendants released than in the competitive case.[49] However, the state could compensate for the cartel by lowering M below the competitive level in order to release on bail the optimal number of defendants.

---

48. Some form of state regulation appears to be the rule. For example, in large metropolitan areas bonds are generally written by agents (bondsmen) of surety companies that are regulated as part of the insurance business. Fees and minimum cash reserves are set by the state. Bondsmen are also licensed in some states. In addition, there exist laws prohibiting bondsmen from giving rebates to attorneys and public officials in exchange for recommending clients, and from soliciting business in courtrooms. See Daniel J. Freed & Patricia M. Wald, *supra* note 38, at 36–38.

49. This would require

$$fM = G_b = H_b + C_b - J_b \tag{i}$$

$$fM \left(1 + \frac{1}{e} \right) = T_b, \tag{ii}$$

where e is the elasticity of the demand curve G_b in Figure 3. With the same number of defendants released in the competitive and monopoly cases, the fees to defendants (fM) are also the same. However, f is larger and M smaller with monopoly than competition.

An Economic Analysis of the Courts

William M. Landes

University of Chicago and National Bureau of Economic Research

"The object of our study, then, is prediction, . . . The prophecies of what the courts will do in fact, and nothing more pretentious, are what I mean by the law." Oliver Wendell Holmes, Jr., The Path of Law (1897).

In the folklore of criminal justice a popular belief is that the accused will have his case decided in a trial. Empirical evidence does not support this belief. Table 1 indicates that most cases are disposed of before trial by either a guilty plea or a dismissal of the charges. What factors determine the choice between a pretrial settlement and a trial? What accounts for the large proportion of settlements compared to trials? How are certain aspects of the criminal justice process such as the bail system and court delay related to the decision to settle or to go to trial? The main

This study has been supported by a grant for the study of law and economics from the National Science Foundation to the National Bureau (Grant Number GS-3314). The views expressed in this essay are not attributable to the National Science Foundation, whose support I gratefully acknowledge. I should like to thank Professors Gary Becker, Solomon Fabricant, Laurence Miller, Sherwin Rosen, Finis Welch and Neil Wallace, and Elisabeth Landes for helpful criticisms. I also received useful comments at seminars at the NBER, Columbia, Rochester, U.C.L.A. and the University of Chicago. Charles H. Berry, Eugene P. Foley, and Eli Goldston provided valuable advice as members of the reading committee of the National Bureau's Board of Directors.

TABLE 1
DISPOSITION OF CRIMINAL CASES

Area (Year)	Number of De- fendants	Trials		Guilty Pleas		Dismissed	
		Num- ber	Per Cent	Num- ber	Per Cent	Num- ber	Per Cent
132 State County Courts (1962)	7,510 [a]	1,394	19	5,293	70	823	11
U.S. District Courts (1967)	31,535	4,208	13	23,131	73	4,196	13

SOURCES. – Lee Silverstein, Defense of the Poor in Criminal Cases in American State Courts, A Field Study and Report (2 v. 1965); Ann. Rep., Admin. Off. of the United States Courts, 1967.

[a] Number of felony defendants in sample.

purpose of this essay is to answer these questions by means of a theoretical and empirical analysis of the criminal justice system using standard tools of economic theory and statistics.

A theoretical model is first developed that identifies the variables relevant to the choice between a settlement and a trial. The basic assumption of the model is that both the prosecutor and the defendant maximize their utility, appropriately defined, subject to a constraint on their resources. It is shown that the decision to settle or to go to trial depends on the probability of conviction by trial, the severity of the crime, the availability and productivity of the prosecutor's and defendant's resources, trial versus settlement costs, and attitudes toward risk. We then analyze the effects of the bail system and court delay on settlements, and consider several proposals for improving the bail system and reducing court delay. These include "preventive detention," monetary compensation to defendants not released on bail, and the imposition of a money price for the use of the courts. The model is further useful in evaluating the frequently made argument that the criminal justice system discriminates against low-income defendants. This proposition is analyzed by relating a defendant's income or wealth to his decision to settle or go to trial, the probability of his conviction, and his sentence if convicted. The interactions of these factors with the bail system and court delay are also examined.

The second part of this study is an empirical analysis from published data on the disposition of cases in state and federal criminal courts.

Multiple regression techniques are used to test the effects on the demand for trials (or conversely, settlements) and on the probability of conviction of the following: (1) pretrial detention; (2) court queues; (3) the size of the potential sentence; (4) judicial expenditures; (5) subsidizing defendants' legal fees; and (6) demographic variables such as population size, region, county income, per cent nonwhite, and urbanization. Finally, in the appendix a theoretical and empirical analysis on the demand for civil cases is presented.

I. THE MODEL

We make the following assumptions.

(1) There are n defendants.

(2) The probability of conviction in a trial for the ith defendant ($i = 1, \ldots, n$) depends on the prosecutor's and defendant's inputs of resources, R_i^* and R_i respectively, into the case. That is,

$$P_i^* = P_i^*(R_i^*, R_i; Z_i)$$

and

$$P_i = P_i(R_i^*, R_i; Z_i), \tag{1}$$

where P_i^* is the prosecutor's and P_i is the defendant's estimates of the probability of conviction by trial. P_i^* can be greater, less than, or equal to P_i. Z_i denotes other factors affecting the level of P_i^* and P_i; for example, the availability of witnesses, the defendant's past record, his alibi, etc. Inputs of R_i^* would tend to raise P_i^* and P_i, while inputs of R_i would tend to lower them so that

$$\frac{\partial P_i^*}{\partial R_i^*} \geq 0 \qquad \frac{\partial P_i^*}{\partial R_i} \leq 0$$

$$\frac{\partial P_i}{\partial R_i^*} \geq 0 \qquad \frac{\partial P_i}{\partial R_i} \leq 0. \tag{2}$$

(3) The sentence, S_i, the defendant would receive if convicted in a trial is known to the prosecutor and defendant and independent of R_i^* and R_i.[1]

---

1. There is some justification for this assumption other than mathematical simplicity since most crimes carry statutory penalties which are presumably known to both parties and independent of R_i^* and R_i. However, statutory penalties usually set a minimum and maximum sentence for the defendant convicted in a trial, and within this range the sentence received would partly depend on R_i^* and R_i. To allow the sentence to be a function of R_i^* and R_i would substantially complicate the model at this point (for example, two sen-

(4) Initially, there is no money charge for the use of the courts nor a nonmoney cost in terms of court delay or queues.

PROSECUTOR

Let the prosecutor's decision rule be to maximize the expected number of convictions weighted by their respective S_i's — he prefers longer to shorter sentences — subject to a constraint on the resources or budget available to his office (B).[2] This decision rule coincides with the social optimum in the following sense. If expected sentences are regarded as prices the community charges for various offenses, then the prosecutor's behavior is equivalent to maximizing the community's "profit" for a given level of prosecution expenditures.

The prosecutor maximizes $E(C)$ where

$$E(C) = \sum_{i=1}^{n} P_i^* S_i + \lambda(B - \sum_{i=1}^{n} R_i^*),$$ (3)

which yields the equilibrium conditions

$$\frac{\partial P_1^*}{\partial R_1^*} \cdot S_1 = \frac{\partial P_2^*}{\partial R_2^*} \cdot S_2 = \cdots, = \frac{\partial P_n^*}{\partial R_n^*} \cdot S_n.$$ (4)

Thus, the prosecutor allocates greater resources to cases, ceteris paribus, where the sentence is greater and where P_i^* is more responsive to changes in R_i^*.[3] If all n defendants need not be prosecuted, one would also predict charges would be dismissed when the prosecutor sees little chance of conviction regardless of his resource input into the trial, or given a conviction he expects a negligible sentence. The formulation of (3) is suffi-

---

tences would have to be included — the defendant's estimate and the prosecutor's estimate) without substantially changing the analysis of the trial versus settlement decision. In a later section on wealth effects, I allow the sentence to be a function of resource inputs.

2. Other decision rules are possible; for example, maximizing the expected number of convictions without weighting by the S_i's. The difficulty here is that the prosecutor, in order to increase his convictions and conserve his resources, would often be willing to drop a murder charge against a suspected murderer if the latter agreed to plead guilty to a minor offense (for example, a traffic violation). A simple way of eliminating this in the model is to weight by the S_i's. (See the analysis of a settlement presented below.) Note that fines could be included in S_i by specifying a rate at which the prosecutor transforms fines into sentences keeping his utility constant.

3. We assume the price of a unit of R_i^* is \$1.00 and $\partial^2 P_i^*/\partial R_i^* < 0$. It should also be noted that (4) does not necessarily have a unique solution unless one assumes that the prosecutor takes as given the defendant's inputs, R_i's. If he readjusts his inputs of R_i^* to changes or anticipated changes in any of the R_i's, then the defendants may in turn readjust their R_i's, and so forth. This process need not converge to a unique solution.

ciently general to give the prosecutor discretion over the type of charge brought against each defendant. The charge selected would be one that maximized $E(C)$. Further, the maximization of $E(C)$ together with the assumption that $\partial P_i^*/\partial R_i^* \geq 0$ imply (possibly unrealistically) that the prosecutor would suppress any evidence that reduces the probability of conviction.

Scarce resources provide an incentive for the prosecutor to avoid a trial and negotiate a pretrial settlement with the defendant. From (3) and (4) it follows that if the prosecutor's transaction costs of a settlement equal his optimal resource expenditure on a trial, he would be willing to offer the suspect a reduction in the sentence below S_i in exchange for a plea of guilty (which makes $P_i^* = P_i = 1$).[4] However, since trial costs probably exceed these transaction costs, he would be willing to offer a further sentence reduction as the savings in resources can be used to increase the conviction probabilities in other cases. If ΔS_i denotes the sentence reduction that is a positive function of the difference between the prosecutor's trial costs and transaction costs of a settlement, then

$$So_i = P_i^* S_i - \Delta S_i, \tag{5}$$

where So_i is the minimum sentence the prosecutor is willing to offer the defendant for a guilty plea.[5] From (5) we note that the terms offered the defendant will be more favorable the lower P_i^* and S_i, and the greater the prosecutor's resource saving from a settlement. Finally, suppose that certain cases bring the prosecutor considerable notoriety only if a trial occurs. If notoriety were desired, the sentence variable, S_i, could be increased by a notoriety factor (for example $S_i(1 + j_i)$ where j_i is a positive function of the amount of notoriety and is ≥ 0). Hence in some cases So_i could be greater than $P_i^* S_i$ and even S_i. Unless otherwise stated, we assume $So_i < P_i^* S_i$.

---

4. The prosecutor's transaction costs of a settlement would equal his time spent explaining the terms of the offer to the suspect and judge, paperwork in his office, etc. These costs will generally be less than his total costs of reaching a settlement since the latter may involve substantial negotiating or bargaining costs in order to arrive at a sentence more preferred than the minimum sentence he is willing to offer in a settlement.

5. A settlement that releases resources from any one case will increase the R_i^*'s in other cases. Thus, the R_i^*'s that initially satisfy (4) are not the final equilibrium values because adjustments take place as cases are settled. Moreover, these adjustments raise the So's in cases not yet settled. I largely ignore these secondary effects in the analysis.

DEFENDANT

If the defendant goes to trial, the outcome is either of two mutually exclusive states: a conviction state with an endowment Wc defined as

$$Wc = W - s \cdot S - r \cdot R \tag{6a}$$

or a nonconviction state with an endowment Wn defined as

$$Wn = W - r \cdot R. \tag{6b}$$

W is his wealth endowment prior to arrest, s equals the present value of the average pecuniary and nonpecuniary losses per unit of jail sentence, r is the average price of a unit of R, and S and R are defined as before.[6] I assume Wc is nonnegative.

Let U be a continuous utility function over the defendant's endowment. His expected utility from going to trial is then

$$E(U) = PU(Wc) + (1 - P)U(Wn). \tag{7}$$

Since inputs of R lower P, Wc and Wn, the defendant would select a level of R to maximize $E(U)$ such that

$$-P'[U(Wn) - U(Wc)] = r[PU'(Wc) + (1 - P)U'(Wn)], \tag{8}$$

where $P' = dP/dR$ and U' denotes the marginal utility (>0) of the endowment in each state.[7] The left-hand side of (8) represents marginal returns of R and the right-hand side, marginal costs of R.[8] An analysis of the determinants of the optimal R is presented later.

---

6. The subscript i is deleted, since it is explicit that we are now dealing with one defendant.

7. The qualification stated in footnote 3 regarding the prosecutor's equilibrium inputs of R^* also applies to the defendant's equilibrium inputs of R.

8. The second-order condition for the optimum R requires that the rate of change of marginal returns be less than the rate of change of marginal cost. That is,

$$-P''[U(Wn) - U(Wc)] + rP'[U'(Wn) - U'(Wc)] <$$

$$-rP'[U'(Wn) - U'(Wc)] - r^2[PU''(Wc) + (1 - P)U''(Wn)],$$

where $P'' = d^2P/dR^2$, and $U'' = $ the rate of change of U'. P'' is assumed >0 to indicate diminishing marginal product of R in reducing P. If $U'' = 0$, the last three terms above are zero and hence marginal returns are falling while marginal costs are constant. If $U'' \neq 0$,

TRIAL VERSUS SETTLEMENT

Let $r \cdot \hat{R}$ equal the defendant's transaction costs of a settlement.[9] Note that the defendant's trial costs, $r \cdot R$, are greater than $r \cdot \hat{R}$ because a defendant going to trial will in the process of rejecting a settlement incur most of the costs in $r \cdot \hat{R}$, and in addition he has expenditures on the trial. The defendant would choose between a trial or settlement on the basis of whether his expected utility from the former, $E(U)$, were greater or less than his utility from the latter. Similarly, the prosecutor would choose the alternative that maximizes his conviction function, $E(C)$. Therefore, a necessary condition for a settlement is that both the defendant and prosecutor simultaneously gain from a settlement compared to their expected trial outcomes. This requires that

$$\pi = U(W - s \cdot So - r \cdot \hat{R}) - E(U) > 0, \tag{9}$$

because one can then find a negotiated sentence somewhat greater than So, the minimum offer of the prosecutor, that leaves the defendant with a utility from a settlement greater than $E(U)$ and at the same time increases $E(C)$ for the prosecutor above its value in a trial. Although (9) explicitly allows for the prosecutor's and defendant's transaction costs of a settlement, the attempt to reach mutually acceptable terms may in certain cases involve substantial bargaining costs that are large enough to prevent a settlement even though $\pi > 0$. In spite of this qualification, I will assume that $\pi > 0$ is not only a necessary but also a sufficient condition for a settlement. Alternatively, $\pi < 0$ is a necessary and sufficient condition for a trial. These conditions are Pareto optimal in that if $\pi > 0$, both parties expect to gain from a settlement, and if $\pi < 0$, both parties expect to gain from a trial.

We can derive the following implications from (9) regarding the likelihood of settling and the resulting sentence.

1. Although the precise sentence in a pretrial settlement is indeterminate, it must lie between the extremes defined by (9). Within this range it would depend on the relative bargaining strengths of the parties involved. In general, one would expect a smaller negotiated sentence the

---

marginal costs may be rising, falling or constant with increases in R since the two terms on the right-hand side are of opposite sign. Similarly, when $U'' < 0$, marginal returns may actually rise since $rP'[U'(Wn) - U'(Wc)]$ is positive but when $U'' > 0$, marginal returns must fall.

9. Similar to the definition of the prosecutor's transaction costs (see *supra* note 4), $r\hat{R}$ would be generally less than the defendant's total costs of negotiating a settlement since $r\hat{R}$ excludes bargaining costs.

smaller the probability of conviction in a trial. A smaller P raises $E(U)$ and thus lowers the maximum sentence accepted by the defendant, while a smaller P^* reduces the minimum acceptable to the prosecutor. For identical reasons, a lower sentence if convicted by trial, S, should lead to a lower negotiated sentence.

2. π will be positive and a settlement chosen whenever

$$s \cdot So < r(R - \hat{R}),   \tag{10}$$

since this implies $U(W - s \cdot So - r\hat{R}) > U(Wn)$, and by definition $U(Wn) \geq E(U)$. This result is independent of the defendant's attitude toward risk and his estimate of the conviction probability, because regardless of the trial outcome he is always better off with a settlement. (10) implies that a trial is less likely for offenses with small expected sentences (since So depends on S and P^*) relative to the defendant's differential cost of going to trial, $r(R - \hat{R})$.[10] Except when explicitly stated to the contrary, I now assume $s \cdot So > r(R - \hat{R})$ so that Wn is greater than $(W - s \cdot So - r\hat{R})$.

3. If both parties agree on the probability of conviction by trial ($P^* = P$), a settlement will take place for defendants who are risk averse ($U'' < 0$) or risk neutral ($U'' = 0$).[11] When $P^* = P$, one can show that a trial is equivalent to an unfair gamble (that is, the expected trial endowment is less than the settlement endowment).[12] Risk neutral suspects maximize their expected endowment and, therefore, refuse the trial "gamble," and a fortiori risk averse suspects also refuse the "gamble." On the other hand, a trial can still occur for a risk preferrer ($U'' > 0$) even though $P^* = P$.[13]

---

10. This provides an explanation of why many persons plead guilty to traffic violations instead of spending considerable time in traffic court disputing them.

11. U'' denotes the rate of change of U' with respect to one's endowment.

12. A trial is an unfair gamble if

$$(W - s \cdot So - r\hat{R}) - [P \cdot Wc + (1 - P)Wn] > 0,   \tag{i}$$

which can be rewritten as

$$s \cdot \Delta S + r(R - \hat{R}) > 0,   \tag{ii}$$

using (5), (6a, 6b) and the assumption $P^* = P$. Since we have assumed $s \cdot \Delta S$ and $r(R - \hat{R})$ are both positive, (ii) holds and the gamble is unfair.

13. Given risk preference, a negative π, which leads to a trial, would be more likely the greater the preference for risk, the larger $r\hat{R}$, and the smaller $s \cdot \Delta S$ and rR. To prove this differentiate (9) partially with respect to these variables. The partial derivatives are negative for $r\hat{R}$, and positive for $s \cdot \Delta S$ and rR, indicating that π falls with respect to increases in $r\hat{R}$ and decreases in $s \cdot \Delta S$ and rR.

4. Suppose the prosecutor and defendant differ in their estimates of the trial conviction probability. If $P^* < P$, a trial becomes an even less favorable gamble in comparison to $P^* = P$, and hence risk averse and risk neutral suspects would continue to settle.[14] Risk preferrers are also more likely to settle since π in (9) rises. $P^* > P$ is the more interesting case because this provides an explanation in addition to risk preference of why trials occur. When $P^* > P$ a trial becomes a more favorable gamble compared to $P^* = P$, and hence π falls, increasing the chances of a trial. Moreover, if $P^* > P$, one can show that the likelihood of a trial is generally greater for defendants accused of crimes that carry stronger penalties.[15]

Several additional points are worth noting in regard to the settlement versus trial decision:

5. The greater the savings in costs from a settlement, other things the same, the smaller So and $r\hat{R}$, and the more likely a settlement. This suggests that policy measures designed to eliminate or subsidize the defendant's legal fees, which in turn reduce the cost differential between a trial and a settlement, will increase the proportion of trials.

6. Suppose a not-guilty verdict in a trial produces pecuniary and nonpecuniary returns to the defendant. This would raise $E(U)$ and make a trial more likely. Similarly, publicity gains to the prosecutor from a trial would raise So, as previously noted, and also make a trial more likely.

7. The question of whether the defendant did in fact commit the crime he is charged with does not explicitly enter the analysis. The prosecutor and defendant have been assumed to react to the probability of

---

14. As P^* falls, So falls, which in turn increases $(W - s \cdot So - r\hat{R})$. Similarly, the increase in P lowers $[PWc + (1 - P)Wn]$. Thus, the value of (i) in footnote 12 rises relative to the case where $P^* = P$. Since (i) is already >0 when $P^* = P$, it is obviously >0 when $P^* < P$.

15. Differentiating π with respect to S and noting that $So = P^* \cdot S - \Delta S$ (see (5)) yields $\partial\pi/\partial S \lessgtr 0$ according as

$$\frac{P}{P^*} \lessgtr \frac{U'(W - s \cdot So - r\hat{R})}{U'(Wc)}. \tag{i}$$

$\partial\pi/\partial S < 0$ when $U'' \geqslant 0$ since $U'(W - s \cdot So - r\hat{R}) \geqslant U'(Wc)$ and $P < P^*$. Thus, risk preferring and risk neutral defendants are more likely to go to trial as S rises given $P^* > P$. When $U'' < 0$ risk aversion), both sides of (i) are <1, and the sign of $\partial\pi/\partial S$ is indeterminate. However, if the degree of risk aversion is weak (the right-hand side of (i) is close to one), risk averters are also more likely to go to trial as S rises.

In another sense, the likelihood of a trial is *always* greater for large than for small sentences. We have already shown in (10) that a trial will not occur when $s \cdot So$ is less than the difference in costs between a trial and a settlement, $r(R - \hat{R})$. Thus, for very small sentences $r(R - \hat{R})$ is likely to dominate and a settlement will take place.

conviction and other variables in choosing between settling and going to trial, while their behavior has not been directly influenced by the actual guilt or innocence of the defendant. However, this factor may enter in two ways. First, the amount and quality of the evidence against the defendant seems likely to diminish in the case of an innocent person. This would reduce the probability of conviction in a trial or even lead the prosecutor to dismiss charges more readily since P^* may be close to zero. Second, an innocent person may have an aversion to lying so that he would have a greater reluctance to plead guilty to an offense than a guilty person. This can be interpreted as imposing psychic losses on a guilty plea for an innocent suspect which would reduce $U(W - s \cdot So - r\hat{R})$ in (9) and hence increase the likelihood of a trial.

8. We observed in the introduction that a large fraction of cases are settled before trial. Our analysis predicts this if in most cases the prosecutor and suspect agree on the expected outcome of a trial, the costs of a trial to both parties exceed their settlement costs, and suspects are generally risk averse in their trial versus settlement choice.

WEALTH AND SENTENCE EFFECTS

In this section two further questions are considered. (1) Do the resources (R) invested by the defendant in a trial rise as the sentence increases? (2) Do the resources invested increase with the level of the defendant's initial endowment or wealth? The latter question is directly related to the widespread claim that the criminal justice system works less favorably for low income suspects than for affluent ones,[16] because if the defendant's investment of resources rises with wealth, then both the probability of conviction in a trial and a negotiated sentence would tend to be lower for wealthier defendants.

To determine the effect of an increase in the sentence, we take the total differential of the first-order condition in (8) with respect to S and R.[17] This yields $dR/dS \gtreqless 0$ according as

---

16. See Patricia M. Wald, Poverty and Criminal Justice, in U.S. Pres. Comm'n on Law Enforcement and Admin. of Justice, Task Force on the Admin. of Justice, Task Force Report: The Courts, at 139, app. C (1967).

17. The differential is

$$\frac{dR}{ds} = \frac{s[P'U'(Wc) - rPU''(Wc)]}{-P''[U(Wn) - U(Wc)] + 2rP'[U'(Wn) - U'(Wc)] + r^2[PU''(Wc) + (1 - P)U''(Wn)]}.$$

The second-order condition for $E(U)$ to be a maximum requires that the denominator be <0. Hence, $dR/dS \gtreqless 0$ as $P'U'(Wc) - rPU''(Wc) \lesseqgtr 0$.

$$\frac{-P'}{r \cdot P} \gtrless - \frac{U''(Wc)}{U'(Wc)}, \tag{11}$$

where $-U''(Wc)/U'(Wc)$ is a measure of absolute risk aversion. From (11) it follows that $dR/dS > 0$ for defendants who are risk preferrers or risk neutral. If defendants are risk averse, the sign of dR/dS is uncertain. It is more likely to be positive the more responsive P to increases in R, the lower r, and the smaller the level of absolute risk aversion.[18] In sum, for a group of defendants differing in their attitudes toward risk, we might expect to find a greater investment of resources on average for defendants charged with crimes carrying longer sentences. Note that this need not lead to an observed negative relation between the probability of conviction and the severity of the crime since we have previously shown that an increase in the potential sentence also induces the prosecutor to allocate more resources to the case.

The value of one's time is generally related positively to one's income and wealth. In consequence, an increase in the defendant's wealth will lead to an increase both in r and s, the prices per unit of R and S respectively. To show this for r, let R be produced by both inputs of market goods such as the services of lawyers, expert witnesses, etc., and inputs of one's time. The optimal input combination is where the marginal products of the inputs over their respective marginal factor costs are equal. Since defendants with greater wealth attach higher prices to their time input, they would not only substitute more market intensive methods of producing R, but would also have a higher r.[19] Moreover, it follows from the equilibrium condition in (8) that a rise in r will lead to fewer inputs of R. In contrast, the increase in s as wealth rises will usually result in an increase in R.[20] Thus, to predict the net effect of an increase in wealth,

---

18. (11) may also be rewritten as

$$\frac{e}{rR/Wc} \gtreqless -Wc \frac{U''(Wc)}{U'(Wc)},$$

where e is the elasticity of P with respect to R, rR/Wc is the share of R in the suspect's conviction wealth, and $-WcU''(Wc)/U'(Wc)$ is a measure of relative risk aversion. The value of the latter is often argued to hover around 1. (See Kenneth Arrow, Aspects of the Theory of Risk-Bearing, 33–37 (1965).) Thus, if rR/Wc were small, one would expect $dR/dS > 0$ for risk averse suspects.

19. If higher income or wealth defendants are more productive in their use of time to produce R, then the marginal product of time would be positively related to income. This would work to offset the substitution of market inputs for time as income and wealth rose. Further, r need not increase with wealth.

20. The condition under which $dR/dS > 0$ is identical to that for $dR/dS > 0$ in (11).

which increases both r and s, one would have to determine the relative magnitudes of these two offsetting forces. In addition, a change in wealth even if s and r were to remain constant may change the equilibrium input of R if tastes for risk depend on wealth. We analyze below the case of risk neutrality and in the mathematical appendix we consider nonneutral tastes for risk.

The total differential of (8) with respect to W and R, assuming risk neutrality, gives $dR/dW \gtreqless 0$ according as

$$-P'E_s \gtreqless E_r \frac{r}{s \cdot S}, \tag{12}$$

where $E_s = \partial s/\partial W(W/s)$ and $E_r = \partial r/\partial W(W/r)$. E_r will be <1 since the price of market inputs is unaffected and some substitution of market inputs for time takes place as wealth rises. E_s can be assumed equal to 1 because as a first approximation the per unit value of time in jail is proportional to wealth. The optimality condition for R (see (8)) becomes with risk neutrality $-P' = r/s \cdot S$, and, therefore, dR/dW will be positive when $E_s > E_r$.[21] Thus, the amount of resources invested in a trial would tend to rise and the probability of conviction would tend to fall with increases in wealth. Note that this result also implies a lower negotiated sentence for wealthier defendants.[22]

Suppose that the penalty for conviction is not a jail sentence but instead a money fine. E_s would equal zero with a fine since changes in the value of time do not alter the dollar value of a fine, and dR/dW would be negative. Therefore, the effect of wealth on R reverses when penalties

---

21. An identical result holds when R affects not only P but also S. With risk neutrality, the first-order condition for the optimal R becomes

$$-P'(s \cdot S) - P(s \cdot S') = r, \tag{i}$$

where $S' = \partial S/\partial R \le 0$. The total differential of (i) with respect to W and R yields $dR/dW \gtreqless 0$ as

$$E_s[-P'(s \cdot S) - P(s \cdot S')] \gtreqless E_r r, \tag{ii}$$

which gives $dR/dW \gtreqless 0$ as

$$E_s \gtreqless E_r. \tag{iii}$$

22. An increase in R that is anticipated by the prosecutor would lower P^* and hence his minimum offer, S_o, while the reduction in P would raise the defendant's expected utility from a trial and lower the maximum sentence he would accept to settle. Other things the same, these forces should work to lower the negotiated sentence.

are in terms of money and not time for risk neutral defendants.[23] Once risk aversion or preference is introduced, the effect of changes in wealth on R cannot in general be specified unless one has explicit knowledge of additional parameters of the defendant's utility function. Nevertheless, one can presume that if the deviation from risk neutrality is small, the effects of wealth on R will follow the effects for risk neutrality.

II. SOME APPLICATIONS

THE BAIL SYSTEM

In the United States the typical procedure for bail is that shortly after the defendant's arrest a bond is set as security for his appearance at trial. If the defendant can post the amount of the bond through a deposit of cash or other assets, or have a professional bondsman do it for him, he is released until trial. The bondsman's fee runs about 10 per cent of the value of the bail bond. If the defendant does not meet the bail requirement, he remains in jail. The bond is generally forfeited should the released defendant fail to appear at trial.

Several implications of the bail system can be derived from our model.

1. Bail costs would be deducted from the defendant's endowment, W, so that both $U(W - s \cdot So - r\hat{R})$ and $E(U)$ in (9) would fall. For defendants released on bail there would be no obvious change in π (since equal dollar amounts are subtracted from $(W - s \cdot So - r\hat{R})$, Wc and Wn) and hence no reason to expect a change in their use of trials compared to settlements. Bail costs for defendants not released would equal the opportunity cost of their time in prison plus losses from restrictions on their consumption and freedom. These costs would be greater for a trial than a settlement because the delay in reaching trial generally exceeds the time taken to negotiate a settlement.[24] This in turn would lower $E(U)$

---

23. G. S. Becker, Crime and Punishment: An Economic Approach, this volume, presents a similar argument without presenting a proof. However, he argues that the incentive to use time to reduce the probability of a sentence is unrelated to earnings, and the incentive to use money to reduce the probability of a fine is also unrelated to earnings. These results would follow when in the former case R is produced solely by time and in the latter case R is produced solely by market inputs. However, once R is produced by both time and market inputs there is always an incentive to substitute market inputs for time as earnings rise.

24. Empirically, the time difference appears to be positive. For example, in the 89 United States district courts the median queues in 1967 were as follows: jury trial = 5.7 months; court trial = 3.9 months, and settlement (guilty plea) = 1.9 months. See, 1967 Ann. Rep. Admin. Off. of the United States Courts, 269–71, table D6.

relative to $U(W - s \cdot So - r\hat{R})$ in (9), raise π and make a settlement more likely for defendants not released on bail. Thus, given a positive time differential between a trial and settlement one would predict proportionately more settlements among defendants not released than those released on bail.[25]

2. The defendant in jail is restricted in his use of resources to reduce the probability of conviction. This can be interpreted as either raising the costs or lowering the marginal products of his market and time inputs. For example, in the case of market inputs, detention would hamper consultation with lawyers, and in the case of time inputs, the defendant would have greater (even prohibitive) difficulty in seeking out witnesses and in engaging in other investigatory activities. These factors increase the marginal cost of producing a given R and lower the defendant's input of R.[26] Thus, other things the same, the probability of conviction by trial should be greater for defendants not making bail than for those making bail.[27] As noted earlier, a higher probability of conviction by trial also leads to worse terms in a settlement. One should add that for these reasons the prosecutor always has an incentive to request the judge to set high bail charges.

3. Finally, if making bail is positively correlated with income, then

---

25. Two additional points should be noted. (a) If the defendant not released on bail were given credit toward his sentence for time in prison prior to disposition of his case, the only bail deduction in (9) would be from Wn, the defendant's endowment if he is not convicted. π would still rise. However, the rise in π would be negatively related to the probability of conviction. In the limit, if the probability of conviction equaled 1, court delay would leave π unchanged. (b) Bail costs of defendants released on bail will generally *not* be greater for a trial than a settlement. The bondsman's fee is independent of whether the defendant goes to trial or accepts a settlement, and a majority of felony defendants who make bail use bondsmen. (See, Lee Silverstein, Bail in the State Courts – A Field Study and Report, 50 Minn. L. Rev. 621, 647–52 (1966).) And the returns from assets (except cash) used as security for bail bonds will continue to be received by the owner.

26. Defendants not making bail may have available added resources for legal services that would have been used to finance bail. These can offset the higher costs of R so that the probability of conviction need not increase. However, it is also possible that their resources will decline should the loss in income (excluding a consumption allowance) exceed the cost of financing bail. In the latter case, capital market difficulties would presumably have prevented their release.

27. Critics of the bail system have recognized this point. For example, see Report of the Att'y Gen. Comm. on Poverty & the Admin. of Fed. Crim. Just. 74–76 (1963). Also note that the increase in cost of R for jailed defendants may be partly offset by the greater availability of "legal" advice from other inmates. However, if this factor were sufficiently important, one would observe defendants who were able to meet bail requirements accepting pretrial detention instead.

the effects of pretrial jailing, cited above, would fall most heavily on low-income defendants.

Proposals for bail reform generally focus on eliminating income as an indirect criterion of pretrial release. The Federal Bail Reform Act of 1966 requires that criminal defendants in federal courts (which cover a small minority of criminal defendants) be released prior to trial unless there is reason to believe they would flee. The "President's Commission" suggests placing greater reliance on release of defendants without bail, accompanied by certain restrictions on their behavior (for example, restrictions on travel, associations), while simultaneously confining suspects whose release would pose a significant threat to the community, regardless of their financial ability to make bail,[28] the latter provision being a form of "preventive detention." If these reforms were to result in the pretrial release of more defendants and more low-income ones we would predict the following: a decline in the negative correlations between income and the effects of pretrial jailing outlined above; a reduction in the fraction of defendants convicted since fewer defendants would be restricted in their use of R; and an increase in the demand for trials as differential bail costs between a trial and settlement go to zero for more defendants.[29] The latter would probably increase court delay.

These reforms leave persons detained in the same position as before and, moreover, their position relative to defendants released may worsen if the latter group does not pay for their release. Suppose those detained were paid a monetary compensation that increased with the length of their detention. We could then eliminate much of the discriminatory aspects of the bail system while still detaining persons believed to be dangerous. A higher marginal cost of R for detained suspects would still be present, but they would have additional resources to mitigate the adverse effects of this on the probability of conviction. Compensation would reduce the defendant's incentive for a settlement as the differential bail costs between a trial and settlement decline and approach zero for full compensation. If compensation were paid out of the prosecutor's budget, the latter's incentive for a settlement would increase given that the payment were greater for a trial than a settlement. This in turn would lower his minimum offer, So, and raise $U(W - So - r\hat{R})$ in (9). Hence, the incentive

---

28. U.S. Pres. Comm'n on Law Enforcement and Admin. of Justice, Task Force on the Admin. of Justice, Task Force Report: The Courts, at 38–40 (1967). [Hereinafter, The Courts.]

29. Other effects could be added. For instance, a predicted increase in crime from reducing the average probability of conviction, and a savings in resources used for pretrial detention.

for a settlement need not fall with compensation. Note as So falls this tends to reduce the positive difference between negotiated sentences for defendants not released compared to defendants released on bail.[30]

COURT DELAY

It is widely recognized that the courts are burdened with a larger volume of cases than they can efficiently handle. The results are often long delays prior to trial, and hasty considerations when cases reach trial.[31] This is not surprising since users pay a nominal money fee, if any, and a queue develops to ration the supply.

To understand the implications of nonmoney and money pricing on the demand for courts, assume initially there is a money price, M, paid by the loser that clears the market.[32] We also assume that the prosecutor's budget is not increased to cover these court costs. M affects both the prosecutor's and defendant's demand for trial. First, it reduces the minimum sentence offered by the prosecutor, So in (5), by a positive function of $(1 - P^*) \cdot M$. This, in turn, raises π in (9) and increases the likelihood of a settlement. Second, it lowers the defendant's wealth if convicted by trial, Wc, by an amount equal to M, reducing $E(U)$ and raising π in (9). This also increases the chance of a settlement. The larger is M, the greater the increase in π, and the more settlements that take place. Thus, a downward sloping demand curve for the courts is generated. Further, one can venture from the analysis of (9) that as M rises, the reduction in quantity demanded of trials (hereafter, trial demand) will be primarily from cases where there is not a significant disagreement between the prosecutor and defendant over the probability of conviction, and where the sentence if convicted by trial tends to be small.[33] Put differently, cases that still go to trial as M rises are where there are significant disagreements over the probability of conviction and where penalties are severe. Moreover, changing the allocation of the payment of M has little effect on the above results, since whether the loser or winner pays M, or both share M, a money price always increases π in (9) and reduces trial demand.

---

30. For a detailed analysis of alternative bail systems see my paper, The Bail System: An Economic Approach, this volume.

31. The Courts, *supra* note 28, at 80–90.

32. This does not mean that defendants are immediately brought to trial. Some time is required by both defendant and prosecutor to prepare a case for trial. Current delays are alleged to run considerably in excess of this.

33. Optimal values of P^*, P, R^* and R may change as M rises since the prosecutor and defendant must now allocate some resources to losses from expected court fees.

Compare this pricing scheme with one in which the courts are heavily subsidized, taking the extreme example of a zero money price. As M goes to zero, So and Wc rise, π falls and without an increase in supply, trial demand would exceed supply. Let us assume trial dates are allocated on the basis of waiting time since arraignment and a trial queue develops. The queue will reach an equilibrium size because, as we will show, trial demand is a decreasing function of waiting or queueing time. An increase in the queue imposes losses on the prosecutor as it (a) reduces the number of convictions in the current year from cases commenced in that year by delaying trial convictions,[34] and (b) ties up resources in a case for a longer period of time. These losses increase as the queue lengthens, inducing the prosecutor to offer a lower sentence in exchange for a guilty plea. Although $U(W - s \cdot So - r\hat{R})$ in (9) then rises (as So falls) the incentive for the defendant to settle as the queue grows will depend on whether or not he is released on bail. For defendants not released, the longer the queue the higher the bail costs of a trial and hence the lower their expected utility from a trial.[35] This factor, together with the response of the prosecutor, leads to the prediction that the demand for trials will fall as the queue lengthens for defendants not released on bail. On the other hand, for defendants released on bail the net effect on their expected utility of an increase in the queue is unclear. The discounted loss from a sentence received in a trial would diminish or increase as the penalty is pushed into the future, depending on whether earnings are rising at a slower or faster rate than the defendant's discount rate. In addition, the defendant's earnings may be adversely affected during the period he is free on bail due to his being under indictment. If on balance their expected utility falls or remains constant and the prosecutor's losses rise, one would expect an increase in π and a reduction in trial demand as the queue lengthens for defendants free on bail. However, one would predict that the demand for trials among defendants released would be less responsive to an increase in the queue than the demand among defendants not released, since the

---

34. Even if the prosecutor had no time preference with respect to convictions, an increase in the queue would still impose losses on him. For example, suppose the prosecutor is in office for 5 years. An increase in the queue during his tenure would lead to fewer convictions and a lower weighted conviction function than a constant queue because he will have left to his successor a greater stock of cases than his predecessor had left to him.

35. This would be partially offset by giving credit towards the eventual sentence for time spent in jail awaiting trial. Wc would be unchanged as the queue lengthened, providing the time spent in jail awaiting trial was less than S, but Wn would still fall. Hence, $E(U)$ would continue to fall as the queue increased.

cost of an increase in the queue is greater for the latter than the former group.

These points are illustrated in Figure 1, where Q_t = trial queue, Q_p = pretrial settlement queue, and T = fraction of trials per unit of time. D_1 and D_2 denote the trial demand curves for defendants not released and released on bail, respectively. Assume initially that there is no money charge for trials, the number of defendants not released on bail equals the number released, and credit against one's sentence is not given for pretrial detention. When $(Q_t - Q_p) = 0$, T would be the same for defendants released and not released, since the differential bail costs between a trial and settlement are zero for both groups. As $(Q_t - Q_p)$ rises, due to a reduction in supply of trial services, the differential bail costs rise by a greater amount for the not released than for the released defendants and hence the reduction in trials will tend to be greater for the former than the latter group. Thus, D_1 diverges from D_2 as $(Q_t - Q_p)$ increases. If the equilibrium queue initially equaled $\bar{Q}$, T would equal T_1 for defendants not released and T_2 for defendants released. Suppose a money charge for trials is established that is sufficient to reduce $(Q_t - Q_p)$ to zero, keeping the number of trials constant. As a first approximation, the demand curves for trials of the released and not released defendants would be identical because the differential bail costs between a trial and settlement are now

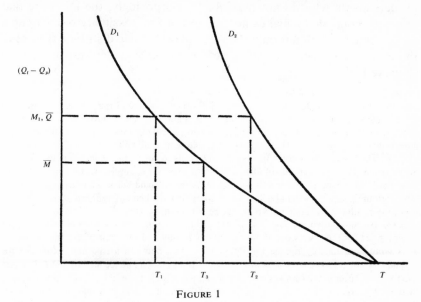

FIGURE 1

zero for both groups.[36] If the defendant's trial fee were set at M_1, a price that equals the maximum amount that defendants who are not released would pay at the margin for the same number of trials in order to reduce $(Q_t - Q_p)$ to zero, the aggregate number of trials demanded would be less than the available supply as $2T_1 < T_1 + T_2$.[37] In order for demand to be equated with supply, the defendant's court fee must be less than M. Let $\bar{M}$ in Figure 1 equal the market clearing court fee. At $\bar{M}$ the fraction of trials for each group would equal T_3 and by assumption, $2T_3 = T_1 + T_2$. Thus, a money charge for the courts that kept constant the number of trials can lead to an increase in the use of the courts on the part of defendants not released on bail, and a reduction in use among defendants released on bail. Moreover, if the supply curve of trials were positively sloped with respect to a money price, one would also expect an increase in the total number of trials.

In sum, we should note that although a zero money price is often advocated as a means of not discouraging low-income defendants from using the courts, its effect can be the opposite. A zero price operating with a bail system that tends to detain in jail low-income defendants will discourage the latter group from going to trial. In contrast, an appropriate money price may reduce the demand for the courts of defendants released on bail, and by reducing the trial queue can increase the use of the courts by defendants who do not make bail.[38] Surprisingly, the literature that criticizes court delay makes no mention of the possibility of charging a money price, which not only reduces delay, but can distribute the use of the courts more equally among defendants independent of their ability to make bail.

---

36. Note that the demand curves may differ. For example, if the average wealth of released defendants exceeds that of jailed defendants and the wealth elasticity of trial demand is not zero, then the demand curve of the former group will be to the right of D_1. However, as long as it is still to the left of D_2, the results that follow will still hold.

37. The prosecutor's court fee as $(Q_t - Q_p)$ falls to zero must be large enough to keep So constant. If other methods of allocating court fees (for example, winner or loser pays) were used, we could no longer assume that D_1 is the demand curve when trials are priced. Although the geometry would become more complicated when different pricing schemes are used, the results of the analysis would not be substantially altered.

38. An alternative scheme that would produce similar results is to continue a zero money price for the courts but allow defendants to buy and sell their places on the queue. This would presumably reduce the differential costs between a trial and settlement for defendants not released on bail relative to those released, and hence lead to a shift in court use from the latter to the former group. For example, if $\$X =$ the equilibrium price for a place in the queue that makes $(Q_t - Q_p) = 0$, the differential trial cost would be $\$X$ for both defendants released and not released, and their trial demands would be approximately equal.

III. EMPIRICAL ANALYSIS

In the legal area readily accessible and systematically collected data are quite limited. However, two sources of data were found that make it possible to test a number of the important hypotheses in the theoretical model. The first source is an American Bar Foundation (ABF) study, in which over 11,000 felony defendants in 1962 were sampled from state court dockets in nearly 200 counties.[39] From this sample we can estimate for several counties within most states the number of defendants released on bail and their average bail charge, the number going to trial, and the number dismissed, acquitted and sentenced. The second major source of data is for the 89 U.S. district courts where annually published statistics on civil and criminal cases are available.[40] These data contain information of civil and criminal court queues, the number of cases going to trial, the disposition of cases, and the number of criminal defendants receiving subsidized legal services. It should be added that most criminal defendants have their cases decided in state not in U.S. courts. In 1962 about 300,000 persons were charged with felonies in the state courts, while about 30,000 criminal defendants annually have their cases disposed in the U.S. district courts.[41]

THE DEMAND FOR TRIALS

The theoretical analysis suggests the following demand function for criminal trials:

$$T = f(B, Q_t, Q_p, S, D, U), \tag{13}$$

---

39. Lee Silverstein, Defense of the Poor in Criminal Cases in American State Courts, A Field Study and Report (2 v. 1965). Note that a felony is generally defined as any crime punishable by imprisonment of more than one year.

40. See various years of the Ann. Rep. Admin. Off. of the United States Courts and Fed. Offenders in the United States District Courts 1967.

41. Lee Silverstein, *supra* note 39, at 7–8 and Ann. Rep., Admin. Off. of the United States Courts, *supra* note 40. The types of offenses also differ in the state and U.S. courts. Offenses in the U.S. courts include forgery, counterfeiting, interstate transportation of stolen goods and vehicles, postal theft, and violation of immigration laws, liquor laws and other federal statutes, while it includes few cases of murder, assault, robbery, and other "violent" crimes. The latter types of offenses are concentrated in state courts. The one exception is the U.S. district court in the District of Columbia which handles all criminal offenses in the area. In the empirical analysis of the U.S. Courts I have excluded the District of Columbia in order to have comparable offenses across districts.

where T is the fraction of defendants going to trial, B is the fraction of defendants released on bail, Q_t and Q_p are the average trial and pretrial settlement queues respectively, S is the average sentence if convicted by trial, D is the average cost differential between a trial and settlement, and U is the combined effect of all other factors.[42] We would predict on the basis of our model that B, Q_p, and S will have positive effects on T, while Q_t and D will have negative effects on T. Unfortunately, data limitations prevent us from estimating the partial effects of these variables in a single equation. The ABF sample of state county courts has no data on queues or cost differentials between trials and settlements, while the data for the U.S. courts contain no information on bail. Therefore, the analysis will use the ABF data to test bail effects, and the U.S. data to test queue effects. At the same time we will point out possible biases and alternative interpretations of the results that arise from leaving out either the bail or queue variables.

STATE COUNTY COURTS

Least-squares multiple regression equations were estimated across state county courts in 1962. These equations were of the following general form:

$$T = \alpha + \beta_1 B + \beta_2 S + \beta_3 Pop + \beta_4 Re + \beta_5 NW + \beta_6 Ur + \beta_7 Y + u. \quad (14)$$

The variables in (14) are defined as follows:

T: the fraction of defendants in a county court whose cases were disposed of by trial in 1962. Cases where a plea of guilty was made at time of trial are not counted as trials.

B: the fraction of defendants in each county released on bail in 1962.

S: the average time served of first-released prisoners in 1964 who had sentences of one year or longer. S is an estimate of the average sentence, if convicted by trial, of felony defendants in 1962. Releases in 1964 are used because the average time served in state prisons of first-released prisoners was about two years, and hence 1964 should be the average release year for defendants sentenced in 1962.

---

42. U would include factors derived from the π function (equation (9)) such as the distribution of estimates of the probability of conviction by trial, and attitudes toward risk. I have not been able to directly measure these variables and hence they are largely ignored in the empirical analysis. U also includes several demographic variables that will be specified in the statistical estimation of (13).

Pop: county population in 1960.

Re: region dummy variable that equals 1 for counties in South and 0 for non-South counties.

NW: per cent nonwhite population in county in 1960.

Ur: per cent urban population in county in 1960.

Y: median family income in county in 1959.

Weighted regressions on T are presented in Table 2 for counties in the U.S., the non-South and South.[43] In the U.S. and non-South equations (2.1–2.2) the regression coefficients of the bail variable have the predicted positive sign and are always highly significant, while in the South the coefficient is not significantly different from zero. Before discussing these results in greater detail, an interesting interpretation can be given to the bail regression coefficient. T can be written as

$$T = \frac{\lambda_1 N_1 + \lambda_2 N_2}{N}, \tag{15}$$

where N is the number of defendants, N_1 is the number not released on bail, and N_2 is the number released. λ_1 and λ_2 are the average propensities to go to trial of the not released and released group respectively. The theory predicts that $\lambda_2 > \lambda_1$, providing that the trial queue is longer than the settlement queue. Since $N_1/N + N_2/N = 1$ and $N_2/N = B$, (15) can be rewritten as

$$T = \lambda_1 + (\lambda_2 - \lambda_1)B. \tag{16}$$

Therefore, from a set of observations on T and B, the intercept in a simple regression of T on B would be an estimate of λ_1 and the beta coefficient on B would be an estimate of $(\lambda_2 - \lambda_1)$. A positive beta coefficient would be consistent with the prediction that $\lambda_2 > \lambda_1$. The interpretations of these regression coefficients are modified with the addition of other independent variables, X_i, which enter the regression indirectly through their influence on λ_1 and λ_2. For example, let

$$\lambda_1 = c_1 + \sum_{i=2}^{j} \beta_i X_i \tag{17}$$

---

43. Observations were weighted by the $\sqrt{n}$ where n is the number of defendants sampled in each county. The range of n is from 3 to 349 with a mean of 58, and n generally rises with the size of the county population. Weighted regressions were computed because of the likelihood of larger variances in the residuals as n declined. However, unweighted regressions were also computed, and as it turned out, the weighting made little difference in the results.

TABLE 2
Weighted Regressions and t-Values for Criminal Trials in 1962, State County Courts [a]

Equation Number	Area	Counties	Dependent Variable	Regression Coefficients and t-Values [b]								R²[c]
				α	B	S	Pop	Re	NW	Ur	Y	
2.1	U.S.	132	T	-.065	.348	-.0002	.037	.098	.014	.062	-.002	.26
				(.624)	(4.071)	(.087)	(3.312)	(2.723)	(.106)	(.709)	(.101)	
2.2	N.S.	100	T	.002	.498	.003	.038		-.217	.129	-.043	.45
				(.027)	(6.521)	(1.515)	(4.263)		(1.548)	(1.513)	(2.552)	
2.3	South	32	T	.229	-.012	-.009	.463		.109	-.570	.095	.48
				(.833)	(.059)	(1.746)	(3.215)		(.488)	(2.716)	(2.042)	

SOURCES.— T and B from Lee Silverstein, Defense of the Poor in Criminal Cases in American State Courts, A Field Study and Report (2 v. 1965); Pop, NW, Ur and Y from U.S. Bureau of the Census, County and City Data Book 1962; S from U.S. Bureau of Prisons, National Prisoner Statistics Detailed Reports: State Admissions and Releases, 1964, table R-5.

[a] Although the ABF sample covered nearly 200 counties, many had to be excluded because there was no reporting on the number of defendants who made bail. I have no reason to believe that the group of excluded counties would have differed systematically from the counties included in the regression equation. Two counties in New Jersey were excluded because no data on S were available for New Jersey.

[b] t-values in parentheses.

[c] All R²'s are unadjusted in Table 2 and all other tables unless explicitly stated to the contrary.

186

and

$$\lambda_2 = c_2 + \sum_{i=2}^{j} \alpha_i X_i. \tag{18}$$

By substitution into (16) we have,

$$T = c_1 + (c_2 - c_1)B + \sum_{i=2}^{j} \beta_i X_i + \sum_{i=2}^{j} (\alpha_i - \beta_i)B \cdot X_i. \tag{19}$$

Estimates of equation (19) were not successful because of the large amount of multicollinearity resulting from the inclusion of interaction variables. This tended to eliminate statistical significance from any of the independent variables. However, if we set $\alpha_i = \beta_i$ for all $_i = 2,$———, j, the interaction variables drop out and (19) reduces to the form of equations estimated in Table 2. It also follows from (17) and (18) that when $\alpha_i = \beta_i$ the regression coefficient on B is a measure of $(\lambda_2 - \lambda_1)$, the difference in trial propensities between defendants released and not released on bail.

Estimates of $(\lambda_2 - \lambda_1)$ from Table 2 for the U.S. and non-South imply, for example, that the release of an additional 20 defendants on bail, other things the same, would lead to a desired increase of about 7 to 10 trials as a result of the reduction in trial costs associated with making bail. One can also get a rough idea of the increased demand for trial if the existing bail system were replaced with a system of preventive detention that released all defendants except a few "hard-core" criminal suspects (for example, 10 per cent). The weighted means of T and B are about .18 and .45 respectively. Therefore, the release of additional defendants to bring the number released to 90 per cent would lead to an increase in the fraction desiring trials from 18 per cent to between 34 and 40 per cent, or roughly a 100 per cent increase in desired trials.[44]

Although no direct measures of trial queues are available in the ABF data, longer trial queues are generally thought to exist in large urban areas. If the county population variable is interpreted as an imperfect proxy for the difference between trial queues and settlement queues, the sign of the regression coefficient on the population variable would depend on the relative strength of two opposing forces. On the one hand, longer queues discourage trials, but on the other hand, longer queues may

---

44. This is the increase in trials desired with no change in the trial queue. With an increased demand and unchanged court capacity the queue would presumably grow so that the actual increase in T would be less than the desired increase. In fact, if the courts were fully employed, the queue would grow until the costs of waiting were just sufficient to make desired trials equal to the previous level of trials.

be the result of an increased demand for trials. In Table 2, the coefficient on the population variable is positive and significant in all regressions, which suggests that the positive association of trials with queues dominates.

Further evidence on the effects of population size appears in Table 3 where separate regressions are given for counties in the non-South with populations greater than 450,000, between 100,000 and 450,000, and less than 100,000, and in the South with populations greater than 200,000 and less than 108,000. In Table 3 not only does the bail variable continue to have a positive effect on trials in all non-South equations, but its coefficient (or ($\lambda_2 - \lambda_1$)) has a systematically greater value as county size rises (.09 in eq. 3.3, .31 in eq. 3.2, and .75 in eq. 3.1), which is precisely what one would expect if ($Q_t - Q_p$) was positively correlated with county population.[45] ($\lambda_2 - \lambda_1$) is statistically significant in the non-South except in counties of less than 100,000. This result could be observed if the difference between ($Q_t - Q_p$) was negligible in small counties. Moreover, the empirical finding that the coefficient on the bail variable increases as county population size rises is indirect evidence that ($Q_t - Q_p$) is in fact larger in counties with bigger populations.

Let us briefly consider the empirical results for the South. The three regression coefficients on the bail variable in the South in Tables 2 and 3, were negative and not significantly different than zero. One possible explanation is that ($Q_t - Q_p$) is negligible for counties sampled in the South so that ($\lambda_2 - \lambda_1$) would approach zero, and hence the regression coefficients on bail would not be significant.[46] A second explanation is that greater measurement errors in the bail variable may exist in the South compared to the non-South, which would lower the value of regression coefficients on bail in the South relative to the non-South. Along these lines it might be argued that justice is more informally administered in the South, particularly in rural areas, and this would produce poorer records on bail. (A similar argument may be used to rationalize the non-significant but positive bail coefficient in non-Southern counties of less than 100,000.) However, it is questionable whether this argument should be given much weight since a nonsignificant bail variable was also ob-

---

45. If we refer to Figure 1, *supra*, we note that at a given value of ($Q_t - Q_p$) the difference getween D_2 and D_1 equals $\lambda_2 - \lambda_1$ and as ($Q_t - Q_p$) increases, $\lambda_2 - \lambda_1$ increases due to the increase in bail costs of defendants not released compared to defendants released.

46. Data for the federal courts indicate that queues are somewhat lower in the South. In 1966, the mean civil Q_t's were 22.0 and 15.7 months for the non-South and South, and the mean criminal Q_t's were 6.3 and 5.3 months in the two areas. However, ($Q_t - Q_p$) for criminal cases was 3.8 and 3.5 months in the non-South and South.

TABLE 3

WEIGHTED REGRESSIONS AND t-VALUES FOR CRIMINAL TRIALS IN 1962 BY COUNTY POPULATIONS, STATE COUNTY COURTS

Equation Number	Area	Counties	Dependent Variable	Regression Coefficients and t-Values							
				α	B	S	Pop	NW	Ur	Y	R^2
3.1	Non-South >450,000	30	T	.312 (1.011)	.750 (4.589)	.004 (.923)	.045 (2.864)	-.479 (1.778)	-.063 (.238)	-.081 (2.468)	.37
3.2	Non-South 100–450,000	27	T	-.041 (.200)	.309 (2.619)	.001 (.223)	.101 (.493)	.114 (.157)	-.120 (.616)	.014 (.430)	.31
3.3	Non-South <100,000	43	T	.151 (1.777)	.085 (1.126)	-.001 (.895)	.044 (.084)	.010 (.058)	.099 (1.556)	-.026 (1.562)	.17
3.4	South >200,000	17	T	-.194 (.417)	-.010 (.036)	-.016 (2.667)	.524 (2.674)	.590 (2.249)	-.642 (1.394)	.188 (3.633)	.81
3.5	South <108,000	15	T	.255 (.783)	-.186 (.775)	.0001 (.013)	-4.269 (2.402)	-.252 (.974)	-.067 (.342)	.088 (1.200)	.59

SOURCE.—Table 2, *supra*.

189

served for the South in counties with populations greater than 200,000.

Although a sufficient explanation is not available for the South, the overall results of Tables 2 and 3 give strong support to the hypothesis that the frequency of trials is greater among defendants released on bail than those not released. A positive and statistically significant relationship between bail and trials was observed for the U.S. and the non-South, and the latter region included more than three-fourths of our observations. This finding is consistent with the prediction of the theoretical model that the costs of going to trial compared to settling are increased by not making bail, which in turn reduces the likelihood of a trial.

Several additional comments on the results in Tables 2 and 3 are in order. (1) It might be argued that the bail variable is a proxy for wealth so that a finding that T increases with B is due to differences in wealth and not to greater trial costs for those not released. First, there is nothing in the theoretical analysis that indicates that wealth directly affects the choice between a trial and a settlement. If wealth were positively correlated with the ability to make bail, one would observe wealthier defendants going to trial, but the theoretical explanation lies with differences in costs not differences in wealth. Second, the empirical analysis of the U.S. courts in the next section contains indirect estimates of a defendant's wealth which show that increases in wealth have no observable positive effect on trials. (2) A second criticism, which if valid would weaken my conclusion that increases in B lead to increases in T, is that spurious correlation exists between B and T. The argument can be made that defendants planning to plead guilty will not be willing to incur the costs of making bail, while those planning to go to trial will incur these costs. If this were true, an increase in T would lead to an observed increase in B and not the reverse. Although this argument has some plausibility, it has a defect. A defendant planning a guilty plea presumably desires the most favorable terms in a settlement. We showed in the model that one effect of not making bail is to raise the probability of conviction in a trial, which in turn results in worse settlement terms. Therefore, it is not obvious that the defendant planning to settle will find it any less desirable to post bail than the defendant planning a trial, since both suffer losses from not being released on bail. (3) The regression coefficients on the sentence variable, S, do not support the hypothesis that the likelihood of a trial is greater for defendants accused of crimes carrying longer sentences. In 4 of 8 equations in Tables 2 and 3 the sign of S was positive, and in only one equation (3.4), where S had a negative effect, was the variable significant. The inconclusive behavior of S may partly be attributed to the data. The theoretical analysis calls for a variable that measures the average severity of offenses for defendants sampled in each county in 1962, while data limitations have forced us to use the average time served by all felons in a state who were first released in 1964. Fortunately, the regressions for the U.S. courts provide us with a stronger test of the sentence hypothesis because data on sentences in the U.S. courts correspond more closely to the theoretical requirements. (4) The NW, Ur and Y variables, which are included in the regressions of Tables 2 and 3, should be viewed as demographic characteristics of counties rather than as indicators of socioeconomic classes of defendants, since the relation of these variables to defendants may be remote. There are no prior expectations on the effects of these variables on trials, and their regression coefficients do not show a consistent pattern. In Table 2 Y and NW have negative effects on T in the non-South and positive effects in the South, while Ur has a positive effect in the non-South and a negative effect in the South. About two-thirds of the NW, Ur and Y regression coefficients are not statistically significant.[47]

U.S. COURTS

Least-squares regression equations were estimated across U.S. district courts in 1967 of the following form:

$$T_1 = \alpha + \beta_1 Q_t + \beta_2 Q_p + \beta_3 S + \beta_4 D + \beta_5 Re + \mu. \tag{20}$$

All variables are in natural logs except Re and hence the regression coefficients are elasticity measures. The variables in (20) are defined as follows:

T_1: ratio of defendants whose cases were disposed of by trials during 1967 to the total number of defendants disposed of in 1967. Regressions were also fitted on T_2 which equals the ratio of trials to defendants for 1968.

Q_t: weighted average of median time intervals from filing to disposition by court trial and by jury trial in 1967, where weights are the proportion of court and jury trials respectively.

Q_p: median time interval from filing to disposition by a plea of guilty in 1967.

S: weighted average of sentences received by convicted defendants whose

---

47. Regressions were also estimated without the NW, Ur and Y variables. The regression results for the bail, population, and sentence variables were largely unaffected.

cases were disposed of in 1967, where weights are the proportion of convicted defendants receiving each type of sentence.[48]

D: proportion of criminal defendants disposed of in 1967 who are assigned counsel by the court under provisions of the Federal Criminal Justice Act of 1964. The Act provides for counsel when defendants are unable to pay all or part of their legal fees.[49] Thus, D is a direct measure of the fraction of defendants with subsidized legal counsel. Since the ability to pay for counsel is related to the defendant's wealth, D would also serve as a rough measure of the fraction of defendants with low incomes or wealth.

Re: region dummy variable where 1 is assigned to district courts in the South and 0 to district courts in the non-South.

Data on Q_t are available for only 44 of 89 district courts in 1967 (see note b to Table 4), while data on Q_t and Q_p are not available for other years. Regressions were first estimated for the 44 districts in 1967. However, in order to incorporate observations for the remaining districts, and to work with years other than 1967, a proxy variable for Q_t was used that can be computed for all years and districts. The proxy for Q_t in year m is the ratio of pending cases (Pc) at the end of year m-1 to the average annual number of cases that go to trial ($\bar{T}$) in years m and m-1. One would expect Pc to estimate the backlog and $\bar{T}$ to roughly measure the availability of trial services, and hence $Pc/\bar{T}$ should serve as a measure of Q_t even though not all pending cases eventually go to trial.[50] The accuracy of

---

48. Obvious problems arise in evaluating a diversity of sentences that include imprisonment, fines, probation with and without supervision, suspended sentence, etc. The Administrative Office of the U.S. Courts has devised a common set of values for these sentences (see Fed. Offenders, *supra* note 40, at 4) that assign 0 to suspended sentences and probation without supervision, 1–4 for fines and various terms of probation with supervision, and 3–50 for imprisonment with sentences that range from 1 to more than 120 months. Although higher values are generally given to more severe sentences, the method is still arbitrary. For example, why all fines and probation with supervision from 1 to 12 months are both assigned the value 1 is never explained. Nevertheless, the use of this variable as an estimate of the average potential sentences of accused defendants in each district seems preferable to using just the mean prison sentence, since the latter group includes only 38 per cent of all defendants disposed of in 1967, while the former group includes 77 per cent. Both measures suffer because they exclude defendants not convicted when the relevant theoretical variable is the average potential sentence faced by all defendants before disposition of their case.

49. See The Courts, *supra* note 28, at 59–61.

50. There were 10,771 pending criminal cases in the beginning of fiscal year 1967, and 3,924 trials in the 1967 fiscal year. Since the average trial queue is about six months, this would suggest as a first approximation that roughly one-half of the trials in 1967 were from pending cases in the beginning of the year. Thus, about 20 per cent of pending cases would go to trial.

TABLE 4

WEIGHTED REGRESSIONS [a] AND t-VALUES FOR CRIMINAL TRIALS IN U.S. DISTRICT COURTS, 1960, 1967 AND 1968

Equation Number	Year	Districts	Dependent Variable	Regression Coefficients and t-Values								
				α	Q_t [b]	Q_p	$P_c/\bar{T}$	S	D	Re	$E(T)$ [c]	R^2
4.1	1967	44	T_1	-2.814 (4.853)	-.246 (1.666)	.629 (4.201)		.610 (2.255)	.392 (2.529)	.159 (1.249)		.61
4.2	1967	44	T_1	-2.646 (6.321)		.608 (6.027)	-.407 (5.698)	.413 (1.976)	.151 (1.199)	-.039 (.379)		.78
4.3	1968	44	T_2	-1.999 (3.533)	-2.50 (1.803)	.591 (3.788)		.296 (1.116)	.461 (3.166)	.095 (.822)		.57
4.4	1968	44	T_2	-1.880 (3.920)		.532 (4.494)	-.311 (3.849)	.143 (.598)	.349 (2.627)	-.047 (.430)		.67
4.5	1967	89	T_1	-2.750 (6.894)		.578 (5.882)	-.463 (6.573)	.495 (2.518)	.194 (1.620)	-.087 (.856)		.66
4.6 [d]	1960	86	T	-.365 (.323)			-.410 (5.142)	.315 (1.246)		.037 (.293)	1.287 (3.954)	.42
4.7 [e]	1960	43	T	1.294 (.996)			-.208 (2.338)	.242 (.805)		.054 (.372)	1.958 (5.751)	.58

[See following page for Notes.]

193

NOTES TO TABLE 4

SOURCES. $-T_1$, Q_t, Q_p, $Pc/\bar{T}$ for equations 4.1 through 4.5 are from 1967 Ann. Rep., Admin. Office of the United States Courts, tables D6, D1, C7; T_2 for equations 4.1 through 4.5 is from 1968 Ann. Rep., Admin. Office of the United States Courts, table D6; S and W for equations 4.1 through 4.5 are from Fed. Offenders in the United States District Courts 1967, tables D10, D11; T, $Pc/\bar{T}$, $E(T)$ in equations 4.6 and 4.7 are from 1960 Ann. Rep. Admin. Office of the United States Courts tables C7, D1, D3, D4; S for equations 4.6 and 4.7 is from U.S. Bureau of Prisons, Federal Prisons 1960, table 20.

ᵃ Weighted by $\sqrt{n}$ where n is the number of defendants disposed (equations 4.1 through 4.5) and the number of cases commenced (equations 4.6 and 4.7). All variables except Re are in natural logarithms.

ᵇ Q_t is the district average of the median court trial queue and median jury trial queue. Data on either median were available only if there were at least 25 observations for that type of trial. 44 out of 89 districts had figures on at least one of two trial queues. Since most trials are jury trials (about 67 per cent), 29 out of the above 44 districts did not publish any information on court trial queues. The latter were estimated by assuming the ratio of the court trial to jury trial queue in the circuit (the 89 district courts are divided into ten circuits) was equal to the ratio in the district. Information was available on the aggregated circuit level, and hence the median court trial queue in a district could be directly estimated. Estimates were generally required in districts that had a small proportion of court relative to jury trials. Therefore, any errors in estimating the court trial queue would have a small effect on the weighted average Q_t. Finally, note that in 5 districts the queue for court trials but not jury trials was available. The procedure described above was then used to estimate the jury trial queue.

ᶜ $E(T)$ in the ith district equals $\sum_{j=1}^{16} T_j^* O_{ji}$ where T_j^* is the proportion of defendants in the jth offense category whose cases were disposed of by trial for all districts taken together in 1960, and O_{ji} is the proportion of defendants accused of the jth offense in district i. There were 16 offense categories. Thus, variations in $E(T)$ across districts are due solely to differences in the composition of offenses. $E(T)$ was devised to take account of the possibility that differences in the fraction of trials across districts were the result of $E(T)$ rather than the queue. Data did not permit a similar calculation for 1967–68.

ᵈ In 1960 there were 86 district courts. By 1967 there were 89 district courts as several were eliminated and new ones were added. There are several small differences between the 1960 and 1967 data. They are: (1) T is the ratio of the number of cases that went to trial over the number of cases commenced in 1960. This differs from 1967 where the trial data are for defendants not cases, and the denominator is disposed defendants not commenced cases. In a given year the number of new defendants is about 25 per cent greater than the number of cases commenced, indicating that the number of cases with more than one defendant exceed the number of defendants involved in more than one case. Since this is reflected in the numerator of the trial variable as well, the correlation in a given year between T for cases and defendants would be very high; (2) S in 1960 is the average prison sentence of convicted defendants, and excludes defendants who were fined or put on probation with supervision. The latter groups are included in the 1967 S variable.

ᵉ Regressions computed from districts in 1960 that match those districts in 1967 that had data on Q_t.

$Pc/\bar{T}$ as an estimate of trial queues was checked by running simple regressions of Q_t, Q_p, and $(Q_t - Q_p)$ on $Pc/\bar{T}$.[51] These equations indicate that $Pc/\bar{T}$ is positively and significantly related to Q_t and $(Q_t - Q_p)$, accounting for nearly half the variation in these variables. Although $Pc/\bar{T}$ is also positively related to Q_p, it is substantially more important in explaining variations in Q_t and $(Q_t - Q_p)$. Therefore, $Pc/\bar{T}$ is not merely a measure of general delay in the disposition of criminal cases, but, on the contrary, is a measure of differential delay between trials and guilty pleas. This result allows us to estimate regressions for all 89 district courts in 1967, and to check the stability of the model over time by fitting equations to an earlier year, 1960, in which direct data on queues were absent.

If equation (20) estimates a demand curve for trials, the theoretical analysis predicts that the regression coefficient on Q_t (and $Pc/\bar{T}$) will be negative, and the regression coefficient on Q_p will be positive. However, single-equation estimates may identify a supply curve instead, if the demand for trials varied more than the supply across districts. In the latter case, higher observed values for Q_t would have resulted from shifts to the right in demand curves, giving rise to a positive coefficient on Q_t. Similar behavior would produce a negative coefficient on Q_p if a reduction in guilty pleas lowered Q_p. I have attempted to deal with this identification problem in two ways: (1) Equation (20) includes S and D variables that are expected to lead to shifts in the demand for trials. By holding S and D constant, the likelihood of identifying a demand curve is increased. A region variable, Re, also enters equation (20), but it is not obvious that Re operates more on the demand than supply side of trials. (2) Regressions have been estimated with a 1968 trial variable, T_2, against 1967 values of Q_t and Q_p. If defendants and prosecutors form their expectations about current queues on the basis of last year's queue, then Q_t in 1967 could still be inversely related to T_2 even though demand shifts in 1967 had caused a positive correlation between T_1 and Q_t.

---

51. The regression equations for the 44 districts in 1967 were

$$Q_t = \underset{(14.961)}{1.272} + \underset{(5.689)}{.420(Pc/\bar{T})} \qquad R^2 = .44$$

$$Q_p = \underset{(4.087)}{.489} + \underset{(1.603)}{.167(Pc/\bar{T})} \qquad R^2 = .06$$

$$(Q_t - Q_p) = \underset{(4.155)}{.516} + \underset{(5.844)}{.629(Pc/\bar{T})} \qquad R^2 = .45$$

$Pc/\bar{T}$, Q_t, Q_p, and $(Q_t - Q_p)$ are in natural logs, and all observations are weighted by $\sqrt{n}$ where n is the number of defendants disposed of in each district in 1967.

Regression estimates of equation (20) are presented in Table 4 for the years 1960, 1967, and 1968. In districts where Q_t and Q_p are available, the regression results strongly support the hypothesis that increases in Q_t, holding Q_p constant, have significant negative effects on T_1 and T_2, and increases in Q_p, with Q_t constant, have significant positive effects on T_1 and T_2. When $Pc/\bar{T}$ is substituted for Q_t, in equations 4.2 and 4.4, $Pc/\bar{T}$ has the predicted negative sign and is statistically significant, while Q_p has the same effects on T_1 and T_2 as before.[52] Further, when the sample is expanded to include all 89 districts in equation 4.5, the signs and significance of Q_p and $Pc/\bar{T}$ are similar to the results for the 44 districts. This suggests that any biases in estimating the effects of queues on trial demand due to excluding 45 districts in equations 4.1–4.4 are probably of small magnitude. Estimation of regressions for 1960 indicates that for all districts (equation 4.6) the queue, as measured by $Pc/\bar{T}$, had about the same effects as in 1967 and 1968. However, for districts in 1960 that match the districts in which Q_t were available in 1967 (equation 4.7), the regression coefficient of $Pc/\bar{T}$ was still negative but with a smaller absolute value. The latter partially results from the absence in 1960 of a measure of Q_p. Since Q_p and $Pc/\bar{T}$ are positively correlated, part of the positive effect of Q_p on trials would be picked up by $Pc/\bar{T}$ which, in turn, would diminish the negative effect of $Pc/\bar{T}$ on trials. I have tested this for 1967 by reestimating equation 4.2 without Q_p, which reduces the regression coefficient of $Pc/\bar{T}$ from $-.407$ to $-.331$.

Although the regressions in Table 4 are consistent with the hypothesis on Q_t and Q_p, these results contain an interesting puzzle. In both equations 4.1 and 4.3, trials are substantially more responsive to changes in Q_p than Q_t. One possible explanation is that errors in measurement are more important in Q_t than Q_p. Q_t is based on a sample of defendants that in each district averages less than 25 per cent of the sample size of Q_p, and in addition, Q_t often had to be estimated because either data on the jury trial queue or the court trial queue were absent (see note b in Table 4).[53]

---

52. The significance of Q_p improves with this substitution, and the R^2's rise. The former is due to the substantially higher correlation between Q_p and Q_t than between Q_p and $Pc/\bar{T}$ (.54 compared to .24), while the latter is related to some spurious negative correlation since trials are present in the denominator of $Pc/\bar{T}$ and the numerator of T_1 and T_2. This spurious correlation probably explains why the absolute value of the regression coefficient of $Pc/\bar{T}$ is larger than Q_t.

53. Errors in measurement of Q_t would also bias downward the regression coefficient of Q_p since the regression coefficient of Q_t and the partial correlation between Q_t and Q_p are of opposite signs. See G. C. Chow, Demand for Automobiles in the United States, A Study in Consumer Durables app. I (13 Contributions to Economic Analysis 1957).

The effects on trial demand of the remaining variables in Table 4 may be summarized as follows: (1) S has a positive sign in all regressions as predicted by the theoretical analysis, and is statistically significant in the 1967 equations. The lack of significance in equations 4.3 and 4.4 is probably due to the fact that T_2 denotes defendants going to trial in 1968, whereas S refers to defendants sentenced in 1967. The nonsignificance of S in 1960 reflects the less comprehensive·measure of S in that year. S is the average prison sentence in 1960, while in 1967, S includes defendants who were fined, placed on probation, and sentenced to prison. (2) D measures the fraction of defendants with subsidized legal counsel. These subsidies reduce the cost of a trial relative to a settlement, providing unsubsidized legal fees are greater for the former than the latter, and this in turn increases the demand for trials. The results of Table 4 support this hypothesis. The coefficient on D is positive in all regressions and significant in 4 out of 5 equations. This finding is relevant to the previous analysis of state courts where it was shown that defendants making bail had higher trial propensities. The latter was explained in terms of cost differentials between a trial and settlement that were greater for defendants not making bail. However, an alternative explanation was that wealthy persons were more likely to go to trial, and hence the observed relation between bail and trials resulted from the positive correlation between wealth and the ability to make bail. The analysis of the U.S. courts does not support this view. If differences in wealth per se were an important determinant of trial demand and wealthier defendants were more likely to go to trial, then the coefficient on D would have had a negative sign, since D should be inversely related to the fraction of wealthy defendants in a district. Thus, the results in Table 4, together with the findings for state courts, indicate that the cost differential between trials and settlements, and not differences in wealth among defendants, is an important factor in trial demand.[54] (3) The South dummy variable, Re, had no systematic effect on trials in Table 3, which contrasts with the strong positive effect of Re in the state data. This is not surprising, since the region effect in the state courts may have picked up the effect of lower trial queues in the South, whereas queues were held constant in the U.S. courts.

---

54. If one still believed that wealth was an important variable in trial demand, then the observed positive coefficients on D would show that wealthier defendants were *less* likely to go to trial. This contradicts the results of the state data which showed that wealthier defendants were *more* likely to go to trial. One final note is that if wealth were a determinant of the ability to make bail in the U.S. courts, then the coefficient on D could have a negative sign. However, the Bail Reform Act (to the extent it is effective) would have reduced or eliminated the correlation between wealth and the ability to make bail.

The Probability of Conviction

STATE COUNTY COURTS

The theoretical analysis predicted that if the defendant were not released on bail, the costs of his resource inputs would rise, leading to a reduction in these inputs and an increase in the probability of conviction. Therefore, a decline in the fraction of defendants making bail should result in an increase in the fraction of defendants convicted. A major difficulty in testing this hypothesis relates to the direction of causation between the bail and conviction variables. At the time bail is set a prima facie case is often made against the accused. If the preliminary evidence points to his guilt, a higher bail bond is likely to be set, which would lower his chance of being released. Hence, a selection process would take place before the final disposition of cases whereby defendants with a higher probability of conviction would be less likely to make bail. I have attempted to deal with this problem by including as independent variables both the fraction of defendants released on bail (B) and the average money bail charge (C) in regressions on the fraction of defendants convicted. Since setting a high money bail is a method of detaining a defendant with a high initial probability of conviction, then including C as an independent variable has the effect of holding constant differences across counties in these probabilities.[55] This in turn would remove from the regression coefficient on B any negative correlation due to higher conviction probabilities reducing the fraction of defendants released on bail.

Weighted regression equations of the form

$$P = \alpha + \beta_1 B + \beta_2 Pop + \beta_3 R_e + \beta_4 NW + \beta_5 Ur + \beta_6 Y + \beta_7 C + \beta_8 T + u$$

(21)

are presented in Table 5. B, Pop, Re, NW, Ur, Y and T are defined as before (see pp. 184–85) and P and C are defined as follows:

P: the fraction of felony defendants sentenced to prison in each county. Some convicted felony defendants received only fines so that P understates the total

---

55. The inclusion of C is only an approximation to holding constant variations in the probabilities because C may reflect other factors as well. For example, the severity of the offense, variations in the fraction of defendants not appearing for trial, attitudes of judges, etc.

TABLE 5

WEIGHTED REGRESSIONS AND t-VALUES FOR CRIMINAL CONVICTIONS IN 1962, 70 COUNTY COURTS IN U.S.

Equation Number	Dependent Variable	Regression Coefficients and t-Values									R^2
		α	B	Pop	Re	NW	Ur	Y	C	T	
5.1	P	.683 (4.771)	-.438 (3.821)	.010 (.748)	.063 (1.141)	-.127 (.809)	.076 (.581)	-.006 (.235)			.23
5.2	P	.655 (4.545)	-.369 (2.917)	.007 (.544)	.062 (1.129)	-.142 (.909)	.105 (.800)	-.019 (.663)	.015 (1.280)		.25
5.3	P	.676 (4.808)	-.247 (1.822)	.020 (1.447)	.051 (.947)	-.090 (.585)	.056 (.431)	-.017 (.632)	.011 (.989)	-.289 (2.130)	.30
5.4	$Ds + A$	.076 (.641)	.227 (1.978)	-.019 (1.566)	.033 (.719)	.010 (.074)	.103 (.940)	-.031 (1.330)	.015 (1.520)	-.299 (2.600)	.30
5.5	Ds	.115 (1.044)	.150 (1.408)	-.012 (1.114)	.063 (1.482)	-.042 (.348)	.101 (.994)	-.031 (1.440)	.013 (1.442)	.011 (.101)	.19
5.6	A	-.039 (1.019)	.077 (2.089)	-.006 (1.653)	-.030 (2.039)	.052 (1.236)	.002 (.056)	.0002 (.020)	.002 (.565)	.288 (7.789)	.67
5.7	P [a]	.824 (7.409)	-.430 (4.307)	.016 (1.283)	-.073 (1.729)	.091 (.631)	.014 (.147)	-.028 (1.292)			.17

SOURCES.—See Table 2 *supra*, for all variables except C. C is from Lee Silverstein, Bail in the State Courts—A Field Study and Report, 50 Minn. L. Rev. 621, tables 2, 3 & 4 (1966).

[a] Equation 5.7 is for all 132 counties where data on B are available whereas equations 5.1 through 5.6 are for 70 counties where data on C are available.

number of defendants receiving penalties. However, data available in a few counties indicate that the fraction of defendants receiving only fines was negligible.

C: average dollar amount of bail set for defendants in each county.

The negative and statistically significant effect of *B* in equation 5.1 reflects in part the negative correlation described above that runs from *P* to *B*. *C* has a positive effect on *P* in equation 5.2, suggesting that defendants with greater conviction probabilities had *C* set at higher amounts.[56] As expected both the absolute value of the regression coefficient on *B* and its significance are reduced when *C* is entered. We have previously shown that defendants released on bail have greater propensities to go to trial. One would like to determine to what extent the observed effect of *B* on *P* in 5.2 is due to differences in the method of disposition of cases (that is, trials versus settlements) between defendants released and not released on bail. In equation 5.3 a trial variable (*T*) has been added. *T* further reduces the regression coefficient of *B* and its significance because defendants going to trial are less likely to be sentenced to prison (that is, the regression coefficient on *T* is negative and significant) and more likely to make bail. In sum, the results of equations 5.1–5.3 support the hypothesis that the probability of conviction is increased for a defendant when he is not released on bail. At the mean values of *P* and *B* (both are about .5) the regression coefficient on *B* in 5.3 implies that the frequency of prison convictions is .38 for defendants released on bail and .62 for defendants not released, holding *C* and *T* constant. Observe that the coefficient of *B* is reduced by about 40 per cent when *C* and *T* are held constant — 15 per cent due to *C* and 25 per cent due to *T*.

Regressions are also presented in Table 5 on the fraction of defendants dismissed (*Ds*) and the fraction acquitted (*A*). These results confirm the previous findings that defendants released on bail are less likely to be convicted. The regression coefficients on *B* are positive in all three equations where *C* and *T* are held constant, and statistically significant in two. Note that 15 per cent of defendants in the sample were acquitted or dismissed, 50 per cent were sentenced to prison, while the remaining 35 per cent were generally given suspended sentences or placed on probation. The latter type of sentences, where the defendant's costs are small

---

56. Data on *C* are available in only 70 of the 132 counties used in analysis of trials in county courts. The exclusion of 62 counties does not create any obvious biases since a regression computed for all 132 counties without *C* (equation 5.7) yields similar coefficients to equation 5.1.

in comparison to prison sentences, should probably be viewed as non-convictions. For this reason P would be a better measure of convictions than $1 - (Ds + A)$. The positive though nonsignificant coefficients on C in the Ds and A regressions suggest that increases in defendants sentenced to prison as C rises, which are found in equations 5.2 and 5.3, come from a reduction in probations and suspended sentences rather than from fewer dismissals and acquittals.

Other findings in Table 5 may be summarized as follows. (1) The population variable generally has a positive effect on convictions, indicating that longer trial queues across counties tend to increase the fraction of convictions. One should be cautious with this interpretation because of the uncertain relation between queues and population size and the lack of strong statistical significance of the population variable. (2) The demographic variables, NW, Ur and Y are not statistically significant in any regression. (3) An additional problem relates to the interpretation of the regression coefficient of B. Although a negative effect of B on convictions is found, this could be due to a greater average wealth rather than to a lower cost of resources for defendants released on bail. The relationship between wealth and convictions will be examined in the analysis of the U.S. court data.

Data on judicial expenditures in 1966–67 are available for twenty counties with populations greater than 450,000. A reasonable assumption is that these expenditures are positively correlated with the size of the prosecutor's budget in a county. We would then predict from the theoretical analysis that the proportion of defendants convicted would be greater in counties with larger judicial expenditures per defendant. This hypothesis is consistent with findings in Table 6 where judicial expenditures, denoted by J, have a positive effect on convictions in all regressions.[57] The primary effect of an increase in J is to reduce the proportion of cases dismissed, while there is no significant effect on acquittals. Moreover, the increase in the fraction of defendants going to prison as J rises can be accounted for solely by a reduction in dismissals. At the mean values of J, Ds and P, a 15 per cent rise in J reduces Ds from .13 to .11 and increases P from about .50 to .52. Thus, the major economizing move as judicial expenditures fall is to reduce the number of cases prosecuted – hence an increase in dismissals.

---

57. J is not divided by the number of defendants in a county because this information is not available. However, population size, which is probably positively correlated with the number of defendants in a county, is held constant in the regression equations.

TABLE 6

WEIGHTED REGRESSIONS AND t-VALUES FOR CRIMINAL CONVICTIONS IN 1962, 20 COUNTY COURTS IN U.S.

Equation Number	Dependent Variable		Regression Coefficients and t-Values										R^2
		α	B	Pop	Re	NW	Ur	Y	C	T	J	
6.1	P	.813 (1.841)	−.539 (1.495)	.028 (1.208)	−.033 (.262)	.399 (.869)	−.120 (.222)	.013 (.172)	−.015 (.603)	−.378 (1.487)		.55
6.2	P	.396 (.851)	−.369 (1.079)	−.011 (.350)	.147 (.975)	.249 (.584)	−.554 (1.011)	.123 (1.347)	−.008 (.365)	−.255 (1.066)	.007 (1.796)	.67
6.3	$Ds+A$	.903 (2.887)	.042 (.182)	.042 (2.035)	−.157 (1.539)	−.124 (.433)	.904 (2.453)	−.257 (4.191)	.017 (1.155)	.186 (1.145)	−.011 (4.052)	.82
6.4	Ds	1.013 (3.308)	−.141 (.626)	.045 (2.237)	−.125 (1.255)	−.097 (.344)	.775 (2.149)	−.241 (4.010)	.010 (.643)	−.088 (.555)	−.010 (3.862)	.76
6.5	A	−.110 (.755)	.183 (1.704)	−.003 (.333)	−.032 (.663)	−.028 (.206)	.129 (.747)	−.016 (.565)	.008 (1.126)	.275 (3.617)	−.001 (.579)	.82

SOURCES.— See Tables 2 and 5, *supra*, for variables except J. J is from U.S. Bureau of the Census, Criminal Justice Expenditure and Employment for Selected Large Governmental Units 1966–1967, tables 16 & 20 (State and Local Gov't Special Studies No. 51, 1969).

U.S. COURTS

Two conviction variables are used in regressions computed across U.S. district courts in 1967.

P: the fraction of defendants sentenced to prison.
F: the fraction of defendants receiving a fine only.

Prison sentences were more numerous than fines as the weighted means of P and F were .38 and .07 respectively in the 89 districts.

Of considerable interest in Table 7 is the behavior of the variable D, the proportion of defendants assigned counsel by the court. D has a positive and significant effect on P, and a negative though nonsignificant effect on F in all equations. This suggests that increases in wealth of defendants reduce (increase) the frequency of convictions for offenses carrying prison sentences (fines) since D serves as a proxy variable for the fraction of lower income defendants in a district (see p. 192). These findings are consistent with a "wealth" hypothesis developed in the theoretical section which predicted for risk neutral defendants that (a) when penalties were in the form of jail sentences a rise in wealth would lead to an increase in the defendant's resource inputs and a subsequent fall in the probability of conviction and (b) when penalties are in the form of fines an increase in wealth would lower his inputs and raise the probability of conviction. A related interpretation of the increase in P as D rises is that court-assigned lawyers are less effective and less able than privately hired lawyers. This is not at variance with the "wealth" hypothesis because more able lawyers can be counted as more units of the defendant's resource inputs than less able ones. However, the ability explanation would also predict that privately hired lawyers would reduce the conviction rate on fines, and the reverse is found in Table 7.[58]

An increase in delay between a trial and settlement is associated with an increase in the fraction of defendants sentenced to prison. The coefficients are positive for Qt and $Pc/\bar{T}$ and negative for Qp in the P regressions in Table 7. We also observed in the state data that the population

---

58. A possible reconciliation is that more able lawyers are able to lower the defendant's conviction costs by shifting penalties from prison sentences to fines. This explanation would be consistent with both a positive effect of D on P and a negative effect of D on F. Another possible interpretation of the observed effects of D on P and F is that in districts where wealth is higher (and hence D lower) the types of crimes committed are more likely to be those carrying fines rather than jail sentences.

TABLE 7
WEIGHTED REGRESSIONS AND t-VALUES FOR CRIMINAL CONVICTIONS IN U.S. DISTRICT COURTS,[a] 1967

Equation Number	Districts	Dependent Variable	Regression Coefficients and t-Values							
			α	Q_t	Q_p	$Pc/\bar{T}$	D	Re	T_1	R^2
7.1	89	P	.593 (11.730)		−.096 (3.587)	.022 (1.069)	.086 (3.226)	.032 (1.319)	.046 (1.858)	.34
7.2	89	F	−.057 (1.711)		.061 (3.469)	−.012 (.875)	−.026 (1.471)	−.027 (1.707)	−.040 (2.441)	.27
7.3	44	P	.612 (6.217)		−.119 (2.656)	.030 (.955)	.081 (2.049)	.028 (.852)	.049 (.984)	.37
7.4	44	P	.502 (6.825)	.094 (2.717)	−.154 (3.815)		.086 (2.378)	.021 (.701)	.042 (1.232)	.46
7.5	44	F	.015 (.292)		.050 (2.227)	−.002 (.149)	−.012 (.591)	−.019 (1.151)	−.005 (.204)	.32
7.6	44	F	.018 (.449)	.002 (.108)	.047 (2.149)		−.011 (.558)	−.019 (1.158)	−.002 (.104)	.32

SOURCES.—See Table 4, *supra*, for all variables except P and F. P and F are from Federal Offenders in the United States District Courts 1967, table D10.

[a] All variables are in natural log form, except P, F, and Re.

variable (interpreted as a proxy for trial delay) had a positive effect on convictions. One reason for the positive association between trial delay and prison convictions may be that the prosecutor becomes more selective with respect to the cases he prosecutes as trial delay increases. That is, he selects from an inventory of cases the ones he believes to have the greatest probability of conviction and the highest sentences if convicted in order to maximize his weighted conviction function. Moreover, if the prosecutor views fines as light penalties in comparison to jail sentences,[59] we would expect a negative relation between trial delay and the frequency of defendants fined. The equations on F give some support to this hypothesis although the regression coefficients on the Qt and $Pc/\bar{T}$ variables are not significant.

IV. SUMMARY AND CONCLUSIONS

The model developed in this essay utilizes two behavioral assumptions: the prosecutor maximizes the expected number of convictions weighted by their sentences, subject to a budget constraint, and the defendant maximizes the expected utility of his endowments in various states of the world. Both participants can influence the probability of conviction by their input of resources into the case, and cases are disposed of either by a trial or a voluntary pretrial settlement between the prosecutor and defendant. A settlement results in either a dismissal or a guilty plea. The major implications of the model are the following:

    1. A settlement is more likely to take place (a) the smaller the sentence if convicted by trial, (b) the greater the resource costs of a trial compared to a settlement, (c) the greater the defendant's aversion to risk, and (d) the greater the defendant's estimate of the probability of conviction by trial relative to the prosecutor's estimate. We further showed that if the defendant and prosecutor agree on the expected outcome of a trial, a decision to go to trial is analogous to accepting an unfair gamble. In this instance, a settlement would result for risk neutral and risk averse defendants.

    2. The defendant's investment of resources into his case is related both to the sentence if convicted by trial and to wealth. Generally, the

---

59. The Administrative Office of the U.S. Courts assigns the value 1 to fines and 3 to imprisonment of 1 to 6 months in calculating a weighted average of the severity of all sentences (see Fed. Offenders, *supra* note 40, at 35, table 10 and note 48, *supra*). This indirectly suggests that fines are of small magnitude compared to jail sentences of a few months.

resource investment is greater for crimes carrying larger sentences. Under the special assumption of risk neutrality (or presumably where the deviation from risk neutrality is small), increases in the defendant's wealth lead to greater resource investments when penalties are jail sentences and to smaller investments when penalties are money fines.

3. Court delays increase the opportunity costs of a trial compared to a settlement for defendants not released on bail. This leads to a smaller likelihood of going to trial for these defendants than for defendants released on bail. The greater the court delay the greater the difference in trial demand between the two groups. Pretrial detention also raises the marginal costs of the defendant's resources and hence lowers his input. Therefore, defendants not released on bail are likely to have higher conviction probabilities in a trial and receive longer sentences if they settle than defendants released on bail. If making bail is a positive function of wealth, then the effects of pretrial jailing fall primarily on low-income defendants. We argued that paying a defendant not released on bail for time spent in jail prior to disposition of his case, or alternatively, crediting him for this time towards his eventual sentence and paying him only if he is not convicted would eliminate much of the "discriminatory" aspects of the current bail system.

4. In the absence of money pricing for the courts a trial queue arises to ration the limited supply. An equilibrium queue is reached because trial costs increase with the length of the queue. Queues could be reduced by charging a money price for trials, which reduces demand, leading to more settlements. Various methods of allocating the court fee—loser pays, winner pays, defendant and prosecutor share the cost—are consistent with a downward sloping demand curve for trials. Pricing trials will not only reduce delay but can also distribute trials more equally among defendants independent of their ability to make bail.

Available data on criminal defendants in state county courts and in U.S. district courts enabled us to test a number of the hypotheses developed in the theoretical analysis. Multiple regressions were estimated for various cross sections in selected years from 1957 to 1968. The principal findings of the empirical analysis may be summarized as follows.

1. The propensity to go to trial was smaller for defendants not released on bail than defendants released, holding constant the average sentence and several demographic variables. This was observed for state county courts in the United States as a whole, and the non-South. Moreover, results from the U.S. district courts indirectly indicate that increases in wealth do not increase trial demand. Thus, the observed relation between bail and trials in state courts is probably due to cost dif-

ferences as predicted by the model rather than to differences in wealth that are positively correlated with the ability to make bail.

2. The absolute difference in trial propensities between defendants released and not released on bail increased as county population rose. One explanation for this finding is that court delay is greater in counties with larger populations. Note that direct measures of court delay were not available for the state courts.

3. Trial demand was negatively related to trial delay and positively related to settlement delay across U.S. district courts for 1960, 1967, and 1968. Thus, as the queue differential between a trial and settlement increased, the demand for trials fell.

4. Subsidizing defendant's legal fees in the U.S. district courts increased the demand for trials. This is consistent with the hypothesis that as the cost differential between a trial and settlement falls, the demand for trials increases.

5. District courts in which the average sentence was greater had proportionately more trials as predicted by the model. However, the results for the sentence variable in the county courts were inconclusive. The latter may be due to the crudity of the sentence variable used in counties.

6. The probability of conviction as measured by the proportion of defendants sentenced to prison was greater for defendants not released on bail than for defendants released on bail in county courts. This was observed in regressions which held constant, among other factors, both the size of money bail and the method of disposition (that is, trial or settlement). Money bail was included as an independent variable to reduce spurious correlation between the conviction and bail variables since defendants who were more likely to be convicted were also likely to have bail set at higher amounts, reducing their chance of release on bail. Regressions using the proportion of defendants acquitted and dismissed as the dependent variable supported the finding that defendants not released on bail were more likely to be convicted.

7. Convictions leading to prison sentences were lower in districts where estimates of the average wealth were higher, while convictions resulting in monetary fines were greater where average wealth was higher. One interpretation of this result is that the effect of wealth on the defendant's investment of resources into his case depended on whether penalties were jail sentences or fines.

8. Conviction rates were higher in district courts where trial delay was greater, and in county courts where judicial expenditures were larger. The former may result from a greater selectivity on the part of

the prosecutor with respect to cases he prosecutes as the backlog increases. The latter was consistent with the hypothesis that the size of the prosecutor's budget determined the proportion of defendants convicted.

APPENDIX A

CIVIL CASES

We can extend our model to make it applicable to civil cases. The plaintiff replaces the prosecutor. Damages replace sentences. Both the plaintiff and defendant maximize their expected utility. It is assumed that civil trials decide both the question of the defendant's liability and the amount of damages. Only the defendant's guilt was at issue in criminal cases; the sentence if convicted was fixed and known prior to trial. A similar assumption for damages is not justified because statutory penalties generally do not exist for various types of civil suits. This modification requires that the plaintiff and defendant form expectations not only on the probability of the defendant being found liable, but also on the size of damages. With these changes, the analysis of civil cases remains quite similar to the model for criminal cases. To avoid excessive duplication I present only a brief outline of the civil model and its more important results.

In civil suits the plaintiff and defendant each select a level of resource inputs that maximizes his expected utility in the event of a trial. The plaintiff's inputs raise both the estimates of the probability that the defendant will be found liable and the amount of damages awarded in a trial, while the defendant's inputs lower these estimates. The plaintiff will determine a settlement payment ($= X$) that yields him the same utility as his expected utility from a trial. X would be the minimum sum accepted by the plaintiff to settle. If the payment of X by the defendant yields him a higher utility than his expected utility from a trial, a settlement will take place. This follows because one can find a payment somewhat greater than X that gives both parties a higher utility from a settlement than their expected utilities from a trial. It can further be shown that a settlement is likely when the following factors are present: (1) both parties have similar expectations on the probability that the defendant will be found liable in a trial; (2) both parties have similar estimates of the damages, given that the defendant is found liable in a trial; (3) neither party has strong preferences for risk; (4) the costs of a trial including lawyer's fees, time costs of the plaintiff and defendant, court fees, etc., exceed the costs of a settlement. Alternatively, the more dissimilar the plaintiff's and defendant's estimates of liability and damages (providing the plaintiff's estimates are higher), the greater their preference for risk, and the lower court costs relative to settlement costs, the more likely a trial.[60]

---

60. This result is similar to one derived by R. H. Coase, The Problem of Social Cost, 3 J. Law & Econ. 1 (1960). Coase shows that with well-defined property rights, and in the absence of transaction costs, a private agreement will be reached between individuals that

The analysis of charging a money price for the courts, as opposed to queuing costs, is similar for civil and criminal cases. For example, a money price (M) will raise the maximum settlement offered by the defendant in a civil suit and lower the minimum settlement accepted by the plaintiff. M narrows the gap between what the defendant offers and what the plaintiff is willing to accept (providing the former was initially less than the latter sum), and increases the likelihood of a settlement. Moreover, the greater M the fewer civil cases that go to trial. As M falls to zero, the demand for trials will increase and a queue is likely to develop. The queue rations demand in the following way. As the queue lengthens, the discounted value of damages awarded in a trial falls. This would lower both the amount the plaintiff will accept and the amount the defendant will offer in a settlement. However, there are probably some costs to the defendant from trial delay. For example, his ability to dispose of assets (particularly if they are directly involved in the suit) and his ability to obtain funds in the capital market may be adversely affected by his being involved in litigation. If, on the average, the gains and costs of delay to the defendant offset each other, or the costs dominate, then the defendant's settlement offer would remain constant or increase as delay increases. The net effect would be a reduction in desired trials as the queue lengthened, since the defendant's settlement offer remains constant or increases while the plaintiff reduces the amount he is willing to accept.

There are several additional points on court delay that should be noted. (1) The analysis of queueing in civil cases is almost identical to criminal cases where the defendant is released on bail. In the latter, the prosecutor reduces his minimum sentence offer as delay increases, while the defendant's response is affected by two offsetting forces. Delay pushes his potential sentence from a trial further into the future, reducing its present value, while simultaneously his current earnings may be adversely affected by being under indictment. (2) A system analogous to the bail system could be instituted for civil cases. This would require, for example, defendants in civil suits to either pay a sum to the court per unit of time, or forgo the returns from all or part of their assets by depositing them with the court during the period between filing and disposition of the case. One effect of this procedure would be to make trial demand more responsive to a change in the queue as the costs of delay rise to the defendant. This is similar to the greater responsiveness of criminal trial demand for defendants not released on bail relative to those released. (3) A requirement that the defendant pay interest on any sum awarded the plaintiff in a trial would have little effect on trial demand or court queues. Interest payments would raise both the defendant's settlement offer and the minimum sum acceptable to the plaintiff in a settlement. Hence, as a first ap-

---

internalizes externalities. If we interpret the absence of transaction costs in civil cases as the availability of information on damages at zero cost and zero bargaining costs of a settlement, and we generalize Coase's notion of well-defined property rights to include identical expectations over property rights or liability decisions in a trial, then Coase's theorem on private agreements would also include pretrial settlements in the absence of risk preference.

proximation it would not close the gap between the defendant's offer and the plaintiff's acceptance sum and, therefore, would have no effect on the trial versus settlement decision. (4) Differences in the rate at which the plaintiff and defendant discount future damages awarded at a trial can give rise to differences in the response of trial demand to a change in the queue. The higher the plaintiff's discount rate relative to the defendant's, the larger the plaintiff's losses and the smaller the defendant's gains from an increase in the queue. This, in turn, would reduce the sum acceptable to the plaintiff by a greater amount than it reduces the defendant's offer, making a settlement more likely.

We can test the hypothesis that the demand for civil trials is negatively related to the length of the trial queue. The statistical specification of the demand function is

$$T = \alpha + \beta_1 Q_t^* + \beta_2 E(T) + \beta_3 Re + \mu. \tag{22}$$

Data were from the 86 U.S. district courts in 1957–61. The variables are in natural log form except Re and are defined as follows:

T: The ratio of the number of trials from cases that commenced in 1957 over the number of cases commenced in 1957.[61]

Q_t^*: Estimate of the expected trial queue in 1957 where Q_t^* is an exponentially declining weighted average of 1957, 1956, and 1955 median trial queues.[62] Q_t, the median trial queue in 1956, was also used as an estimate of the expected trial queue.

---

61. A frequency distribution of civil cases by length of time from filing to disposition by trial is published for each year from 1957 to 1961. (After 1961 only median trial queues are available.) This allows us to trace over time the eventual disposition (that is, trial or settlement) of cases commenced in 1957 assuming all of the latter cases are disposed of within four years from the date of filing. Since civil trial queues average about one-and-one-half years in the U.S. courts, a frequency distribution of trials is an important advantage in estimating T. For example, if the number of trials in a given year were used as the numerator of T, it would be difficult to choose an appropriate denominator for T because the trials were from cases commenced over several different time periods with an average queueing time to trial of one-and-one-half years. Moreover, it would be equally difficult to choose a value for the expected trial queue. Frequency distributions of trials are not available for criminal cases, but the above problems are not as great since criminal queues average about six months.

62. Derived from the assumption that persons form expectations of future queues on the basis of past expectation and adjustment based on ratio of current value to previous expected value. That is,

$$Q_{t_y}^* = Q_{t_{(y-1)}}^* [Q_{t_y} / Q_{t_{(y-1)}}^*]^\gamma \tag{i}$$

where Q_t^*'s are expected and Q_t's are actual median queues in a district, y is the year, and γ is the adjustment coefficient. (i) can be rewritten as the following infinite series:

E(T): Expected fraction of trials in a district are estimated by dividing civil cases commenced in each district in 1957 into five broad groups, and then multiplying each group by the fraction of trials in that group for all U.S. district courts in 1957.[63] Therefore, the inclusion of $E(T)$ allows us to hold constant differences in the distribution of types of cases across districts.

Re: Region dummy variable that equals 1 for district courts in South and 0 for non-South district courts.

Table 8 presents regression estimates of equation (22). Separate regressions were also computed for districts in the non-South and South. All regression coefficients on Q_i^* and Q_t have the predicted negative signs, are highly significant, and are of similar magnitude. In sum, these results support the hypothesis that the demand for trials is negatively related to the size of the trial queue.

A difficulty in interpreting the findings of Table 8 arises from the way in which the trial variable is measured. An unknown number of civil cases that would come under the jurisdiction of the U.S. courts are settled before they are filed. Since these cases are excluded from the denominator of T, the true proportion of civil cases going to trial in a district each year is less than the observed fraction. This measurement error in T will not bias the regression coefficients if the error is uncorrelated with the independent variables. However, we can show that the error

$$Q_{t_y}^* = Q_{t_y}^\gamma \cdot Q_{t_{(y-1)}}^{\gamma(1-\gamma)}, \ldots \cdot Q_{t_{(y-\infty)}}^{\gamma(1-\gamma)\infty} \tag{ii}$$

Q_i^* in 1957 was approximated in the empirical analysis by using three previous values for Q_t. In logs this becomes

$$\log Q_{t57}^* = \gamma \log Q_{t57} + \gamma(1-\gamma) \log Q_{t56} + \gamma(1-\gamma)^2 \log Q_{t55}. \tag{iii}$$

γ was initially set equal to .4, but to have the weights sum to 1 all weights were proportionally raised by a factor of 1.2755.

63. Fraction of trials for various categories are as follows:

1. U.S. Plaintiff (excludes land condemnation and forfeiture cases)   .031
2. U.S. Defendant (ex. habeas corpus)   .188
3. Federal Question (ex. habeas corpus)   .123
4. Diversity   .151
5. Admiralty   .081

Note that 53,343 civil cases were commenced in 1957 in 86 U.S. District Courts and the number of cases excluded above were 4,613. These were excluded because data on queues and trials for each district do not include these types of cases. Note that when the U.S. government is involved in a suit as a defendant there is much greater likelihood of a trial than when the U.S. is the plaintiff. One explanation is that the costs to the defendant from delay (that offset the gains from the reduction in the present value of a trial settlement), such as his inability to dispose of assets or to obtain funds in the capital markets, may not be present when the defendant is the U.S. government. Hence, for a given queue one would expect more trials when the U.S. government is the defendant than when it is the plaintiff.

TABLE 8

WEIGHTED REGRESSION EQUATIONS [a] AND t-VALUES FOR CIVIL TRIALS IN
U.S. DISTRICT COURTS, 1957–61

Equation Number	Area	Dis- tricts	α	Q_t^*	Q_t	$E(T)$	Re	R²
					Regression Coefficients and t-Values			
8.1	U.S.	86	−.307	−.410		.354	−.337	.28
			(.413)	(5.444)		(1.051)	(4.014)	
8.2	U.S.		−.422		−.369	.352	−.314	.27
			(.563)		(5.188)	(1.032)	(3.757)	
8.3	Non-South	52	.164	−.429		.546		.45
			(.238)	(6.033)		(1.770)		
8.4	Non-South		.196		−.400	.596		.46
			(.285)		(6.079)	(1.940)		
8.5	South	34	−2.005	−.376		−.255		.12
			(1.087)	(2.080)		(.288)		
8.6	South		−2.399		−.323	−.386		.10
			(1.283)		(1.818)	(.420)		

SOURCES. – 1956–1962 Ann. Rep., Admin. Off. of the United States Courts, tables C1, C3 and C5.

[a] Each observation weighted by $\sqrt{n}$ where n equals the number of cases commenced in 1957.

in T is likely to be positively correlated with the trial queue, and this in turn will bias downward the absolute value of the queue elasticities.[64]

In Table 8 $E(T)$ has a positive and significant effect on T in the U.S. and non-South, but a negative and nonsignificant effect in the South. Overall, $E(T)$ was less important than trial queues in explaining variations in T across districts. Re which is significant at the .01 level indicates that the fraction of civil trials was about 30 per cent lower in the South holding the queue and $E(T)$ constant. This result is puzzling in view of the finding that Re had no significant effect on the

---

64. Let t = the number of trials in a district, F = the number of cases filed, and C = the number of cases filed plus those settled before filing. Further, assume that $K \cdot F = C$, where $K > 1$. Suppose the relationship between t/C and Q_t^* is

$$t/C = Q_t^{*\beta} e^{\mu}, \tag{i}$$

while the estimating equation is

$$t/F = Q_t^{*\hat{\beta}} e^{\hat{\mu}}, \tag{ii}$$

where μ and $\hat{\mu}$ are error terms. (ii) can be rewritten as

$$\log K + \log (t/C) = \hat{\beta} \log Q_t^* + \hat{\mu}. \tag{iii}$$

Let $E = \log K$, $Y = \log (t/C)$ and $X = \log Q_t^*$, and let e, y, and x denote deviations from

demand for criminal trials in the U.S. courts. A possible explanation is that the average size of damages in civil suits in the South is considerably lower than in the non-South. Thus, the negative effect on T of lower damages would be picked up by the Re variable.

APPENDIX B

MATHEMATICAL NOTES: WEALTH EFFECTS

In this section we analyze the effect of changes in W on R when the defendant has nonneutral tastes for risk. Risk aversion is assumed. The case of risk preference can easily be worked out from the example of risk aversion. Inputs of R are assumed to reduce both P and S (that is, $S' = \partial S/\partial R < 0$) in contrast to the assumption in Section I that S was a constant and independent of R.

The first- and second-order conditions for $E(U)$ to be a maximum may be written, respectively, as

$$-P'[U(Wn) - U(Wc)] - sS'PU'(Wc) - r[PU'(Wc) + (1 - P)U'(Wn)] = 0 \quad (23)$$

and

$$-R''[U(Wn) - U(Wc)] + 2rP'[U'(Wn) - U'(Wc)] + r^2[PU''(Wc)$$
$$+ (1 - P)U''(Wn)] - 2sS'P'U'(Wc) - sS''PU'(Wc)$$
$$+ 2rsS'PU''(Wc) + (sS')^2PU''(Wc) < 0. \quad (24)$$

Relative risk aversion at Wn is defined as follows:

$$A(Wn) = -WnU''(Wn)/U'(Wn). \quad (25)$$

$A(Wc)$ is similarly defined at Wc. Taking the total differential of (23) with respect to W and R, noting that (24) is negative, and substituting $A(Wn)$ and $A(Wc)$ gives $dR/dW \gtrless 0$ as

$$U'(Wn)\left[-P'k - r'(1 - P) + \frac{r(1 - P)A(Wn)k}{Wn}\right]$$
$$+ U'(Wc)\left[P'm - s'S'P + \frac{sS'PA(Wc)m}{Wc} - r'P + \frac{rPA(Wc)m}{Wc}\right] \gtrless 0, \quad (26)$$

---

their respective means. The least-squares estimator of $\hat{\beta}$ is

$$\hat{\beta} = \beta + \frac{\Sigma xe}{\Sigma x^2}, \quad \text{(iv)}$$

which will be an unbiased estimator of β only if Cov $(x, e) = 0$. However, it is more likely that as Q_t^* rises, K will also rise, since the incentives to settle (both before and after filing) increase with the size of Q_t^*. This implies that Cov $(x, e) > 0$. Given that β and $\hat{\beta}$ are negative, this would result in $|\hat{\beta}|$ underestimating $|\beta|$.

where $r' = \partial r/\partial W > 0$, $s' = \partial s/\partial W$, $k = (1 - r'R)$ and $m = (1 - s'S - r'R)$. Note that $0 < k < 1$, $0 < m < 1$ and $k > m$. m and k are both positive because an increase in W must increase both Wn and Wc. Even with further simplifying assumptions the sign of (26) is indeterminate. For example, suppose $A(Wn) = A(Wc) = 1$ and let $Er = r'(W/r)$ and $Es = s'(W/s)$ where $0 \leq Er, Es \leq 1$. This gives $dR/dW \gtrless 0$.

$$\frac{U'(Wn)}{U'(Wc)} \gtrless Wn \frac{\begin{bmatrix} -P'(W - E_sS - E_rrR)Wc \\ - sS'P[W - (E_sWc + E_ssS + E_rrR)] \\ - rP[W - (E_rWc + E_ssS + E_rrR)] \end{bmatrix}}{Wc[-P'(W - E_rrR)Wn + r(1 - P)(1 - E_r)W]}. \tag{27}$$

The sign of dR/dW cannot be determined from (27) without additional information about the defendant's utility function, the elasticities of s and r with respect to W, and the productivity of R in reducing S. If $E_s = E_r = 1$, (27) becomes

$$\frac{U'(Wn)}{U'(Wc)} \gtrless \frac{Wc}{Wn}. \tag{28}$$

In the special case of a Bernoulli utility function, where the utility of wealth equals its logarithm, then $dR/dW = 0$, since $U'(Wn)/U'(Wc) = Wc/Wn$.

In general, the effects of changes in wealth on the defendant's input of resources are indeterminate once nonneutral tastes for risk are introduced. This conclusion is valid even when the strong assumption is made that relative risk aversion equals one for all levels of the defendant's wealth. Nevertheless, one still presumes that if the deviation from risk neutrality is small, the effects of wealth on R will be similar to those for risk neutrality.

The Behavior of Administrative Agencies

Richard A. Posner

University of Chicago and National Bureau of Economic Research

Administrative agencies are an increasingly prominent feature of the legal system. This article presents a model of the behavior of such agencies that can be tested empirically and the results of some preliminary empirical tests.[1] The model is designed to predict how a rational utility-maximizing agency divides its attention among cases having different characteristics. Part I develops the model, discusses and tests some empirical implications, and compares the implications of the model with alternative models. Part II uses the model developed in Part I as the basis for an empirical examination of a long-standing issue in administrative law — whether combining prosecution and adjudication in the same agency contaminates adjudication.

I wish to express my gratitude to George J. Stigler for his many helpful suggestions. Helpful comments on previous drafts were also made by Gary S. Becker, Kenneth Culp Davis, Owen M. Fiss, Julius G. Getman, William M. Landes, Bernard D. Meltzer, and the participants in the Industrial Organization Workshop of the University of Chicago. The National Bureau of Economic Research provided financial support under a grant from the National Science Foundation for research in law and economics.

1. I use the term "administrative agency" broadly to include any law-enforcement agency whether or not independent of the executive branch of government. The model developed here, however, is limited to the prosecutorial activities of administrative agencies. Much of the analysis is applicable to conventional criminal law enforcement.

I. A MODEL OF THE BEHAVIOR OF ADMINISTRATIVE AGENCIES

A. THE SIMPLE MODEL

The agency's goal is assumed to be to maximize the utility of its law-enforcement activity. The utility (or more precisely expected utility) of an individual case is the public benefit, if prosecuted successfully, discounted (multiplied) by the probability of successful prosecution. Discounting is required in order to reflect the fact that a case is less worthwhile if, all other things being equal, there is a smaller chance of the agency's winning it.[2] For simplicity, the agency is assumed to bring only two types of cases (the cases within each type being homogeneous) and the number of cases of each type is fixed. Both assumptions are unrealistic but only the second has analytical significance and it will be relaxed later.

The agency maximizes expected utility by investing resources, mostly lawyers' time, in prosecuting violators. The effectiveness of its expenditures in enhancing the probability of successful prosecution and hence utility of a case depends significantly on how much money the defendant decides to spend in defending the case. Most simply,

$$p = \frac{c}{c + c'}, \tag{1}$$

where p is the probability of the agency's winning, c is the agency's litigation outlays, and c' the defendant's. If the defendant spends nothing on the litigation, the probability of the agency's winning becomes unity, even if the agency spends very little. If the agency spends nothing, the probability of its winning falls to zero. If both parties spend the same amount, the probability of the agency's winning is 50 per cent.

This formulation is too simple, because it assumes that outcome is a function solely of the ratio of the parties' litigation outlays. If the law is well settled in favor of the agency, or the agency a more efficient litigator

---

2. The bringing of unmeritorious cases imposes costs on innocent parties, comforts the guilty, and weakens the deterrent effect of the law. Merit is not a dichotomous property and is approximated by the probability of a successful outcome. The model could be altered to recognize that on occasion a case may have value for an agency even if it ends in defeat.

An earlier mathematical model of law enforcement from which I have borrowed is presented in William M. Landes, An Economic Analysis of the Courts, included in this volume. Compare Alan E. Friedman, Note, An Analysis of Settlement, 22 Stan. L. Rev. 67 (1969).

than the defendant, a smaller expenditure by the agency may have a greater impact on the outcome than a much larger expenditure by the defendant (or vice versa). Equation 1 should be restated as

$$p = e\left(\frac{c}{c + c'}\right),\qquad(2)$$

where e is some factor—it may be a fraction, or it may be larger than one —that measures the effectiveness of the agency's litigation outlays in influencing the outcome of a case in its favor.[3] If e were 1.5, it would follow that the agency had a 75 per cent chance of winning when both parties spent the same amount of money on the case. If e were 2, the agency would have a 67 per cent chance of winning even though the defendant spent twice as much as the agency. However, since p cannot be larger than 1,

$$e < \frac{c + c'}{c}.\qquad(3)$$

In deciding how much money to invest in each type of case, the agency cannot simply keep spending until a dollar of expenditure no longer increases expected utility by a dollar. It is limited to its appropriation from Congress. A budget constraint must therefore be added to the model.

Equations (4) and (5) summarize the model as thus far developed:

$$E(U) = a\,\frac{c_1 e_1}{c_1 + c_1'}\,s_1 + b\,\frac{c_2 e_2}{c_2 + c_2'}\,s_2;\qquad(4)$$

$$ac_1 + bc_2 = B.\qquad(5)$$

a and b are the number of cases of each type; B is the agency's budget; and s_1 and s_2 are the agency's gain, expressed in dollars,[4] from successful

---

3. A better formulation would probably be $p = (c/c + c')^e$. This would avoid the necessity for a restriction on e (other than $e > 0$) to prevent p from exceeding unity, and would permit the proportional impact of e on p to vary with changes in c and c'. James Meginniss has suggested an alternative formulation, $p = e^{c'/c}$, where e is the agency's probability of winning when $c = c'$, that also has desirable properties. Unfortunately, either formulation greatly increases the computational difficulties of the model, and the gain in realism would not appear to have substantial analytical significance (but see text following note 21, *infra*).

4. Although administrative proceedings rarely involve damages or any other readily quantifiable remedy, it is plausible to suppose that an agency ranks its cases, at least implicitly, in accordance with some rough estimate of the dollar equivalent, in public benefits conferred, of a successful prosecution.

prosecution. The budget constraint is expressed as an equation rather than an inequality in view of the notorious reluctance of government bodies to turn back unused funds to the Treasury.

Clearly, the agency's expenditure on a case is in part a function of how much the defendant spends, and the reverse must also be true—the defendant's expenditure is a function in part of the agency's expenditure. Before we can use equations (4) and (5) to find the agency's optimal expenditure on each case, we must know what the defendant is likely to spend. This requires that we construct a model like equation (5) but from the defendant's point of view.

Assume that, before the litigation, the defendant in a case of the second type had a certain wealth position, W. Litigation will produce one of two states of the world. If he wins, his wealth will be diminished only by his litigation expenses; if he loses, his wealth will be diminished by his stakes in the case as well. By discounting each state by the probability of its occurrence, we can express his wealth position after litigation (W') as follows:

$$W' = \frac{c_2' e_2'}{c_2' + c_2} (W - c_2') + \left(1 - \frac{c_2' e_2'}{c_2' + c_2}\right) (W - s_2' - c_2'). \qquad (6)$$

The first expression on the right-hand side of the equation $(c_2' e_2')/(c_2' + c_2)$ is the probability (p_2') that the defendant will win rather than the agency. It should be emphasized that e_2' (and therefore p_2') like e_2 (and therefore p_2) is a subjective term: it is the defendant's estimate of the effectiveness of his expenditures on the outcome of the suit. The parties may have inconsistent estimates. Indeed, as we shall see, without such differences there would be few litigated cases.

The defendant is assumed to operate without a budget constraint. Unlike the agency, he can hire additional legal resources until their marginal product falls to zero.

The reader may wonder why the stakes for the defendant, s_2', are distinguished from the stakes for the agency in the same case, s_2. The reason is that they may not be identical. A clear instance of asymmetry is presented by any monopoly case: the social costs of monopoly exceed the private benefits to the monopolizer.[5] To take another example, an

---

5. The monopolist who cannot discriminate perfectly in price maximizes profits by selling a smaller quantity at a higher price than under competition. His gain—the difference between the monopoly and the competitive price multiplied by the number of units sold—is also a loss to the purchasers of this output. Another loss, which the monopolist does not capture, is the loss to those consumers whom the higher, monopoly price deters from continuing to buy the monopolist's product, and who substitute other products that cost more, or are otherwise less desirable, than the monopolist's product when sold at a competitive price.

order forbidding the mailing of a type of advertising brochure found to be deceptive may be much more costly to a defendant who has already had the brochure printed than to a defendant who has not, yet the order against the second defendant is just as valuable to the agency as the order against the first. Furthermore, an order may have importance to an agency beyond any effect in abating the defendant's illegal conduct: as a precedent. Precedent has a dual significance. It makes it easier for the agency to win the next case (if a similar case), and it may deter others from engaging in like conduct. The dismissal of a case will lack comparable significance to the defendant unless he anticipates frequent future encounters with the agency.[6] Finally, since the benefits of administrative proceedings frequently cannot be quantified, the agency's implicit valuation of the fruits of a successful prosecution may differ substantially from the costs to the defendant.

The first derivative of W' with respect to c_2' is

$$\frac{dW'}{dc_2'} = \frac{c_2 s_2' e_2'}{(c_2' + c_2)^2} - 1.$$ (7)

By setting the derivative equal to zero and solving for c_2', we can discover how much money a defendant in our second type of case should spend in order to maximize his wealth. That expenditure is

$$c_2' = \sqrt{c_2 e_2' s_2'} - c_2,$$ (8)

which implies, not unrealistically, that if the defendant's stakes are relatively small, an increase in c_2 will induce him to reduce his expenditure on the case, while if they are relatively large, it will induce him to increase it.[7]

We may now return to equation (4) and determine the utility-maximizing expenditure of the agency on the same case. By substituting equation (8) into equation (4), solving equation (5) for c_1 and substituting the

---

6. Such asymmetry is not limited to public law enforcement. In accident litigation, for example, the usual defendants – insurance companies – have an interest in precedent that is not shared by the accident claimants. Some evidence on the significance of this asymmetry is presented in Richard A. Posner, A Theory of Negligence, 1 J. Leg. Studies 29, 94–96 (1972).

7. The rate of change of c_2' with respect to c_2 is

$$\frac{\partial c_2'}{\partial c_2} = \frac{\sqrt{e_2' s_2'}}{2\sqrt{c_2}} - 1.$$

This expression is negative (signifying that an increase in c_2 will cause a decrease in c_2') when s_2' is relatively small, and positive when it is relatively large.

result into equation (4), and simplifying, we can restate equation (4) as follows:

$$E(U) = \frac{\sqrt{a}e_1s_1\sqrt{B - bc_2}}{\sqrt{e_1's_1'}} + bs_2\left(\frac{c_2e_2}{\sqrt{c_2e_2's_2'}}\right). \tag{9}$$

The first derivative of $E(U)$ with respect to c_2 is

$$\frac{dE(U)}{dc_2} = \frac{bs_2e_2}{2\sqrt{c_2e_2's_2'}} - \frac{be_1s_1\sqrt{a}}{2\sqrt{e_1's_1'(B - bc_2)}}. \tag{10}$$

By setting the derivative equal to zero and solving for c_2 we discover that the expenditure by the agency on type 2 cases that maximizes the agency's utility is

$$c_2 = \frac{Bs_2^2e_2^2s_1'e_1'}{as_1^2e_1^2s_2'e_2' + bs_2^2e_2^2s_1'e_1'}. \tag{11}$$

An objection to this method of determining the agency's optimum expenditure is that while the agency, in deciding how much to spend on prosecuting a case, takes account of the fact that the defendant's expenditure is a function in part of how much the agency spends, the defendant takes the agency's expenditure as given—he does not consider how the agency might react to a change in his expenditure. The asymmetry is not entirely unrealistic. The position of the parties is asymmetrical. The agency is the moving party in the litigation and controls to a considerable extent its timing and scope. The agency presumably has greater experience with respect to the particular kind of litigation involved than a defendant who appears infrequently before it, although this disparity may be offset to the extent that there are private lawyers who specialize in litigation before the particular agency. Finally, the agency is a bureaucracy in which decisions and procedures presumably tend to be routinized. These factors make it somewhat plausible that the agency, in deciding what to spend on a case, will make a rough estimate of the defendant's likely expenditures (viewed in part as a function of its own expenditures) and the defendant will adjust to the level of the agency's expenditures. If the defendant were assumed to have the same reaction function as the agency's in the model, the optimum expenditure of both parties would be indeterminate.[8]

---

8. This indeterminacy resembles that encountered by attempts to determine an oligopolist's optimum price when he is assumed to act independently but to take account of his rivals' reactions to his price changes. See George J. Stigler, The Theory of Price 217–19 (3d ed. 1966), for a succinct discussion of the problem. An alternative approach to the

For understanding how changes in the characteristics of the agency's two types of cases alter the allocation of resources between them, the ratio between c_2 and c_1 is helpful:

$$\frac{c_2}{c_1} = \frac{s_2^2 e_2^2 s_1' e_1'}{s_1^2 e_1^2 s_2' e_2'}. \tag{12}$$

If B, a, and b are assumed to be constant any increase in c_2 must result in a decrease in c_1, and vice versa. If the agency's stakes (s_1 and s_2) are also held constant, then it is clear from equation (12) that c_2 will fall and c_1 rise if the effectiveness of the agency's expenditures falls in cases of the second type or rises in cases of the first type; if the effectiveness of defendants' expenditures falls in cases of the first type or rises in the second type; or if defendants' stakes rise in the second type of case or fall in the first type.

These factors are independent of the social benefits of successful prosecution of type 2 cases. Even if those benefits are great—let us henceforth assume that s_2 is much larger than s_1—they may be overwhelmed by other factors that a rational utility-maximizing agency must take into account. It is plausible, moreover, that e will be higher in a class of relatively minor violations and s_1' smaller in relation to s_1 than s_2' in relation to s_2. The explanation has to do with precedent. The public benefit from proceeding against a violation may be relatively small because the law is so well settled that the case will have little importance as precedent. Precisely because the law is well settled, however, the probability of successful prosecution, even without a large expenditure of resources, is probably high. The rational agency will be especially attracted to cases that have importance as precedent but in which the monetary stakes are small. The usual defendant is uninterested in whether the outcome of his case will have precedential significance. Since it would be surprising if the precedential significance of a case increased in proportion to the monetary stakes, s_1' is likely to be smaller relative to s_1 than s_2' to s_2.

A frequent criticism of administrative agencies is that they mis-

---

oligopoly problem, and one with some relevance in the present context, is to treat it as a problem of collusive rather than of independent action. See George J. Stigler, A Theory of Oligopoly, 72 J. Pol. Econ. 44 (1964), reprinted in George J. Stigler, The Organization of Industry 39 (1968); Richard A. Posner, Oligopoly and the Antitrust Laws: A Suggested Approach, 21 Stan. L. Rev. 1562 (1969). Like oligopolists, litigants can increase their wealth by agreeing to limit their rivalry, and specifically by agreeing to reduce their expenditures on litigation. Agreements to stipulate rather than litigate facts are a common example—but of this more later.

allocate their resources by bringing mostly small cases.[9] But our model suggests that under plausible assumptions concerning the characteristics of the agency's cases, a perfectly rational, utility-maximizing administrative agency will devote a "disproportionate" amount of its resources to relatively minor cases. Let s_1 and s_1' be $10, e_1 2, e_1' .9, s_2 and s_2' $40, e_2 1.5, e_2' 1, a 20, b 5, and B $50. Solving equation (11) for c_2, and (3) and (8) for c_1, c_2' and c_1', we discover that the agency should spend $3.36 on each case of the second type and $1.66 on each case of the first type. (The defendant's optimum expenditure is found to be $8.44 in a case of the second type and $2.14 in a case of the first type.) Although the aggregate social benefits from cases of each type (*i.e.*, as_1, bs_2) are equal — $200 — the agency devotes two-thirds of its resources to cases of the first type. And although each type 2 case involves four times the social benefits of each type 1 case, the agency spends only twice as much money litigating each case of the former type. This is optimizing behavior rather than a manifestation of stupidity or timidity. The agency's utility would be less if it allocated additional monies from its limited budget to the larger cases.

One factor inducing the agency to devote so many resources to cases of the first type is the higher rate of success in such cases that it anticipates. Another, and related, factor is defendants' relative pessimism about such cases (e_1'). A similar effect would also result if s_2' were higher than s_2, as our earlier analysis suggests it might well be.

Substituting the results of our numerical example into equation (2), we discover that the agency expects to win 87 per cent of its type 1 cases but only 43 per cent of its type 2 cases. The defendants' expectations are inconsistent with the agency's. To determine the objective probability of the agency's winning let us assume that the parties are equally good (or bad) estimators so that the true figure (p) is the mean of their predictions. Thus,

$$\dot{p}_1 = \frac{p_1 + 1 - p_1'}{2}, \qquad (13)$$

from which we can determine that the agency will win 68 per cent of its type 1 cases and 36 per cent of its type 2 cases.

Table 1 presents some additional numerical examples. The last column summarizes the example in the text.

9. See, *e.g.*, ABA Comm'n to Study the Federal Trade Commission, Report, p. 1 (Sept. 15, 1969); Commission on Organization of the Executive Branch of the Government (Hoover Commission), Appendix N, Task Force Report on Regulatory Commissions 119 (Jan. 1949); Philip Elman, Administrative Reform of the Federal Trade Commission, 59 Georgetown L.J. 777, 778 (1971).

TABLE 1
EXAMPLES OF DIFFERENT OPTIMUM EXPENDITURES

	Hypo-thetical 1	Hypo-thetical 2	Hypo-thetical 3	Hypo-thetical 4	Hypo-thetical 5	Hypo-thetical 6
			Independent Variables			
$s_1(\$)$	10	10	10	10	10	10
$s_1'(\$)$	10	10	10	10	10	10
e_1	1	1	2	2	2	2
e_1'	1	1	.9	.9	.9	.9
$s_2(\$)$	40	40	40	40	40	40
$s_2'(\$)$	40	80	50	50	40	40
e_2	1	1	1.7	1.7	1.8	1.5
e_2'	1	1	1.1	1.1	1.1	1
a	20	20	20	20	20	20
b	5	5	5	5	5	5
$B(\$)$	50	50	50	60	60	50
			Dependent Variables			
$c_2(\$)$	5.00	3.33	3.11	3.74	4.78	3.36
$c_2'(\$)$	9.15	13.01	9.97	10.61	9.37	8.44
$c_1(\$)$	1.25	1.67	1.72	2.07	1.81	1.66
$c_1'(\$)$	2.28	2.43	2.21	2.25	2.23	2.14
$ac_1(\$)$	25	33.73	34.45	41.30	36.10	33.20
$bc_2(\$)$	25	16.67	15.55	18.70	23.90	16.80
$p_2(\%)$	35	20	40	44	61	43
$p_1(\%)$	35	41	88	96	90	87
$\dot{p}_2(\%)$	35	20	28	31	44	36
$\dot{p}_1(\%)$	35	41	68	74	70	68

B. EMPIRICAL IMPLICATIONS AND ALTERNATIVE MODELS

Our model has several testable implications. Among them:

1. An agency will probably devote relatively greater resources, in the aggregate, to small cases (as measured by the stakes) than to large.
2. However, it will devote more resources to each large case than to each small one.
3. The dismissal rate will probably be different in different types of cases and lower in the larger cases.
4. The average dismissal rate across all classes of case need not tend toward 50 per cent and may well be lower.

Tables 2 and 3 use data relating to the Federal Trade Commission in a preliminary test of these implications. The results in Table 2, which shows how the FTC allocates its budget among its three classes of case (antitrust cases, deceptive-practice cases, and textile and fur cases), are consistent with the first and second implications. The FTC devotes about one-third as many resources to textile and fur cases as to all other labeling and advertising cases. And it devotes roughly as many resources to all advertising and labeling cases as it does to antitrust, although virtually everyone believes that the Commission's antitrust work involves potentially much greater social benefits than its efforts to prevent mislabeling and false advertising. The ratio of resources devoted to textile and fur cases to resources devoted to antitrust is particularly striking.[10] At the same time the Commission spends more than five times as many resources on the average antitrust case than on the average textile or fur case.

Textile and fur cases are brought under special statutes[11] that require little evidence to establish a violation. In addition, the stakes in such cases are typically small. In our terminology, s and s' (the agency's and the defendant's stakes, respectively) are low; e (the effectiveness of the agency's expenditures in procuring an outcome favorable to it) is high; and e' is low. All of these factors work to reduce c, the agency's optimum expenditure per case, while the high e and low e' make these cases, as a class, relatively more attractive to the agency (assuming it to be a rational utility maximizer) than cases in which the difficulties of establishing a violation are greater. This explains why the expenditure per textile and fur case is low but the aggregate expenditure on the class of these cases high relative to their importance.

Table 3, which compares the dismissal rate in the FTC's antitrust cases with the dismissal rate in all of its cases, supports the third and fourth empirical implications of our model. The dismissal rates in different classes of cases are different; they do not average out to 50 per cent; the

---

10. The ratio of big to little FTC cases is actually overstated in Table 2, since the antitrust category includes the minor provisions of the Robinson-Patman amendments to the Clayton Act, 15 U.S.C. §§ 13(c), (d), and (e) (1970). On the propensity of both the FTC and the Antitrust Division of the Department of Justice to emphasize minor violations, see Richard A. Posner, The Federal Trade Comission, 37 U. Chi. L. Rev. 47 (1969); Richard A. Posner, A Statistical Study of Antitrust Enforcement, 13 J. Law & Econ. 365 (1970). For some other evidence consistent with the implications of the model see id. at 381 (table 11), 382 (table 12); Table 8, infra.

11. Wool Products Labeling Act, 15 U.S.C. § 68 (1970); Fur Products Labeling Act, 15 U.S.C. § 69 (1970); Textile Fiber Products Identification Act, 15 U.S.C. § 70 (1970).

TABLE 2
FTC Budgetary Allocations [a] and Complaints

Period [b]	Antitrust				Deceptive Practices				Textiles and Furs			
	$000	%	Com-plaints	$000 ÷ Com-plaints	$000	%	Com-plaints	$000 ÷ Com-plaints	$000	%	Com-plaints	$000 ÷ Com-plaints
1962	4,003	.54			2,529	.34			882	.12		
1963	4,715	.54			3,009	.35			956	.11		
1964	5,508	.57	95		3,007	.31	126		1,073	.11	85	
1965	6,246	.58	26		3,373	.31	66		1,209	.11	69	
1966	5,937	.55	94		3,633	.34	48		1,272	.12	52	
1967	5,907	.53	24		4,010	.36	108		1,322	.12	89	
1968	5,922	.49			4,631	.38			1,508	.13		
1969	6,131	.48			4,974	.39			1,705	.13		
Total [c]	44,369	.53			29,166	.35			9,927	.12		
1964–67 Total [c]	23,598		239	98	14,023		351	40	4,876		295	17

SOURCES.—1962–1969 FTC Ann. Reps.; U.S. Presidents, Bureau of the Budget, Budget of the United States Government, Appendix fiscal yrs. 1966–1969.

[a] Investigation and litigation only.
[b] Fiscal years.
[c] Or average.

225

TABLE 3
DISMISSAL RATE—FEDERAL TRADE COMMISSION
(Contested Cases Only)

Period	Total Cases	Antitrust Cases [a] Only	Dismissed [b] (%)	Dismissed Antitrust Cases Only (%)
1938	60	4	.12	.25
1941	61	15	.28	.60
1943	32	6	.22	.53
1945	43	6	.21	.33
1946–47	70	7	.21	.43
1949–50	53	10	.17	.40
1951–52	62	3	.19	.33
1955–56	36	12	.19	.25
1959–60	58	7	.12	.29
1965	34	15	.29	.60
Total [c]	509	85	.20	.44

SOURCES.—Federal Trade Commission Decisions, vols. 27, 33, 37, 40, 42–43, 46, 48, 52, 56, 67–68.

[a] Excluding cases brought exclusively under one of the minor Robinson-Patman amendments to the Clayton Act. See note 10, *supra*.

[b] Significant total dismissals, as defined in text, *infra*, p. 240.

[c] Or average.

average is in fact much lower; and the higher dismissal rate is found in the class of larger cases.

Results from a single agency can hardly be considered conclusive; and the classification of cases employed in Tables 2 and 3 is crude. The tests can, however, be refined, and extended to other agencies.

The question arises whether alternative models of the administrative process might not explain the evidence equally well. I believe not. The model implicit in the standard criticism mentioned earlier (agencies spend too much money on small cases) is that administrative agencies are not competent utility maximizers. In that event, however, one would expect the agency either to dismiss a high proportion of cases or suffer reversal at the hands of reviewing courts in a high proportion of cases. In fact the FTC fares extremely well on judicial review.[12]

---

12. See Table 16, *infra*.

Another model characterizes the administrative agencies as tools of effective political groups.[13] An implication of this model that I have discussed elsewhere is that the FTC can be expected to bring a large number of questionable cases to harass the competitors of the firms or groups of firms that dominate the agency.[14] Such cases would rather often end in dismissal, either by the agency in anticipation of adverse court action or by a reviewing court. We would therefore expect—but we do not observe—a high dismissal or reversal rate.

C. The Model Made More Realistic

In this subpart, several severely unrealistic assumptions made in subpart A are progressively relaxed, and we ask what difference relaxing them makes to the predictions derived from the original model.

1. NUMBER OF CASES AS AN ADDITIONAL CHOICE VARIABLE

We assumed that the number of cases of each type brought by the agency was fixed, but in fact the agency, within the limits of its budget, can bring as many or as few of each type of case as it wants. Once we admit n as a choice variable along with c, we must further modify our original model to take account of the fact that the probability of an agency's winning its nth case will decline as n increases, other things being equal. Within any size class of cases, there will be some violations that can be detected and proved with relative ease and others that require much more investigative and litigative effort. Thus, the more cases in the class that the agency decides to bring, the more it will be forced to seek out cases that are more difficult to win with the same expenditure of resources.[15] Figure 1 illustrates this relationship. The area under the curve to the left of the broken line is the cumulative probability (as estimated by the agency) of winning n_1 cases, given equal expenditures per case. If this area is multiplied by s_1, the product is the agency's expected utility from bringing n_1 cases. If it brings more cases its expected utility will increase but at a declining rate.

---

13. See George J. Stigler, The Theory of Economic Regulation, 2 Bell J. Econ. & Management Sci. 3 (1971).

14. See Richard A. Posner, The Federal Trade Commission, *supra* note 10, at 70–71.

15. The negative slope of $p(n)$ is reinforced by two other factors. First, the more cases of a given type an agency brings, the larger will be the body of applicable precedents and this will tend to reduce uncertainty and so increase the proportion of cases that are settled (the determinants of settlement are discussed in detail later): contested cases will be scarcer. Second, bringing more cases is likely to increase the deterrent effect of the law. With the risk of being prosecuted greater, fewer violations will be committed and this will make it more difficult for the agency to find additional violations against which to proceed.

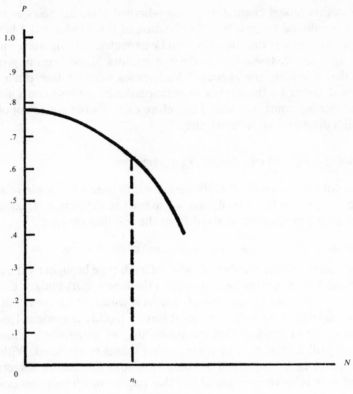

These new assumptions could be incorporated into a revised alge-braic formulation of the agency's utility function, but such a formulation turns out to be quite awkward to manipulate. For our purposes a graphic approach (Figure 2) is sufficient. Dollars, on the vertical axis, are plotted against number of cases on the horizontal axis. Cases of type 1 are to the left of the vertical axis and cases of type 2 to the right. Assume a new agency, groping its way to the optimum combination of c's and n's by a process of trial and error. It begins by selecting a point somewhere to the right of the vertical axis (it could just as well, however, have begun on the left side). That point $(c_2 n_2)$ determines both the number of cases of type 2 that the agency will bring and the expenditure it will make on each such case.[16] The choice of that point also constrains the selection of a

16. The assumption that the agency will spend the same amount of money on cases having different probabilities of success is somewhat arbitrary. Assume that the probability of the agency's winning the first case is .9 and of winning the nth case .6, and that an addi-

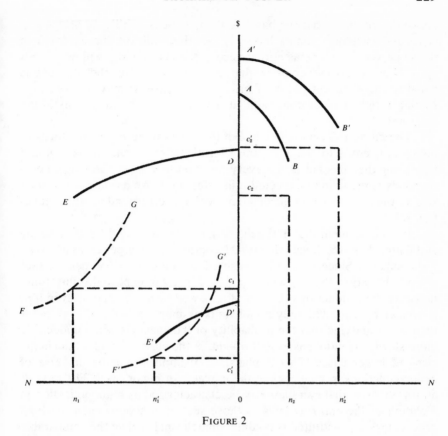

FIGURE 2

point on the left side of the diagram, since B is given and $c_1 n_1 = B - c_2 n_2$.

To every point on either side of the vertical axis, there corresponds a unique function, of the kind depicted in Figure 1 but now multiplied by s, that determines the expected utility of bringing a particular number of cases and spending a particular amount of money on each one. The expected-utility function for $c_2 n_2$ in the diagram is the curve AB. The area

---

tional expenditure of \$1 per case would increase these probabilities by .1. Assuming constant s, the \$1 increment will produce a larger gain in expected utility in the first case than in the second (.1 × .9s, or .09s, compared to .1 × .6s, or .06s). This would seem to suggest that the agency would be better off spending more of the increment on the first case and less on the nth. However, an additional expenditure on a case in which the agency's chances of winning are already high may increase those chances less than the same expenditure would increase the agency's chances in a case where those chances would otherwise be poor. At all events, Figure 2 could be modified to give the c's a negative slope, and the analysis would not be affected.

between that curve and the baseline is the expected utility of bringing n_2 cases and spending c_2 on each one. Notice that while the curve must lie in the same vertical plane as c_2n_2, it need not, and ordinarily will not, touch c_2n_2. There is no presumption that the expenditure on the nth case is equal to the expected utility of bringing that case. It may be lower; assuming a tight budget constraint, it may very well be higher (as in the diagram).

The curve FG on the left side of the diagram represents the locus of points c_1n_1 equal to $B - c_2n_2$, the sum of the rectilinear areas c_1n_1 and c_2n_2 being the constant B. To every point on that curve there again corresponds some unique expected-utility function. We assume the agency selects the c_1n_1 shown in the diagram, with its corresponding utility function DE.

It is no accident that in the diagram c_1 is below c_2 and DE both below and flatter than AB. Recall that type 2 comprises the larger cases and type 1 the smaller. Since c is an increasing function of s, c_2 will usually (not always) be larger than c_1 when $s_2 > s_1$. Since the expected-utility functions are the product of s times p, A may well be higher than E even if p_1 is greater than p_2. The only nonobvious assumption is that DE is flatter than AB, signifying that the probability of the agency's winning declines more slowly, as more cases are brought, in the class of smaller than in the class of larger cases. This is plausible. It implies that the universe of major violations is smaller than the universe of minor ones. The ratio of all transactions that can plausibly be characterized as monopolization in violation of the antitrust laws to those such transactions against which proceedings are instituted is doubtless much smaller than the comparable ratio for consumer frauds. If so, bringing an additional monopolization case (and spending no more money on it than was spent on the last such case) probably involves a larger drop in the probability of a successful outcome for the agency than would bringing an additional fraud case.

Figure 2 illustrates how, on these assumptions, the agency that takes a critic's advice to "reorder its priorities" by bringing more big cases and spending more money on each one may actually reduce its overall effectiveness. By moving to $c_2'n_2'$ [17] the agency increases its expected utility from bringing cases of type 2 to the area under the curve $A'B'$, but this reduces the resources it can devote to cases of type 1 to the locus of points on $F'G'$. Suppose $c_1'n_1'$ is the point that generates the largest expected utility (the area under the curve $D'E'$). Partly because the expected-utility functions for cases of class 1 are flatter than those for cases of class 2 the result of this reallocation of resources is to reduce

---

17. The prime marks here do not refer to defendants' expenditures.

the total expected utility of the agency (the area under $E'D'A'B'$ is smaller than the area under $EDAB$).

Relaxing the assumption that the number of cases of each type brought by the agency is fixed thus reinforces rather than undermines the implications of the primitive model. The analysis that underlies Figure 2 not only suggests why (as we have observed) the FTC brings many more small cases than large but also why it seems to devote excessive resources to small cases in the aggregate.

2. BUDGET AS AN ENDOGENOUS TERM

So far we have assumed that the agency's budget, or overall resources, is an exogenous variable, meaning that it is not affected by changes in the variables that the agency controls, the c's and n's. There is some evidence that administrative agency budgets do in fact contain a large exogenous element,[18] but they cannot be wholly exogenous. The agency that brought no cases or lost every case it brought would surely suffer a reduction in its budget.

To illustrate the consequences of abandoning the assumption that B is exogenous, let us assume that it tends to rise as the agency's work load rises (as discussed more fully later, discussion of work load in fact dominates congressional hearings on appropriations for administrative agencies) but to fall if the agency's batting average ($\dot{p}$) falls (otherwise an agency that wanted a larger budget would bring cases without regard to their merit). The agency and the appropriating body are also interested, presumably, in s, but this does not affect the analysis.

This model has the same implications as Figure 2. As in Figure 2, the agency has an incentive to increase n but this incentive is held in check by the negative impact on p of a higher n if the slope of $p(n)$ is steep. Thus, that slope, which I have suggested provides additional reason for expecting an agency to concentrate major resources on small cases, remains a vital element in the agency's utility function.

3. SETTLEMENTS

Our original model excluded the possibility of a settlement without trial. Not only is this unrealistic, but it invites the objection that the predictions of the primitive model may be incorrect. If, for example, large cases are

---

18. This is strikingly shown in a study by George J. Stigler, who found that changes in agency budgets are much more closely correlated with each other than with differences in the size or rate of growth of the respective industries regulated. George J. Stigler, The Process of Economic Regulation, 17 Antitrust Bull. 207, 218 (1972).

more apt to be settled than small, this would imply that the former are relatively cheap to prosecute, and a rational utility-maximizing agency will therefore allocate greater resources to large cases than the primitive model predicted. We must consider the conditions under which a case will be tried rather than settled.

The minimum offer that a rational plaintiff will accept in settlement of his claim is his expected gain from litigation minus his litigation expenses (which would reduce his net gain from suit) plus the costs of negotiating the settlement. The maximum offer that the defendant will tender is what he expects to owe the plaintiff after the litigation (the stakes to the defendant discounted by the probability, in the defendant's eyes, of the plaintiff's winning) plus his litigation expenses (which he would lose anyway) minus his settlement costs. For a settlement to take place, the plaintiff's minimum settlement price must not exceed the maximum that the defendant is willing to pay. If it is larger there will be no settlement. I assume that settlement cost is some fraction of each party's litigation costs—the same fraction.

The condition for litigation may therefore be expressed as follows:

$$\frac{ces}{c + c'} - c + \frac{c}{k} > s' \left(1 - \frac{e'c'}{c' + c}\right) + c' - \frac{c'}{k}, \tag{14}$$

which simplified (with the help of equation (8)) becomes

$$e > \frac{s'}{s} \left[\sqrt{\frac{e's'}{c}} \, (1 - e') + e' \left(2 - \frac{1}{k}\right)\right]. \tag{15}$$

The larger the ratio of s' to s the likelier a settlement. (The intuitive explanation is that the prospect of a large loss induces the defendant to make an offer that the agency, with the prospect of a relatively small gain from litigation, finds attractive.) And for reasons explained earlier that ratio may be larger in big cases than in small. Notice, however, that when $e' > 1$, the same percentage increase in s and s' will *reduce* the likelihood of settlement by making the first term in brackets a larger negative number.

An increase in settlement costs relative to litigation costs (falling k) reduces the right-hand side of inequality (15): litigation becomes more likely.[19] An increase in e' (the effectiveness of the defendant's litigation outlays) produces a more complex effect, but in general the decline in the first term in brackets will exceed the rise in the second term. However, it is unrealistic to assume that if e' rises e will remain unchanged, for

---

19. For some evidence of this effect see Richard A. Posner, *supra* note 6, at 94–96.

whatever causes the defendant to revise his chances upward should cause the agency to revise its chances downward. We can investigate this possibility by assuming that the sum of the parties' estimates of their chances of prevailing is a constant $((ec)/(c + c') + (e'c')/(c + c') = r)$, so that any increase in e' must be offset by a decrease in e. As shown in the appendix at the end of this article, in the special case where $r = 1$, $k > 1$ (settlement costs are lower than litigation costs), and $s' = s$, there will always be a settlement, whether e' rises or falls. Intuitively, when the parties' estimates sum to 100 per cent, it means that they agree on the outcome, so a settlement can readily be negotiated.[20]

The more interesting case is where $r > 1$. Assuming that k is large and $s' = s$, the condition for litigation is (approximately)

$$\sqrt{e'} < \sqrt{\frac{s}{c}}\,(r - 1). \tag{16}$$

This would seem to indicate that litigation becomes more likely as e' decreases and less likely as it increases. But this is misleading. A decrease in e' and increase in e will produce an increase in c (equation (11)): thus the right-hand side of the inequality will also decrease. What *is* clear is that an increase in r, which measures the divergence of the parties' predictions of success, will increase the likelihood of litigation. An increase in the stakes (s) will also increase the likelihood of litigation—a prediction that has some empirical support.[21]

Thus far we have assumed that the effectiveness of a dollar expended in litigation (e) is a constant that is unaffected by the number of dollars expended, which is unrealistic. In particular, there is probably a threshold below which expenditures on litigation have no, or negligible, effectiveness. If the defendant's threshold expenditure is larger than his stakes in the case, he will not contest the agency's case and the case will be classified as a settlement. To be sure, assuming that the agency has the same threshold, it will not be able to make a credible threat of suing in order to induce the defendant not to contest unless the agency's stakes (unlike the defendant's) exceed the threshold. But since s may be larger than s',

---

20. Assuming (as incidentally I do throughout the paper) that neither party is a risk preferrer. The relevance of attitude toward risk to the likelihood of settlement is discussed in William M. Landes, p. 171.

21. The FTC settles small cases more frequently than large. (Compare Tables 3 *supra* and 12 *infra* with Table A3 in the appendix.) But this could be because the outcome of antitrust cases—the large cases, in our statistics—is less predictable than that of deceptive-practices cases (the small cases in our statistics): the r may be greater.

there will be cases where this condition is fulfilled. These will be small cases, since the threshold litigation expenditure must exceed s'. Here is then another reason for expecting settlements to include a disproportionately large number of *small* cases, consistently with the predictions of the primitive model.

If we solve inequality (15), using the values in our earlier numerical example and assigning a value of 5 to k (signifying that the costs of settlement are one-fifth of the costs of trial) we find that type 1 cases will not be settled. This is not because the parties have different stakes (s_1 and s_1' are the same) but because they disagree sharply about the outcome. The agency estimates the probability of its winning at 87 per cent, while defendants estimate the agency's probability of winning at only 51 per cent. In cases of the second type, where the spread is smaller (the agency estimates its probability of winning at 43 per cent and the defendant estimates the agency's probability of winning at 28 per cent) the parties do settle. Although arbitrary, the numerical example suggests roughly how great a difference there must be between the parties' estimates of probability, given moderate settlement costs and equal stakes, for litigation to occur. Additional examples (again with $k = 5$) are presented in Table 4.

In the numerical example, the larger difference in the parties' estimates of their chances of success was in the smaller case but this is an accident of the numbers. On the one hand, prediction is more difficult the more complex a case is, and complexity is in part a function of size (though even more of novelty). On the other hand, the greater legal resources deployed in the larger case may result in narrowing the area of uncertainty about the outcome.

Our discussion of settlements assumes that the parties cooperate to maximize their joint utility. Our discussion of litigation assumed that

TABLE 4

SETTLED VS. LITIGATED CASES

	Hypo-thetical 1	Hypo-thetical 2	Hypo-thetical 3	Hypo-thetical 4	Hypo-thetical 5	Hypo-thetical 6
Case type 1	S	S	L	L	L	L
Case type 2	S	S	S	S	L	S

SOURCE. – Table 1.

they make independent, noncooperating decisions on their litigation outlays, even though, by agreeing to reduce those outlays, both would be made better off. The dichotomy corresponds at least to casual observation of the operation of the legal system. In a very large class of cases the parties agree to settle in advance of trial and thereby avoid all costs of trial. In cases that are tried, the parties frequently do stipulate to many of the facts essential to the proceeding in order to avoid the costs of having to establish the facts by testimony in court, but such side agreements appear to be less common than settlements and to avoid a smaller proportion of the total costs of going to law. Possibly the transaction costs involved in agreements to curtail the trial process are relatively high, especially since the cases that are not settled—a minority of all cases—are by definition those in which an effort at a meeting of the minds failed. In general, then, a model of cooperative decision making seems more appropriate in the settlement context, and a model of independent decision making more appropriate in the litigation context.

II. DOES COMBINING PROSECUTION AND ADJUDICATION IN THE SAME AGENCY CONTAMINATE ADJUDICATION?

A. THE ELMAN THESIS

An old debate in administrative law—over whether the combination of prosecution and adjudication in a single agency contaminates adjudication[22]—has recently been revived by Philip Elman, a distinguished former member of the Federal Trade Commission. In a recent article, he points to several specific characteristics of an administrative agency that make the combination of these functions likely, in his judgment, to create unfairness:

1. A high rate of dismissals is a confession of ineptitude on the part of the members of the agency, who authorized the bringing of the cases in the first place.
2. It is a rebuff to the staff that investigated and prosecuted the case

---

22. I use "combination of functions" to mean that an agency initiates the cases that it decides, not that members of the Commission participate in the actual prosecution or that members of the prosecutorial staff participate (other than through briefs and oral argument) in the decision. The latter forms of combination have long been considered highly improper, and to my knowledge have never characterized the agencies I shall be discussing.

on the agency's behalf—a staff on which the members of the agency depend.

3. It encourages noncompliance with the statute that they are committed to enforcing.[23]

Although plausible, this reasoning is hardly compelling. It can equally well be argued that an agency will be motivated to review contested cases scrupulously in order to keep the staff on its toes and minimize the likelihood of reversal by a reviewing court. Furthermore, if it is true that an agency measures its success by the number of cease and desist orders entered, it will refuse to dismiss complaints regardless of whether it, its delegate, or a complete outsider brought the case initially.

Nor can we resolve doubt in favor of Professor Elman's position on the ground that it is implicitly based on his extensive personal observation as a member of the Trade Commission. What he observed is that Commission members frequently lack the fair-mindedness expected of judges; and this bears hardly at all on the issue under discussion. Are Federal Trade Commissioners more biased than the average judge? Would they be less biased if they sat on a court rather than on the Commission or if their authority over the issuance of complaints were removed?

B. TESTABLE IMPLICATIONS OF THE ELMAN THESIS

The Elman thesis has several testable implications:

1. An agency in which prosecution and adjudication are separated will dismiss a higher fraction of the cases it decides than one in which these functions are united, other things being equal.

2. When an agency in which these functions are combined does dismiss a complaint, it will tend to do so in a manner that avoids an acknowledgment that the agency erred in initially authorizing the complaint.

3. Such an agency will be more reluctant to dismiss a case in which the issues are primarily factual than one in which the issues are primarily legal.

4. It will be more reluctant to dismiss a big case—big in terms of the amount of agency resources invested in it—than a small one.

5. It will be more reluctant to dismiss a complaint that the current

---

23. See Philip Elman, *supra* note 9, at 810. To similar effect see Richard A. Posner, The Federal Trade Commission, *supra* note 10, at 53.

members of the agency authorized than one authorized by their predecessors.

6. The decrees of an agency in which the functions are combined will be reversed more frequently on judicial review than those of an agency in which the functions are separated.

7. In congressional hearings on an agency's appropriation requests, and in other scrutinies of the agency's performance, the agency's dismissal rate will receive greater emphasis than its rate of reversal on judicial review if prosecution and adjudication are combined in the agency.

These hypotheses can be explored using data from the major federal administrative agencies concerned primarily with the prosecution of law violators—the Federal Trade Commission and the National Labor Relations Board. The Commission has never relaxed its authority over the issuance of complaints. The Labor Board's authority, in contrast, has progressively diminished.[24] Prior to October 1942 all complaints had to be formally approved by the Board. Beginning with that date the Board's Regional Directors were authorized to issue complaints without first notifying the Board or obtaining its approval, unless a novel question of fact or law was presented, and in the first year of operation under the new system 70 per cent of all complaints were issued without a reference to the Board.[25] The Taft-Hartley Act in 1947 carried separation one step further by making the General Counsel of the Board a presidential appointee rather than an employee of the Board and by giving him exclusive authority over the issuance of complaints.[26] This sequence affords interesting opportunities for comparison among different periods of the Labor Board as well as between Board and Commission.

C. THE EMPIRICAL EVIDENCE

1. Elman implies that any bias created by the combination of prosecution and adjudication will show up in a reduced dismissal rate. Our original model supports this view. Substituting equation (8) (defendant's optimum litigation outlay) into equation (13) (the true probability of the agency's winning), and rearranging some terms, we have

---

24. See U.S. Atty. Gen.'s Committee on Administrative Procedure, Administrative Procedure in Government Agencies, S. Doc. No. 8, 77th Cong., 1st Sess. 22–23 (1941); 3 NLRB Ann. Rep. 5 (1938); Ida Klaus, The Taft-Hartley Experiment in Separation of NLRB Functions, 11 Indus. & Lab. Rel. Rev. 371, 372–74 (1958).

25. See 7 NLRB Ann. Rep. 12, n.5 (1942); 8 NLRB Ann. Rep. 13 (1943).

26. See § 2(d) of the National Labor Relations Act, 29 U.S.C. § 153(d) (1970).

$$\dot{p} = \frac{\sqrt{c}}{2\sqrt{s'}} \left(\frac{e + e'}{\sqrt{e'}} \right) + \frac{1 - e'}{2}. \tag{17}$$

The effect of introducing bias in the agency's favor is to increase e and decrease e', making both terms on the right-hand side of the equation larger.

In the more complex model illustrated in Figure 2, the effect on the dismissal rate of an increase in e and a corresponding decrease in e' is not so easy to predict. Typically the immediate consequence will be to shift all of the expected-utility functions upward. If each increases equally and c_1n_1 and c_2n_2 were optimum points before the shift, the agency has no reason to move to different points and p_1 and p_2 (and therefore $\dot{p}_1$ and $\dot{p}_2$) will increase (the dismissal rate will fall). But a change in e and e' could well affect different utility functions differently. In that event the agency might alter its cn points and the new points might involve a larger n and a lower probability of success in the nth case than before the shift. Still, an increase in e accompanied by a decrease in e' will ordinarily reduce the agency's dismissal rate, for the increase in the agency's overall dismissal rate due to bringing some additional cases is unlikely to equal or exceed the decrease in that rate due to a higher e and lower e' in *all* of its cases.

One effect of a declining e' that we do *not* predict is a change in the settlement rate. Any bias introduced by combination of functions would presumably be perceived by both parties roughly equally: the r of inequality (16) would not change.

Table 5 presents dismissal rates for more than 1,100 NLRB unfair labor practice cases and FTC cases, drawn from randomly selected volumes of the agencies' official decisions for various periods since 1938.[27] It reveals that the Commission's dismissal rate has in general been a good deal higher than the Board's both before and after 1947, while the Board's has actually decreased since the creation of the independent General Counsel. Little significance, however, can be ascribed to these

---

27. Decisions are published in these volumes in the chronological order in which they were issued. While a volume of NLRB decisions ordinarily covers no more than two months, an FTC volume will usually cover an entire year's decisions. My procedure was first to select volumes of NLRB decisions at random from various periods, concentrating on the years immediately before and immediately after a change in the Board's structure with respect to separation of functions, and then to select the contemporaneous FTC volume. I omitted the very early years of the Board's decisions on the ground that its early experience might be unrepresentative; however, some evidence on the earliest period is presented in Tables 8 and 11 and note 34, *infra*. I omitted 1969 in the case of the FTC because its decisions for that year had not yet appeared in a printed volume and because it decided very few cases that year.

TABLE 5

DISMISSAL RATE

Agency	Period	Total Cases Con- tested	Cease and Desist Order Entered	Com- plaint Dis- missed in Part or Whole	Com- plaint Dis- missed in Its Entirety	% Dis- missed in Part or Whole	% Dis- missed in Whole
NLRB	1938	33	28	25	5	.76	.15
	1941	18	17	8	1	.44	.06
	1943	26	20	16	6	.62	.23
	1945	16	12	7	4	.44	.25
	1946	27	21	15	6	.56	.22
	1947	20	15	11	5	.55	.25
	Total [a]	140	113	82	27	.59	.19
FTC	1938	60	43	26	16	.43	.27
	1941	61	39	31	22	.51	.36
	1943	32	19	14	13	.44	.41
	1945	43	26	23	17	.53	.40
	1946–47	70	21	56	49	.80	.70
	Total [a]	266	148	150	117	.56	.44
NLRB	1949	38	27	30	11	.79	.29
	1950	52	43	24	9	.46	.17
	1951	57	48	33	9	.58	.16
	1956	57	48	35	9	.61	.16
	1960	105	83	55	22	.52	.21
	1965	103	90	28	13	.27	.13
	1969	70	54	35	16	.50	.23
	Total [a]	482	393	240	89	.50	.18
FTC [b]	1949–50	53	24	38	29	.72	.55
	1951–52	62	41	37	21	.60	.34
	1955–56	36	28	13	8	.36	.22
	1959–60	58	39	36	19	.62	.33
	1965	34	19	18	15	.53	.44
	Total [a]	243	151	141	92	.58	.38

SOURCES. – Decisions and Orders of the National Labor Relations Board, vols. 8, 35, 51, 60, 69, 72, 87, 91, 95, 115, 127, 153, 178; Federal Trade Commission Decisions, vols. 27, 33, 37, 40, 42–43, 46, 48, 52, 56, 67–68.

[a] Or average.

[b] Exclusion of 1969 FTC cases, in this and subsequent tables, is explained in note 27, *supra*.

findings. Table 1 counts as a dismissal any case in which, and for whatever reason, any part of the complaint was dismissed.[28] Many are unimportant partial dismissals. And complaints are frequently dismissed in circumstances where the outcome seems better characterized as a victory for the agency than as a victory for the defendant, such as where the defendant has discontinued the unlawful practice in circumstances where resumption seems highly unlikely.

Table 6 organizes the dismissal data in a more discriminating manner. Dismissals that, for the reasons just stated, are not really significant are excluded. According to Table 6 the NLRB's dismissal rate is approximately the same in the period before and in the period after 1947. If partial dismissals are included the FTC's dismissal rate is lower than the Board's in both periods. If partial dismissals are excluded the Commission's dismissal rate is very slightly higher than the Board's in both periods.

Although the relative dismissal rates of the Labor Board and the Trade Commission do not support the Elman position, neither do they refute it, since p (and hence $1 - p$, the dismissal rate) is, as we know from our model, influenced by variables whose values cannot be assumed to be the same in two so dissimilar agencies as the Labor Board and the Trade Commission.[29] But even if they cannot be used for direct comparison of the agencies, Tables 5 and 6 illuminate our question in two respects.

First, a good deal of the sense that administrative adjudication is biased against defendants may stem from a reaction to the low dismissal rates that characterize administrative adjudication. Instinctively we may think that in a "fair" system of adjudication the dismissal rate would tend toward 50 per cent. Our model of the behavior of administrative agencies shows, however, that a perfectly fair agency might nonetheless dismiss far fewer than 50 per cent of its cases. Tables 5 and 6 reinforce the impression that this is a general feature of administrative adjudication, rather than a distinctive attribute of agencies that have specific sources of contamination such as combination of functions.

---

28. A case in which there was a partial dismissal is counted twice — once in the order column and once in the dismissal column.

29. For this reason I have relegated to the appendix at the end of this article a table that compares the dismissal rate in contested cases brought by the Antitrust Division of the Department of Justice and in contested antitrust cases brought by the FTC — the area of overlap between the jurisdictions of the two agencies. Table A1 shows, for what it is worth, that an antitrust defendant is as likely to convince the Commission to dismiss the complaint against him as he is to convince a court to dismiss a similar complaint brought by the Department, although the functions of prosecution and adjudication are completely separate in antitrust litigation initiated by the Department.

TABLE 6
DISMISSAL RATE – SIGNIFICANT [a] DISMISSALS ONLY

Agency	Period	Total Contested Cases	Significant Dismissals	Significant Total Dismissals Only	% Dismissed	% Dismissed in Entirety
NLRB	1938	33	15	5	.45	.15
	1941	18	4	1	.22	.06
	1943	26	14	6	.54	.23
	1945	16	5	4	.31	.25
	1946	27	11	6	.41	.22
	1947	20	10	5	.50	.25
	Total [b]	140	59	27	.42	.19
FTC	1938	60	12	7	.20	.12
	1941	61	17	17	.28	.28
	1943	32	8	7	.25	.22
	1945	43	11	9	.26	.21
	1946–47	70	18	15	.26	.21
	Total [b]	266	66	55	.25	.21
NLRB	1949	38	26	11	.68	.29
	1950	52	15	9	.29	.17
	1951	57	26	9	.46	.16
	1956	57	30	9	.53	.16
	1960	105	48	22	.46	.21
	1965	103	21	12	.20	.12
	1969	70	29	16	.41	.23
	Total [b]	482	195	88	.40	.18
FTC	1949–50	53	11	9	.21	.17
	1951–52	62	15	12	.24	.19
	1955–56	36	10	7	.28	.19
	1959–60	58	21	7	.36	.12
	1965	34	12	10	.35	.29
	Total [b]	243	69	45	.28	.19

SOURCES. – See Table 5, *supra.*
[a] As defined in text.
[b] Or average.

Second, it may be relevant that the disparity between dismissals and significant dismissals should be so much greater for the Commission than for the Board (indeed, virtually all total dismissals by the Board are significant in my sense of that term). The reason for the disparity is simply that it is not the Board's practice formally to dismiss a complaint when the defendant has discontinued the unlawful practice and resumption is unlikely—the usual ground of "nonsignificant" dismissal of a complaint in its entirety by the Commission. This procedural difference between the agencies is trivial but it is the opposite of what one would expect if Elman were correct, given that it is the Commission, not the Board, that issues as well as adjudicates complaints. Were the Commission highly sensitive to criticisms that dismissal of a complaint was an acknowledgment that the taxpayer's money had been wasted in bringing the case, it would seek wherever possible to avoid characterizing its action in closing a case as a dismissal. The Commission need not issue and print in its official decisions a formal order dismissing the complaint in every case where it finds entry of a formal order to cease and desist to be unnecessary.

Tables 5 and 6 allow a comparison among the several stages of the separation of functions at the Board. Table 7 summarizes the dismissal rates for each of the stages—before 1942, between 1943 and 1947, and since 1947.

The dismissal rate is higher in the two later periods, when prosecution and adjudication were separated, than in the first period, when they were not. This is consistent with Elman's thesis. The dismissal rate in the most recent period, that of formal separation, is lower than in the previous period, that of limited delegation to the Board's staff of authority to issue complaints; this is inconsistent with the thesis. The significance of

TABLE 7
DISMISSAL RATE—SIGNIFICANT [a] DISMISSALS (NLRB)

Period	Total Contested Cases	Significant Dismissals	Significant Total Dismissals Only	% Dismissed	% Dismissed in Entirety
1938–41	51	19	6	.37	.12
1943–47	89	40	21	.45	.24
1949–69	482	195	88	.40	.18

SOURCE.—Table 5, *supra*.
[a] As defined in text.

these findings, however, is impaired by the limitations of our sample. The volumes of the official decisions of the Board from which it was drawn underrepresent the number of dismissals because they omit dismissals by hearing examiners that are not appealed to the Board. We can correct for this omission and also obtain complete statistics of the Board's actions rather than statistics based upon a sample by rearranging certain statistics in the Board's annual reports.[30] Table 8 presents the results of these manipulations. Also, by being limited to unfair labor practices committed by employers, Table 8 corrects for the principal modifications in the law administered by the Labor Board that were made by the Taft-Hartley Act.[31]

Table 8 overrepresents the number of contested orders entered against defendants by including cases in which the defendant filed exceptions to the trial examiner's recommended decision but did not file a brief—a course of action inconsistent with a serious effort to overturn the examiner's decision. (Such cases were omitted from the count of contested cases in the earlier tables.) At all events, there are marked disparities between the results in the previous tables and the results in Table 8. In particular, Table 8 indicates a substantial increase in the dismissal rate, however computed, after 1947. But this may not have been the result of separation of functions. The model developed in Part I of this

---

30. The FTC volumes, in contrast, record all dismissals; and a single volume covers a much longer period in the Commission's decisional process, thus reducing sampling error. All of the periods shown in Tables 5 and 6 of FTC decisions are a full 12 months, with the following exceptions: 1938 (seven months), 1941 (five months), 1943 and 1945 (six months each) and 1946–1947 (18 months).

31. Two related tables are printed in the appendix. Table A2 presents dismissals and withdrawals (often a charge is withdrawn because the Board's staff advises that it will not recommend a complaint) of charges, prior to formal issuance of a complaint, as percentages of total charges pending on the Board's docket. The table is relevant to the possible contention that a higher dismissal rate as a result of separating the prosecutorial and adjudicative functions might manifest itself at the precomplaint stage. Although Table A2 does reveal a rising precomplaint dismissal-withdrawal rate over time, the rate actually fell in the years immediately following the formal separation effected by the Taft-Hartley Act in 1947. A possible explanation for the secular rise in the rate—that a rising proportion of charges is being filed by individuals rather than unions and the proportion of meritorious claims is typically higher among union-initiated than among individually initiated charges—is explored with negative results in Table A2.

Table A3 shows the FTC's dismissal rate as a percentage of all cases, and of all dispositions including informal settlements, to permit comparison with Table 8—although, for reasons noted earlier, a direct comparison between the two agencies is extremely difficult. The caption "stipulations" in Table A3 refers to the only mode of informal settlement for which statistics are regularly reported. Stipulations were discontinued in the early 1960s.

TABLE 8

DISPOSITION OF NLRB EMPLOYER UNFAIR LABOR PRACTICE CASES

Period	Settled Informally	Abandoned [a]	Total	Decided by Board					Dismissed and Abandoned as % of All Dispositions
				Contested	% Contested	Dismissed [b]	% Dismissed	% Contested Cases Dismissed	
1935–36	277	3	65	65	1.00	9	.14	.14	.035
1936–37	1,144	3	55	49	.89	10	.18	.20	.011
1937–38	2,960	39	197	164	.83	6	.03	.04	.014
1938–39	2,072	45	416	241	.58	37	.09	.15	.032
1939–40	1,877	29	550	392	.71	73	.13	.19	.042
1940–41	2,161	17	351	222	.63	43	.12	.19	.024
Total [c]	10,491	136	1,634	1,133	.69	178	.11	.16	.026
1943–44	666	16	230	139	.60	18	.08	.13	.037
1944–45	504	18	200	129	.65	12	.06	.09	.041
1945–46	594	24	262	193	.74	27	.10	.14	.057
1946–47	845	36	211	143	.68	19	.09	.13	.050
Total [c]	2,609	94	903	604	.67	76	.08	.13	.047
1948–49	828	36	217	111	.51	22	.10	.20	.054
1949–50	1,159	29	283	183	.65	37	.13	.20	.045
1950–51	878	44	467	321	.69	57	.12	.18	.075
1951–52	842	26	423	302	.71	71	.17	.24	.067
Total [c]	3,707	135	1,390	917	.66	187	.13	.23	.062
1955–56	428	23	250	202	.81	35	.14	.17	.083
1959–60	1,231	120	907	602	.66	111	.12	.18	.102
1961–62	1,661	123	1,021	817	.80	155	.15	.19	.099
1965–66	2,772	126	780	569	.73	111	.14	.20	.064
1968–69	2,818	149	811	611	.75	171	.21	.28	.085
Total [c]	8,910	541	3,769	2,801	.74	583	.15	.21	.085

SOURCE: 1–6, 9–12, 14–17, 21, 25, 27, 31, 34 NLRB Ann. Reps.
[a] As defined in text.

article predicts a positive correlation between agency resources and number of cases brought. A budget increase might produce an increase in dismissal rate if the change in the number of cases was large in relation to the resource change — if in other words the new resources went mostly to increasing n rather than to increasing c (and hence p). This may be the explanation of the post-1947 increase in the dismissal rate.

A simple index of changes in the Board's resources during the four periods covered by Table 8 can be constructed by first distributing the Board's employees (by means of a simple weighting factor [32]) between its unfair labor practice business and its other business during the period, and then dividing the number of employees thus allocated to unfair labor practices enforcement in each period by the number of unfair labor practice charges lodged with the Board during that period. Table 9 translates the resulting quotients into an index in which the agency's resources in the first period, 1935–41, equals 100.

Table 9 reveals that the agency's resources for dealing with unfair labor practices declined slightly in the period 1943–47 as compared with the prior period and that this decline was attended by a sharp drop in the number of contested cases and in the dismissal rate. In the next period the agency's resources increased, but the number of contested cases increased even more, and the dismissal rate rose. In the latest period, when both resources and the dismissal rate have fallen, the number of contested cases increases so markedly as to suggest a profound change either in the agency's productivity or in the character of its unfair labor practice cases.

According to Table 9, the Board actually expended fewer resources per case in the period 1948–52 than in the previous period — which, quite apart from the higher n, would lead us to predict an increase in the dismissal rate. Figure 3 shows how a reduction in c combined with an even

---

32. The business of the Board consists primarily of two types of cases — unfair labor practice cases and representation cases. Representation cases apparently consume, on average, somewhere between 20 and 40 per cent of the agency resources required by the average unfair labor practice case. See Labor-Federal Security Appropriations Bill for 1948, Hearings before the Subcomm. of the S. Comm. on Appropriations, 80th Cong., 1st Sess. 866 (1947); Departments of Labor and Health, Education, and Welfare Appropriations for 1968, Hearings before a Subcomm. of the H. Comm. on Appropriations, 90th Cong., 1st Sess., pt. 1 at 835 (1967); Departments of Labor, and Health, Education, and Welfare Appropriations for Fiscal Year 1969, Hearings before the Subcomm. of the H. Comm. on Appropriations, 90th Cong., 2d Sess. 481 (1968). I equated representation to unfair labor practice cases at the rate of 3.5 representation cases to one unfair labor practice case. A problem was created by a third class of Board cases, union-authorization cases, which bulked large in the Board's activity in the third period covered by Table 8. I used two exchange rates — 3.5 and 4 — producing the range shown in the table.

greater increase in n (possible because B has increased) could increase the agency's expected utility while reducing the average probability of its winning the cases that it brings.

2. If Elman's thesis is correct, an agency in which prosecution and adjudication are joined should be sensitive to possible criticism of a dismissal as an acknowledgment that the agency erred at the complaint-issuance stage. If so, we would expect such an agency, when it does dismiss a complaint, frequently to do so without acknowledging failure to establish a violation. It may feel compelled to dismiss a complaint that cannot possibly withstand judicial review but it need not cast its dismissal in the form of a potentially damaging admission. A dismissal in which there is no acknowledgment that a violation was not established will be called a "grudging" dismissal.

I have found no grudging dismissals among the decisions of the Board. Table 10, which compares ungrudging with significant dismissals by the FTC, suggests that the grudging dismissal is an important feature of the Commission's decision-making process. That many dismissals of FTC cases, and none of NLRB cases, are grudging may appear to con-

TABLE 9

RESOURCE CONSTRAINT AND DISMISSAL RATE—NLRB UNFAIR
LABOR PRACTICE CASES

Period	Index of Available Resources (1)	Index of Number of Contested Cases (2)	Index (1) ÷ Index (2)	% of Contested Cases Dismissed
1935–41	100	100	1.00	.16
1943–47	97	80	1.21	.13
1948–52	102–107	121	.84–.88	.23
1955–69 [a]	87	296	.29	.21

SOURCES. — See Table 8, *supra;* also U.S. Presidents, Bureau of the Budget, Budget of the United States Government, fiscal yrs. 1935–1969; Hearings before the Subcomm. of the Senate and House Comms. on Appropriations on NLRB appropriations for fiscal yrs. 1935–1969 (earlier hearings are included with the Independent Offices Appropriations Bill hearings from the 77th Cong., 2d Sess. (fiscal yr. 1943) and later are included with the Department of Labor Appropriations Bill hearings).

[a] The years 1955–56, 1959–60, 1961–62, 1965–66, and 1968–69 were used to figure the average for the period.

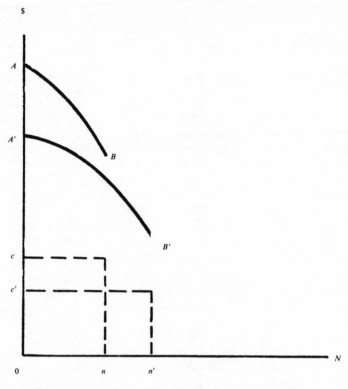

FIGURE 3

firm the Elman thesis. However, grudging dismissals were unknown at the Board even before the first separation of functions in October 1942, and are a much smaller fraction of all FTC significant dismissals after 1945 than until then. Most grudging dismissals are so classified because the Commission gave no reason for its action in dismissing, and this appears to be an aspect of the Commission's early and much criticized reticence about explaining the basis of its decisions, whether punitive or exculpatory.[33] The practice of "blind" dismissals begins to wane in 1946 and disappears after 1952. In the three later periods in Table 10 only two out of 42 significant dismissals (24 total dismissals) are grudging.

---

33. See, *e.g.*, Gerard C. Henderson, The Federal Trade Commission 334–35 (1924), and, with specific reference to the Commission's failure to state the reasons for dismissals, U.S. Atty. Gen.'s Committee on Administrative Procedure, *supra* note 24, at 136–37, and U.S. Atty. Gen.'s Committee on Administrative Procedure, The Federal Trade Commission 63–65 (Monograph No. 6, 1940).

TABLE 10
FORM OF FTC DISMISSALS

Period	Total Contested Cases	% of Ungrudging [a] Dismissals	% of Total Ungrudging Dismissals	Grudging Dismissals as a % of All Significant Dismissals	Grudging Total Dismissals as a % of All Significant Dismissals
1938	60	.10	.03	.50	.71
1941	61	.05	.05	.82	.82
1943	32	.09	.06	.63	.71
1945	43	.07	.05	.73	.78
Total [b]	196	.08	.05	.69	.84
1946–47	70	.20	.16	.22	.27
1949–50	53	.17	.13	.18	.22
1951–52	62	.23	.18	.07	.08
1955–56	36	.28	.19	.00	.00
1959–60	58	.36	.12	.00	.00
1965	34	.29	.24	.17	.20
Total [b]	313	.25	.16	.11	.15

SOURCES. — See Table 5, *supra*.
[a] As defined in text.
[b] Or average.

3. Professor Elman's thesis implies that an agency in which prosecution and adjudication are combined will be less reluctant to dismiss a case in which legal issues predominate than one in which factual issues predominate. Since the scope of judicial review of administrative action is broader with respect to questions of law than with respect to questions of facts, an agency has little to gain by distorting the applicable law whereas it may get away with a certain amount of tendentious fact-finding.

Table 11 attempts to test this implication of the Elman thesis by comparing NLRB dismissal rates at various periods for a type of case — cases in which an employer is charged with discriminating against an employee or employees because of union activities — in which factual questions, primarily motive, predominate. If the Elman thesis is correct, the dismissal rate in discrimination cases should be lower than that in all un-

TABLE 11
DISMISSAL RATE—NLRB DISCRIMINATION CASES

Period	Total Contested Discrimination Cases	Dismissals	Complete Dismissals [a]	% Dismissed	% Dismissed in Entirety
1935–36	42	16	2	.38	.05
1938	29	23	8	.79	.28
1946	26	1	8	.42	.31
1947	17	6	2	.35	.12
Total [b]	114	56	20	.49	.18
1956	30	14	5	.47	.17
1969	29	9	6	.31	.21
Total [b]	59	23	11	.39	.19

SOURCE. – Decisions and Orders of the National Labor Relations Board, vols. 1, 8, 69, 72, 115, 178.
[a] That is, of discrimination count or counts.
[b] Or average.

fair labor practice cases prior to the separations of functions in 1942 or 1947; a comparison with Table 6 shows that it is not.[34]

Table 11 also permits a comparison among dismissal rates at different stages in the Board's evolution that is unaffected by changes either in substantive law (the prohibition against employer discrimination has remained unchanged since the Wagner Act) or in the agency's mix of cases. According to Table 11 the dismissal rate has not been affected by the successive changes in the Board's structure with respect to the separation of functions.

4. It should also follow from the Elman thesis that an agency in which prosecution and adjudication are combined will, other things being equal, dismiss a smaller fraction of *major* cases, so classified by the amount of agency resources consumed in their prosecution, than of minor cases. Criticism of an agency for having wasted the taxpayer's money by bringing an unmeritorious case is more apt to be forthcoming and persuasive when the amount squandered is substantial.

34. The low rate of dismissals in the first year of the Board's operations, 1935–36, is consistent with data obtained for all unfair labor practice cases, but not reported in Table 5 or 6, from the first volume of the Board's decisions. The dismissal rates in that volume are .06 (significant dismissals) and .00 (significant total dismissals).

Unfortunately other things are not equal. Although the FTC does dismiss a higher proportion of its larger cases (the statistics were presented in Table 3), the model developed in Part I of this article suggests that there are reasons for this that have nothing to do with the presence or absence of bias. Table 3 can be made to bear on the present question, however, if another column is added — one showing the percentage of all cases, settled as well as litigated, that are dismissed (Table 12). It appears that in many periods a large fraction of the Commission's antitrust prosecutions, and hence in resource terms a large fraction of the Commission's entire enforcement activity, have not resulted in the entry of remedial orders. So marked a propensity to rule in favor of the defendant is difficult to reconcile with the Elman thesis.

5. The Elman thesis would seem to imply that the members of an agency in which prosecution and adjudication are combined would be less reluctant to dismiss a complaint that had been authorized by their predecessors in office than one they themselves had authorized. In the former case they could not properly be criticized for having initiated a case that lacked merit; in the latter case they could. The low rate of ungrudging

TABLE 12
DISMISSAL RATE — FTC ANTITRUST CASES [a] INCLUDING SETTLED CASES

Period	Total Cases	Percentage Dismissed [b]
1938	19	.05
1941	26	.35
1943	8	.38
1945	9	.22
1946–47	11	.27
Total [c]	73	.25
1949–50	16	.25
1951–52	15	.07
1955–56	32	.09
1959–60	21	.10
1965	34	.26
Total [c]	118	.16

SOURCE. — See Table 3, *supra.*

[a] Excluding cases brought exclusively under one of the minor Robinson-Patman Act amendments. See note 10, *supra.*

[b] Significant total dismissals only, as defined in text.

[c] Or average.

dismissals disclosed by Table 10 for the period up to 1945 may appear to support this hypothesis, for it was a period in which nearly all the cases decided by the members of the Commission had been authorized by the very same members.[35] In subsequent periods the average tenure of the members of the Commission is much shorter.

But an inference that members of the Commission are more prone to dismiss complaints of their predecessors than their own complaints cannot in fact be drawn from these data. As explained earlier, the decline in the proportion of grudging dismissals appears to reflect the gradual adoption of a policy of stating reasons for dismissing a complaint rather than the length of service of the commissioners in relation to the cases they decide. If we ignore, therefore, whether a dismissal is grudging or ungrudging and consider only whether it is significant, we find that the dismissal rate is no higher after 1945, despite the reduction in the commissioners' average length of service.

Further evidence is presented in Tables 13 through 15, which analyze the later periods in detail. The last column in each box in Table 13 shows the percentage dismissed of cases in which all five members of the Commission who decided the case had also been members when the complaint was issued, cases in which four members of the Commission who decided the case had also been members when the complaint was issued, and so on down to zero (*i.e.,* none of the incumbents were members of the Commission when the complaint was issued), in various periods. If members of the Commission are reluctant to dismiss their own complaints but less reluctant to dismiss those of their predecessors the percentage of dismissals should increase as we move down the columns.

If dismissals are grouped according to whether three or more or two or fewer commissioners deciding the case were members of the Commission when the complaint was issued, the dismissal rate is indeed higher in the second group (Table 14). The difference, however, is not statistically significant. Moreover, contrary to the prediction derived from the Elman thesis, the highest rate of dismissal is found where all five members of the Commission were members when the complaint was issued (the number of cases, however, is too small to be significant); and the rate of dismissal is the same where three members of the Commission when the case was decided were members when the complaint was issued as it is where only one present member of the Commission was also a member when the complaint was issued.

---

35. In 1938 the most junior member of the Commission had sat for three years and only two cases decided that year had been instituted prior to his appointment. In 1941 the most junior member had sat for six years; the figure is eight years for 1943 and ten for 1945.

TABLE 13

DISMISSAL [a] RATE AS A FUNCTION OF WHETHER COMMISSIONERS DECIDING CASE WERE MEMBERS WHEN COMPLAINT WAS ISSUED

No. of Commissioners Who Were Members Both When the Complaint Was Issued and When the Case Was Decided [b]	1946–47				1949–50				1951–52			
	Order	Dis.	Total	% Dis.	Order	Dis.	Total	% Dis.	Order	Dis.	Total	% Dis.
5	0	1	1	1.00	0	0	0	–	1	2	3	.67
4	20	7	27	.26	0	0	0	–	11	2	13	.15
3	1	2	3	.67	5	2	7	.29	6	0	6	.00
2	0	1	1	1.00	8	3	11	.27	10	3	13	.23
1	0	0	0	–	11	2	13	.15	11	4	15	.27
0	0	0	0	–	0	0	0	–	2	0	2	.00
Total [c]	21	11	32	.34	24	7	31	.23	41	11	52	.21

No. of Commissioners	1955–56				1959–60				1965			
	Order	Dis.	Total	% Dis.	Order	Dis.	Total	% Dis.	Order	Dis.	Total	% Dis.
5	0	0	0	–	1	1	2	.50	0	0	0	–
4	0	0	0	–	27	6	33	.18	3	0	3	.00
3	5	1	6	.17	9	0	9	.00	10	1	11	.09
2	10	4	14	.29	2	0	2	.00	0	2	2	1.00
1	10	2	12	.17	0	0	0	–	0	0	0	–
0	3	0	3	.00	0	0	0	–	6	5	11	.45
Total [c]	28	7	35	.20	39	7	46	.15	19	8	27	.30

SOURCE.—Federal Trade Commission Decisions, vols. 42–43, 46, 48, 52, 56, 67–68.

[a] "Ungrudging" total dismissals as defined in the text.

[b] Excluding members who dissented from or did not participate in the Commission's decision.

[c] Or average.

TABLE 14
DISMISSAL [a] RATE AS A FUNCTION OF WHETHER COMMISSIONERS
DECIDING CASE WERE MEMBERS WHEN COMPLAINT WAS ISSUED —
SUMMARY OF TABLE 13

No. of Commissioners Who Were Members Both When the Complaint Was Issued and When the Case Was Decided [b]	All Periods			
	Order	Dis.	Total	% Dis.
5	2	4	6	.67
4	61	15	76	.20
3	36	6	42	.14
2	30	13	43	.30
1	32	8	40	.20
0	11	5	16	.31
Total [c]	172	51	223	.23
3–5	99	25	124	.20
0–2	73	26	99	.26

SOURCE. — Table 13, *supra*.

[a] "Ungrudging" total dismissals as defined in the text.

[b] Excluding members who dissented from or did not participate in the Commission's decision.

[c] Or average.

Tables 13 and 14 count only commissioners voting with the majority, either to dismiss or to enter a remedial order. The votes of dissenters are treated separately in Table 15. If members of the Commission were more reluctant to dismiss their own complaints than their predecessors', then we would expect old members (members both when the complaint was issued and when the case was decided) to dissent more frequently when the majority voted to dismiss the complaint than when the majority voted to enter an order. Table 15 indicates, however, that old members voted to dismiss the complaint — their complaint, as it were — 13 times when the majority voted to enter a remedial order, and voted only four times to enter an order when the majority voted to dismiss the complaint.[36]

---

36. It is of course possible for an "old" member voting against the complaint to have dissented from the original action of the Commission in issuing the complaint, in which event his later vote would be no evidence of open-mindedness. Unfortunately, data on vot-

TABLE 15
VOTES OF DISSENTING FTC COMMISSIONERS – 1946–65

| | | Nature of Vote | | | |
| | | For Issuance of Remedial Order | | For Dismissal of Complaint | |
Period	Number	By Commissioner Who Was Member When Complaint Was Issued	By Commissioner Who Was Not Member When Complaint Was Issued	By Commissioner Who Was Member When Complaint Was Issued	By Commissioner Who Was Not Member When Complaint Was Issued
1946–47	3	3	–	–	–
1949–50	–	–	–	–	–
1951–52	3	–	–	3	–
1955–56	9	–	–	9	–
1959–60	–	–	–	–	–
1965	12	1	6	1	4
Total	27	4	6	13	4

SOURCE. – See Table 13, *supra.*

6. If the combination of prosecution and adjudication makes an agency reluctant to dismiss unmeritorious complaints and thus prone to enter unjustified orders, one would expect the orders of such an agency to be reversed more frequently on judicial review than the orders of an agency in which the functions are separated. Table 16 seeks to test this hypothesis by comparing, for a few randomly selected periods, the results of judicial review of FTC cease and desist orders and orders in NLRB unfair labor practice cases. Employer discrimination cases are reported separately to facilitate comparison between the preseparated and the separated Board.

Table 16 shows not only that the FTC has fared consistently better on judicial review than the Board, but also (and more pertinently, since according to our model many factors apart from bias must influence an

---

ing at the complaint-issuance stage are unavailable. It should be noted, however, that under the Elman view the commissioner who voted against issuing the complaint in the first place would still feel considerable pressure to enter a cease and desist order after the trial in order to protect the agency against charges of having wasted the taxpayer's money and in order to prevent the demoralization of the staff.

TABLE 16
JUDICIAL REVIEW OF NLRB AND FTC CEASE AND DESIST ORDERS

Agency	Period	Affirmed	Reversed [a]	Total	% Reversed	Discrimination Cases Affirmed	Discrimination Cases Reversed [a]	Total	% Reversed
NLRB	1943	33	4	37	.11	17	2	19	.11
	1945	35	10	45	.22	9	5	14	.36
	Total [b]	68	14	82	.17	26	7	33	.21
FTC	1944	24	1	25	.04	–	–	–	–
	1945	14	1	15	.07	–	–	–	–
	1946–48	17	5	22	.23	–	–	–	–
	Total [b]	55	7	62	.11	–	–	–	–
NLRB	1962	102	51	153	.33	54	25	79	.32
FTC	1962	19	7	26	.37	–	–	–	–

SOURCES.—Court Decisions Relating to the National Labor Relations Act, vols. 4, 5, 12 and 13; Statutes and Decisions Pertaining to the Federal Trade Commission, vol. 4, 1962 Supp.
[a] Excluding minor modifications in agency's order.
[b] Or average.

agency's p on judicial review) that the Board's record has actually worsened since separation, both generally and with respect to discrimination cases alone. However, Table 16 also reveals secular changes in the outcome of judicial review of agency action that cannot be ascribed to the combination or separation of functions and that may conceal the effect of separation.

7. Finally, an agency in which prosecution and adjudication are combined is, under the Elman thesis, one much concerned about being criticized for dismissing complaints but relatively unconcerned about its record on judicial review. (Were it greatly concerned about its court record it would dismiss all doubtful cases in order to minimize the danger of being reversed by a reviewing court.) This model would be more persuasive were there evidence that an agency like the FTC or NLRB was judged, by those with power over the agency, more by its internal batting average than by its success or failure in the courts. Some places to look for such evidence are the agencies' annual reports, where the agency boasts of its successful performance, presumably using criteria of success persuasive to its intended audience; the agencies' annual appropriation hearings before the House and Senate appropriation subcommittees; and appraisals of the agencies' performance by critics or supporters. A search of these sources reveals, however, many more references to the agency's record on judicial review than to the rate at which either the FTC or the NLRB dismisses complaints.

In one respect, though, dismissals clearly could affect an agency's performance. Congress, the agencies, and their critics all seem greatly concerned with the size of the agency's work load as measured by such quantitative indicia as the number of charges filed with the agency, the number of complaints issued, and the number of decisions. The routine argument advanced for a larger appropriation is that the agency's work load has grown faster than its budget, and an increase in work load is difficult to demonstrate unless some quantitative change can be pointed to. The routine criticism of an agency is that its budget is excessive in relation to its present quantity of work. The effect of a dismissal may be to compel the agency's staff, in similar future cases, to investigate more thoroughly before recommending a complaint and to present more evidence of violation at trial — in short, to expend additional resources in the prosecution of the case. This will reduce the number of cases it can bring with reasonable prospect of success.

Such a process can be seen at work in the FTC in the middle and late 1960s. As Table 3 shows, in 1965 the Commission dismissed 60 per cent of its contested antitrust cases. Many of these decisions established higher standards for proving violations of law than had previously been applied by the Commission. By 1969 we find the American Bar Association's Commission to Study the Federal Trade Commission blasting the Commission for a precipitous decline in its work load as measured by number of investigations, decisions, and other conventional quantitative criteria of activity.[37] The causation is complex but it would seem that one of the reasons for the Commission's decline [38] in number of cases was its change of policy, reflected in the dismissals of the middle 1960s, in the direction of more exacting standards of proof.

This history may influence the Commission's future decisions whether or not to dismiss complaints, in circumstances where a dismissal would increase the difficulty of proving a violation. But it is at least as significant, in appraising the Elman thesis, to observe that the Commission in 1965 was apparently not deterred by such a prospect from dismissing major cases with great frequency.

D. WHY WERE PROSECUTION AND ADJUDICATION SEPARATED AT THE BOARD AND NOT AT THE COMMISSION?

The results of our inquiry into whether the combination of prosecution and adjudication biases an agency's adjudication, although hardly definitive, suggest that it does not. If so, one may wonder why the Board effected a limited separation in 1942, why Congress extended and formalized the separation, apparently at some cost in efficiency,[39] in 1947, and how the FTC has escaped serious pressure for some form of separation.

The congressional hearings preceding enactment of the Taft-Hartley Act developed no firm evidence of bias in adjudication traceable to the combination of functions.[40] And if separation was legislated because combination was thought inherently unfair, it is hard to understand why the combination of functions in the FTC has not only persisted but escaped sustained controversy.

The probable explanation for separation at the Labor Board lies not in the merits of the issue but in its politics. The opposition of the business community to the Wagner Act and its enforcing agency[41] was better or-

---

37. See ABA Comm'n to Study the Federal Trade Commission, *supra* note 9, at 16–26.

38. Which the ABA Commission, however, overstated. See Richard A. Posner, A Statistical Study of Antitrust Enforcement, *supra* note 10, at 370.

39. See 2 Kenneth Culp Davis, Administrative Law Treatise § 13.05, pp. 206–11.

40. See *id.* at § 13.05, pp. 204–5.

41. This opposition is described in Harry A. Millis & Emily Clark Brown, From the Wagner Act to Taft-Hartley – A Study of National Labor Policy and Labor Relations 381–91 (1950).

ganized, more vocal, and more tenacious than the business community's opposition to the FTC and the statutes it enforces has ever been. The costs imposed by the Board on business were probably greater than those imposed by the FTC—this might explain why greater resources were marshaled against the Board than against the Commission. Probably, too, it is easier to organize employers as an effective political pressure group than the diffuse victims of FTC prosecution. At all events, within 12 years of the passage of the Wagner Act the opponents of that Act and of the Board were able, in the Taft-Hartley Act, to effect a major overhaul of the law. Charges of unfairness are a conventional refrain in the litany of political controversy and once the Wagner Act was up for a thorough overhaul it was relatively easy to amend the provisions of the Act relating to the structure of enforcement as well as the substantive law provisions; there has never been a comparable overhaul of the Federal Trade Commission Act. That the separation of functions apparently imposed at least short-term costs in the form of lowered efficiency due to problems of coordination between the Board and the General Counsel provides a sufficient explanation why the Board's opponents should have wanted to bring about a separation of the functions regardless of the actual merits of such a step.

What the last point may suggest is that administrative regulation can perhaps best be understood when elements of the effective-political-group and rational-utility-maximizing models of administrative agency behavior are combined.

APPENDIX

PROOF THAT THE CONDITION FOR LITIGATION
CANNOT BE SATISFIED IF $s = s'$, $k > 1$, AND $r = 1$

$$\frac{ec}{c + c'} + \frac{e'c'}{c' + c} = 1;$$

so

$$e = \frac{\sqrt{e's'}(1 - e')}{\sqrt{c}} + e'.$$

Substituting this equation into inequality (15), the condition for litigation becomes

$$\frac{\sqrt{e's'}(1 - e')}{\sqrt{c}} + e' > \frac{s'e'}{s} \left[\frac{c'}{s'} \left(\frac{1 - e'}{\sqrt{e'}} \right) + 2 - \frac{1}{k} \right].$$

Since $s = s'$, this can be simplified to

$$\frac{\sqrt{e's'}(1 - e')}{\sqrt{c}} + e' > \frac{\sqrt{s'e'}(1 - e')}{\sqrt{c}} + e'\left(2 - \frac{1}{k}\right).$$

Subtracting the first term on the left-hand side of the inequality from both sides, we have

$$e' > e'\left(2 - \frac{1}{k}\right).$$

Since $k > 1$, the right side must exceed the left for any value of e', and the condition for litigation cannot be satisfied.

TABLE A1
RATIO OF SIGNIFICANT DISMISSALS TO REMEDIAL ORDERS, DEPARTMENT OF JUSTICE ANTITRUST DIVISION AND FTC ANTITRUST [a] CASES
(Contested Cases Only)

Agency	Period in Which Case Was Brought	Remedial Order	Dis-missal	Total	% Dis-missed
Antitrust Division	1935–39	15	12	27	.44
	1940–44	51	50	101	.50
	1945–49	26	28	54	.52
	1950–54	38	22	60	.37
	1955–59	58	18	76	.24
	1960–64	63	31	94	.33
	Total [b]	251	161	412	.39
FTC	1935–39	50	36	86	.42
	1940–44	48	23	71	.32
	1945–49	20	12	32	.38
	1950–54	14	10	24	.42
	1955–59	35	22	57	.39
	1960–64	23	14	37	.38
	Total [b]	190	117	307	.38

SOURCE. – Richard A. Posner, A Statistical Study of Antitrust Enforcement, 13 J. Law & Econ. 365, 376 (Table 6), 379 (Table 9), 381 (Table 11), 382 (Table 12).

[a] Excluding cases brought exclusively under the minor Robinson-Patman Act amendments. See note 10, *supra*.

[b] Or average.

TABLE A2
NLRB EMPLOYER UNFAIR LABOR PRACTICE CASES CLOSED AT
PRECOMPLAINT STAGE

Period	Cases Pending	% Withdrawn or Dismissed	% Withdrawn or Dismissed— Excluding Charges Filed by Individuals	% of Charges Filed by Individuals
1935–36	865	.32	N.A.	N.A.
1936–37	3,124	.21	N.A.	N.A.
1937–38	8,213	.31	.29	.08
1938–39	7,132	.25	.24	.09
1939–40	6,836	.33	.30	.11
1940–41	6,981	.30	.28	.09
Total [a]	33,151	.29	.28	.09 [b]
1943–44	3,896	.42	N.A.	.09
1944–45	3,633	.42	N.A.	.09
1945–46	5,126	.40	N.A.	.06
1946–47	6,457	.45	N.A.	.06
Total [a]	19,112	.42	–	.07
1948–49	5,543	.43	N.A.	.38
1949–50	6,635	.43	N.A.	.33
1950–51	8,504	.35	N.A.	.33
1951–52	6,676	.45	N.A.	.27
Total [a]	27,358	.41	–	.33
1955–56	5,326	.57	N.A.	.36
1959–60	11,121	.54	N.A.	.46
1961–62	12,186	.50	N.A.	.38
1965–66	15,632	.44	N.A.	.29
1968–69	17,559	.47	N.A.	.34
Total [a]	61,824	.49	–	.36

SOURCE. – See Table 8, *supra.*
[a] Or average.
[b] Excluding 1935–1937.

TABLE A3
DISPOSITION OF FTC CASES

| | | | | | Order and Dismissals | | | |
Period [a]	Stipulations [b]	Total	Contested	% Contested	Dismissed [c]	% Dismissed	% of Contested Cases Dismissed	% of All Dispositions Dismissed
1938	313	148	60	.41	7	.05	.12	.015
1941	204	179	61	.34	17	.09	.28	.044
1943	173	62	32	.52	7	.11	.22	.030
1945	188	94	43	.46	9	.10	.21	.032
1946–47	202	156	70	.45	15	.10	.21	.042
Total [d]	1,080	639	266	.42	55	.09	.21	.032
1949–50	164	106	53	.50	9	.08	.17	.033
1951–52	151	154	62	.40	12	.08	.19	.039
1955–56	158	180	36	.20	7	.04	.19	.021
1959–60	104	352	58	.16	7	.02	.12	.015
1965	–	136	34	.25	10	.07	.29	–
Total [d]	577	928	243	.26	45	.05	.19	.026 [e]

SOURCE.—See Table 5, *supra.*

[a] All 12 months except 1938 (7 months), 1941 (5 months), 1943 (6 months), 1945 (6 months) and 1946–47 (18 months).

[b] Term explained in note 31, *supra.*

[c] "Significant" total dismissals, as defined in text.

[d] Or average.

[e] Excluding 1965.

261

Index